DOVER · THRIFT · EDITIONS

Politics

ARISTOTLE

Translated by
BENJAMIN JOWETT

With Introduction, Analysis, and Index by
H. W. C. Davis

DOVER PUBLICATIONS, INC.
Mineola, New York

DOVER THRIFT EDITIONS

GENERAL EDITOR: PAUL NEGRI
EDITOR OF THIS VOLUME: JOHN BERSETH

Copyright

Copyright © 2000 by Dover Publications, Inc.
All rights reserved under Pan American and International Copyright Conventions.

Bibliographical Note

This Dover edition, first published in 2000, is an unabridged reprint of the Benjamin Jowett translation (1885) of *Politics*, as published in the standard Oxford University Press edition (1905). Also included are that edition's Introduction, Analysis, and Index, by H. W. C. Davis.

Library of Congress Cataloging-in-Publication Data

Aristotle.
    [Politics. English]
    Politics / Aristotle ; translated by Benjamin Jowett ; with introduction, analysis, and index by H. W. C. Davis.
        p. cm. — (Dover thrift editions)
    ISBN 0-486-41424-8 (pbk.)
    1. Political science—Early works to 1800. I. Jowett, Benjamin, 1817–1893. II. Title. III. Series.

JC71.A41 J6 2000
320'.01'1—dc21

                                                00-031841

Manufactured in the United States of America
Dover Publications, Inc., 31 East 2nd Street, Mineola, N.Y. 11501

Publisher's Note

THE CLASSICAL SCHOLAR Benjamin Jowett (1817–1893) was noted not only as an outstanding teacher at Oxford, where he was master of Balliol College from 1870 until 1893, but also for four widely read translations from the Greek: the *Dialogues of Plato* (1871), Thucydides' *History* (1881), Aristotle's *Politics* (1885), and Plato's *Republic* (1894). Jowett's translation of *Politics* was lauded as "an English classic" by a fellow scholar, Harris W. Rackham of Cambridge University. To the present day it has continued to be a standard source for students and scholars alike.

This edition's Introduction, Analysis, and Index for Jowett's translation of Aristotle's *Politics* is the work of H. W. C. Davis (1874–1928), fellow of Balliol College and Regius Professor of Modern History at Oxford. Davis's Introduction gives a brief account of Aristotle's life and with admirable clarity places *Politics* in the context of the great philosopher's other work.

The numbers in the margins of every page of Jowett's translation refer to the book (Roman numerals), chapter (large Arabic numerals), and section (small Arabic numerals) of the text. They identify the cross references in many of the footnotes and provide useful points of division in the text. As noted in the Introduction, the four-digit numbers alongside the text refer to the definitive edition of Aristotle's work compiled (1831–36) by the German philologist A. I. Bekker.

CONTENTS

INTRODUCTION

THE life of Aristotle, so far as it illustrates this treatise, may be summarized in a few words. He was by birth a Greek, but a native of the small city of Stageira which stood upon the fringe of the Greek world; he was therefore well fitted by his origin to be an impartial, yet sympathetic critic, of the more famous city-states of Greece. In his youth he studied philosophy at Athens under Plato, thus coming at the most impressionable period of his life into close relations with the profoundest thinker whom Greece had yet produced. After the death of Plato (347), he quitted Athens to spend some years in the service of the new race of monarchs whose mission it was to diffuse Greek culture through the East and at the same time to complete the destruction of all that was most valuable and characteristic in the political life of Greece. At the court of Hermias, the obscure tyrant of the obscure city of Atarneus, Aristotle had the opportunity of observing the once great, but then decadent, despotism of Persia, to which he makes some references in the *Politics*. In 343 or 342 he migrated to Macedonia, joined the court of Philip, and acted for three years or so as tutor to the youthful Alexander. The results of his experience in Macedonia, and the drift of the political teaching which he gave to his pupil may perhaps be inferred from the comments which, in several passages of the *Politics*, he passes on monarchies and tyrannies. About the year 335, on the eve of Alexander's great campaigns of conquest, the philosopher turned his back on Macedonia; we may infer from what he says of empires, that while he realized their possible services to civilization, he was still more alive to the dangers, moral and other, which beset the path of a military and aggressive state. His sympathies were with the past, not the future; with Sparta and Athens rather than with Macedon; with Plato rather than with Alexander. Settling down at Athens, he became the leader of a philosophic school, the director of a brilliant academy; but he incurred the odium to which a friend of Macedon was naturally exposed in the city of Demosthenes. In 323, after the death of his pupil and patron, he was driven into exile by a prosecution for impiety which, if he had faced it, would probably have brought upon his head the fate of Socrates. He died in the following year at Chalcis, a Macedonian stronghold. The semi-barbarians, of whose future he doubted, had been more generous to him than the Greeks, whose highest thought it had been his life-work to interpret and to vindicate.

Of his literary work in general this is not the place to speak. It is enough to say that he aimed at expounding in the light of his own philosophic principles all the sciences which were then recognized, and that he followed consistently the method, of which the *Politics* are a conspicuous illustration, of combining induction with deductive reasoning from first principles, and of testing his own conclusions by a comparison with popular opinions and those of other teachers. Encyclopaedic knowledge has never, before or since, gone hand in hand with a logic so masculine or with speculation so profound. But it is in dealing with the moral rather than the natural sciences that he is greatest, most adequately equipped with facts, and most interested in his subject. Of his work in the moral sciences the final results are incorporated in the *Nicomachean Ethics* and the *Politics*. The two treatises are intimately connected. In the *Ethics* he discusses the nature of individual happiness or well-being; in the *Politics* he treats of the state as one of the chief means through which the individual attains to happiness. The object of the *Politics* is both practical and speculative; to explain the nature of the ideal city in which the end of happiness may be completely realized; to suggest some methods of making existent states more useful to the individual citizen than they were in Aristotle's time, or had been in the past.

Aristotle is not, strictly speaking, the founder of political science. In the age of Pericles, and earlier still, statesmen and philosophers had theorized about the origin of society, the relative merits of various constitutions, and other kindred topics. Though Socrates was more concerned with ethics than with politics, he applied the powerful solvent of his dialectic to many of the political ideas which were fashionable in his day. The conceptions of utility as the ideal which the statesman should pursue, and of scientific knowledge as the indispensable equipment of the statesman, would seem to have had their birth in the Socratic circle. Plato, the pupil of Socrates, not content with developing the suggestions of his master and with giving to the Socratic formulae a deeper meaning, essayed a more systematic discussion of the nature of the state and its right organization. In the *Republic* he describes the state as it would appear if founded and governed by philosophers; in the *Laws* he offered to the statesmen of his age a model more practicable and more nearly related to the experience of the past; a model which the legislator for a new colony might follow without undue violence to Greek prejudices and opinions. Although the views of Plato are sharply, and not always justly, criticized by Aristotle, the influence of the *Republic* and the *Laws* is perceptible in many places of the *Politics* where they are not mentioned.

The *Politics*, in fact, would not be so valuable as they are if they expressed the views of an individual man of genius and nothing more. Here as elsewhere it is not the least of Aristotle's merits that he epitomized the best thoughts of a nation and of a stage in human history. He respected the political thinkers of the past, both the statesmen and the theorists; he was loth to admit that any institution or polity which had stood the test of time could be altogether bad. Hence he appears before us as a mediator in the controversies of his own and the preceding ages. It is his wish to lay bare the grain of truth which exists at the core of every political practice and belief. He interprets even those ideals with which he is least in sympathy. And so we learn from him what the various types of the city-state signified to the Greek mind; we are admitted under his guidance to the penetralia of their political thought.

The history of the Greek city-state we can study for our-selves, with fewer sources of information, it is true, than Aristotle had at his command, but also with a more critical appreciation of their value and a more scientific method of interpretation than was to be learned in Athenian schools of the fourth century. We are too in a better position than Aristotle to see the true place of the city-state in the evolution of society, to appreciate its limitations, to condemn its evils, and to draw the moral from its failure. We know, what he does not appear to have suspected, that the careers of his Macedonian patrons had sealed the death-warrant of the community which he regarded as the highest that human skill was capable of framing. Ampler experience has shown us that slavery is not the indispensable basis of a civilization, nor commerce always degrading to the individual and destruc-tive of national morality. In the modern world we have before us communities which, in defiance of his prophecies, have become extensive without becoming disunited. By his own methods of induction and comparison we can refute some of the laws which he regarded as immutable.

Still we must start from Aristotle. His account of the city-state may be supplemented and corrected, but not superseded. The governing ideas of any polity are always best expressed by those to whom they stand for the absolute and final truth; and there is no form of polity which the student of political science should study with more care than the city-state. Just because it is comparatively simple, just because it is unlike the states with which we are personally acquainted, it contains the key to many modern problems. Aristotle is the best interpreter of an essential link in the chain of political development.

But he is something more than this, more than a Greek who states the case of Greece. He is also a philosopher and a student of human nature. His views as to the origin and ultimate structure of society, as to the aims of civic life, as to the mutual obligations of the state and the individual, as to the nature of political justice, all have a value which is independent of his historical position. It is often difficult to follow his discussions of these and cognate subjects. His arguments are stated with extreme conciseness, and the train of thought which leads him from one topic to another is often far from clear. But those who have the patience to wrestle with his text will find in it theories of perennial value, and refutations of fallacies which are always re-emerging. Nor is it merely from his more abstract disquisitions that such lessons are to be extracted. While there could be no greater mistake than to apply his criticisms of democracies and aristocracies to modern governments which go by the same names, without stopping to enquire how far the names have changed their meanings, it is on the other hand often apparent that these criticisms, when the necessary qualifications have been made, are as true of the present as they were of Greece. Of this an illustration may be found in the account of revolutions and their causes which forms the fifth book of the *Politics*.

The *Politics* should probably be regarded as an unfinished work. There are not infrequent repetitions ; some subjects which the author promises to treat are never treated ; and we are sometimes at a loss for the connecting link between successive books or parts of the same book. The traditional order of the books is probably not that which Aristotle contemplated, and has been altered by most editors. The present translation follows the order of Bekker's first edition; the numbering of the books in his octavo edition of 1878 has been given in brackets wherever it differs from that of the first. None of the rearrangements which have been suggested are completely satisfactory. Whichever of them is adopted, the reader will find that positions assumed at an earlier are only proved at a later stage of the argument. The *Politics* should be treated as a quarry of arguments and theories rather than as an artistically constructed piece of literature. It is best studied by the collection and comparison of all the passages which bear upon the same topic. It is hoped that for this purpose the subject-headings in the Index, which is abridged from that of the translator, may be of service. A brief analysis is prefixed to the translation with the object of explaining the thread of the argument, where such a thread exists, of indicating the natural divisions of the text, and of enumerating the chief topics of discussion.

The thanks of the editor are due to the Master of Balliol for his kindness in revising the proof of this Introduction.

H. W. C. DAVIS.

BOOK I.

cc. 1, 2. *Definition and structure of the State.*

The state is the highest form of community and aims at the highest good. How it differs from other communities will appear if we examine the parts of which it is composed (c. 1). It consists of villages which consist of households. The household is founded upon the two relations of male and female, of master and slave; it exists to satisfy man's daily needs. The village, a wider community, satisfies a wider range of needs. The state aims at satisfying all the needs of men. Men form states to secure a bare subsistence; but the ultimate object of the state is the good life. The naturalness of the state is proved by the faculty of speech in man. In the order of Nature the state precedes the household and the individual. It is founded on a natural impulse, that towards political association (c. 2).

cc. 3–13. *Household economy. The Slave. Property. Children and Wives.*

Let us discuss the household, since the state is composed of households (c. 3). First as to slavery. The slave is a piece of property which is animate, and useful for action rather than for production (c. 4). Slavery is natural; in every department of the natural universe we find the relation of ruler and subject. There are human beings who, without possessing reason, understand it. These are natural slaves (c. 5). But we find persons in slavery who are not natural slaves. Hence slavery itself is condemned by some; but they are wrong. The natural slave benefits by subjection to a master (c. 6). The art of ruling slaves differs from that of ruling free men but calls for no detailed description; any one who is a natural master can acquire it for himself (c. 7).

As to property and the modes of acquiring it. This subject concerns us in so far as property is an indispensable substratum to the household (c. 8). But we do not need that form of finance which accumulates wealth for its own sake. This is unnatural finance. It has been made possible by the invention of coined money. It accumulates money by means of exchange. Natural and unnatural finance are often treated as though they were the same, but differ in their aims (c. 9); also in their subject matter; for natural finance is only concerned with the fruits of the earth and animals (c. 10). Natural finance is necessary to the householder; he must therefore know about live stock, agriculture, possibly about the exchange of the products of the earth, such as wood and minerals, for money. Special treatises on finance exist, and the subject should be specially studied by statesmen (c. 11).

Lastly, we must discuss and distinguish the relations of husband to wife, of father to child (c. 12). In household management persons call for more attention than things; free persons for more than slaves. Slaves are only capable of an inferior kind of virtue. Socrates was wrong in denying that there are several kinds of virtue. Still the slave must be trained in virtue. The education of the free man will be subsequently discussed (c. 13).

BOOK II.

cc. 1–8. *Ideal Commonwealths—Plato, Phaleas, Hippodamus.*

To ascertain the nature of the ideal state we should start by examining both the best states of history and the best that theorists have imagined. Otherwise we might waste our time over problems which others have already solved.

Among theorists, Plato in the *Republic* raises the most fundamental questions. He desires to abolish private property and the family (c. 1). But the end which he has in view is wrong. He wishes to make all his citizens absolutely alike; but the differentiation of functions is a law of nature. There can be too much unity in a state (c. 2). And the means by which he would promote unity are wrong. The abolition of property will produce, not remove, dissension. Communism of wives and children will destroy natural affection (c. 3). Other objections can be raised; but this is the fatal one (c. 4). To descend to details. The advantages to be expected from communism of property would be better secured if private property were used in a liberal spirit to relieve the wants of others. Private property makes men happier, and enables them to cultivate such virtues as generosity. The *Republic* makes unity the result of uniformity among the citizens, which is not the case. The good sense of mankind has always been against Plato, and experiment would show that his idea is impracticable (c. 5).

Plato sketched another ideal state in the *Laws*; it was meant to be more practicable than the other. In the *Laws* he abandoned communism, but otherwise upheld the leading ideas of the earlier treatise, except that he made the new state larger and too large. He forgot to discuss foreign relations, and to fix a limit of private property, and to restrict the increase of population, and to distinguish between ruler and subject. The form of government which he proposed was bad (c. 6).

Phaleas of Chalcedon made equal distribution of property the main feature of his scheme. This would be difficult to effect, and would not meet the evils which Phaleas had in mind. Dissensions arise from deeper causes than inequality of wealth. His state would be weak against foreign foes. His reforms would anger the rich and not satisfy the poor (c. 7).

Hippodamus, who was not a practical politician, aimed at symmetry. In his state there were to be three classes, three kinds of landed property, three sorts of laws. He also proposed to (1) create a Court of Appeal, (2) let juries qualify their verdicts, (3) reward those who made discoveries of public utility. His classes and his property system were badly devised. Qualified verdicts are impossible since jurymen may not confer together. The law about discoveries would encourage men to tamper with the Constitution. Now laws when obsolete and absurd should be changed; but needless changes diminish the respect for law (c. 8).

cc. 9–12. *The best existent states—Sparta, Crete, and Carthage—Greek lawgivers.*

The Spartans cannot manage their serf population. Their women are too influential and too luxurious. Their property system has concentrated all wealth in a few hands. Hence the citizen body has decreased. There are points to criticize in the Ephorate, the Senate, the Kingship, the common meals, the Admiralty. The Spartan and his state are only fit for war. Yet even in war Sparta is hampered by the want of a financial system (c. 9).

The Cretan cities resemble Sparta in their constitutions, but are more primitive. Their common meals are better managed. But the Cosmi are worse than the Ephors. The Cretan constitution is a narrow and factious oligarchy; the cities are saved from destruction only by their inaccessibility (c. 10).

The Carthaginian polity is highly praised, and not without reason. It may be compared with the Spartan; it is an oligarchy with some democratic features. It lays stress upon wealth; in Carthage all offices are bought and sold. Also, one man may hold several offices together. These are bad features. But the discontent of the people is soothed by schemes of emigration (c. 11).

Of lawgivers, Solon was the best; conservative when possible, and a moderate democrat. About Philolaus, Charondas, Phaleas, Draco, Pittacus, and Androdamas there is little to be said (c. 12).

BOOK III.

cc. 1–5. *The Citizen, civic virtue, and the civic body.*

How are we to define a citizen? He is more than a mere denizen; private rights do not make a citizen. He is ordinarily one who possesses political power; who sits on juries and in the assembly. But it is hard to find a definition which applies to all so-called citizens. To define him as the son of citizen parents is futile (c. 1). Some say that his civic rights must have been justly acquired. But he is a citizen who has political power, however acquired (c. 2). Similarly the state is defined by reference to the distribution of political power; when the mode of distribution is changed a new state comes into existence (c. 3).

The good citizen may not be a good man; the good citizen is one who does good service to his state, and this state may be bad in principle. In a constitutional state the good citizen knows both how to rule and how to obey. The good man is one who is fitted to rule. But the citizen in a constitutional state learns to rule by obeying orders. Therefore citizenship in such a state is a moral training (c. 4).

Mechanics will not be citizens in the best state. Extreme democracies, and some oligarchies, neglect this rule. But circumstances oblige them to do this. They have no choice (c. 5).

cc. 6–13. *The Classification of Constitutions*; *Democracy and Oligarchy*; *Kingship*.

The aims of the state are two; to satisfy man's social instinct, and to fit him for the good life. Political rule differs from that over slaves in aiming primarily at the good of those who are ruled (c. 6). Constitutions are bad or good according as the common welfare is, or is not, their aim. Of good Constitutions there are three: Monarchy, Aristocracy, and Polity. Of bad there are also three: Tyranny, Oligarchy, Extreme Democracy. The bad are perversions of the good (c. 7).

Democracies and Oligarchies are not made by the numerical proportion of the rulers to the ruled. Democracy is the rule of the poor; oligarchy is that of the rich (c. 8). Democrats take Equality for their motto; oligarchs believe that political rights should be unequal and proportionate to wealth. But both sides miss the true object of the state, which is virtue. Those who do most to promote virtue deserve the greatest share of power (c. 9). On the same principle, Justice is not the will of the majority or of the wealthier, but that course of action which the moral aim of the state requires (c. 10). But are the Many or the Few likely to be the better rulers? It would be unreasonable to give the highest offices to the Many. But they have a faculty of criticism which fits them for deliberative and judicial power. The good critic need not be an expert; experts are sometimes bad judges. Moreover, the Many have a greater stake in the city than the Few. But the governing body, whether Few or Many, must be held in check by the laws (c. 11). On what principle should political power be distributed? Granted that equals deserve equal shares; who are these equals? Obviously those who are equally able to be of service to the state (c. 12). Hence there is something in the claims advanced by the wealthy, the free born, the noble, the highly gifted. But no one of these classes should be allowed to rule the rest. A state should consist of men who are equal, or nearly so, in wealth, in birth, in moral and intellectual excellence. The principle which underlies Ostracism is plausible. But in the ideal state, if a pre-eminent individual be found, he should be made a king (c. 13).

cc. 14–18. *The Forms of Monarchy.*

Of Monarchy there are five kinds, (1) the Spartan, (2) the Barbarian, (3) the elective dictatorship, (4) the Heroic, (5) Absolute Kingship (c. 14). The last of these forms might appear the best polity to some; that is, if the king acts as the embodiment of law. For he will dispense from the law in the spirit of the law. But this power would be less abused if reserved for the Many. Monarchy arose to meet the needs of primitive society; it is now obsolete and on various grounds objectionable (c. 15). It tends to become hereditary; it subjects equals to the rule of an equal. The individual monarch may be misled by his passions, and no single man can attend to all the duties of government (c. 16). One case alone can be imagined in which Absolute Kingship would be just (c. 17).

Let us consider the origin and nature of the best polity, now that we have agreed not to call Absolute Kingship the best (c. 18).

BOOK IV (VI).

cc. 1–10. *Variations of the main types of Constitutions.*

Political science should study (1) the ideal state, (2) those states which may be the best obtainable under special circumstances, and even (3) those which are essentially bad. For the statesman must sometimes make the best of a bad Constitution (c. 1). Of our six main types of state, Kingship and Aristocracy have been discussed (cf. Bk. III, c. 14 fol.). Let us begin by dealing with the other four and their divisions, enquiring also when and why they may be desirable (c. 2).

First as to Democracy and Oligarchy. The common view that Democracy and Oligarchy should be taken as the main types of Constitution is at variance with our own view and wrong (c. 3). So is the view that the numerical proportion of rulers to ruled makes the difference between these two types; in a Democracy the Many are also the poor, in an Oligarchy the Few are also the wealthy. In every state the distinction between rich and poor is the most fundamental of class-divisions. Still Oligarchy and Democracy are important types; and their variations arise from differences in the character of the rich and the poor by whom they are ruled.

Of Democracies there are four kinds. The worst, ex·

treme Democracy, is that in which all offices are open to all, and the will of the people overrides all law (c. 4). Of Oligarchies too there are four kinds; the worst is that in which offices are hereditary and the magistrates uncontrolled by law (c. 5). These variations arise under circumstances which may be briefly described (c. 6).

Of Aristocracy in the strict sense there is but one form, that in which the best men alone are citizens (c. 7).

Polity is a compromise between Democracy and Oligarchy, but inclines to the Democratic side. Many so-called Aristocracies are really Polities (c. 8). There are different ways of effecting the compromise which makes a Polity. The Laconian Constitution is an example of a successful compromise (c. 9).

Tyranny is of three kinds: (1) the barbarian despotism, and (2) the elective dictatorship have already been discussed; in both there is rule according to law over willing subjects. But in (3) the strict form of tyranny, there is the lawless rule of one man over unwilling subjects (c. 10).

cc. 11–13. *Of the Best State both in general and under special circumstances.*

For the average city-state the best constitution will be a mean between the rule of rich and poor; the middle-class will be supreme. No state will be well administered unless the middle-class holds sway. The middle-class is stronger in large than in small states. Hence in Greece it has rarely attained to power; especially as democracy and oligarchy were aided by the influence of the leading states (c. 11). No constitution can dispense with the support of the strongest class in the state. Hence Democracy and Oligarchy are the only constitutions possible in some states. But in these cases the legislator should conciliate the middle-class (c. 12). Whatever form of constitution be adopted there are expedients to be noted which may help in preserving it (c. 13).

cc. 14–16. *How to proceed in framing a Constitution.*

The legislator must pay attention to three subjects in particular; (*a*) The Deliberative Assembly which is different in each form of constitution (c. 14). (*b*) The Executive. Here he must know what offices are indispensable and which of them may be conveniently combined in the person of one magistrate; also whether the same offices should be supreme in every state; also which of the twelve or more methods of making appointments should be adopted in each case (c. 15). (*c*) The Courts of Law. Here he must consider the kinds of law-courts, their spheres of action, their methods of procedure (c. 16).

BOOK V (VIII).

cc. 1–4. *Of Revolutions, and their causes in general.*

Ordinary states are founded on erroneous ideas of justice, which lead to discontent and revolution. Of revolutions some are made to introduce a new Constitution, others to modify the old, others to put the working of the Constitution in new hands. Both Democracy and Oligarchy contain inherent flaws which lead to revolution, but Democracy is the more stable of the two types (c. 1).

We may distinguish between the frame of mind which fosters revolution, the objects for which it is started, and the provocative causes (c. 2). The latter deserve a more detailed account (c. 3). Trifles may be the occasion but are never

the true cause of a sedition. One common cause is the
aggrandizement of a particular class; another is a feud between rich and poor when they are evenly balanced and
there is no middle-class to mediate. As to the manner of
effecting a revolution : it may be carried through by force or
fraud (c. 4).

cc. 5–12. *Revolutions in particular States, and how
revolutions may be avoided.*

(*a*) In Democracies revolutions may arise from a persecu-
tion of the rich; or when a demagogue becomes a general, or
when politicians compete for the favour of the mob (c. 5).
(*b*) In Oligarchies the people may rebel against oppression ;
ambitious oligarchs may conspire, or appeal to the people,
or set up a tyrant. Oligarchies are seldom destroyed except
by the feuds of their own members; unless they employ
a mercenary captain, who may become a tyrant (c. 6). (*c*)
In Aristocracies and Polities the injustice of the ruling class
may lead to revolution, but less often in Polities. Aristocracies may also be ruined by an unprivileged class, or an
ambitious man of talent. Aristocracies tend to become
oligarchies. Also they are liable to gradual dissolution;
which is true of Polities as well (c. 7).

The best precautions against sedition are these : to avoid
illegality and frauds upon the unprivileged; to maintain good
feeling between rulers and ruled; to watch destructive agen-
cies; to alter property qualifications from time to time; to let
no individual or class become too powerful; not to let magistracies be a source of gain ; to beware of class-oppression (c. 8).
In all magistrates we should require loyalty, ability, and justice; we should not carry the principle of the constitution

to extremes; we should educate the citizens in the spirit of a constitution (c. 9).

(*d*) The causes which destroy and the means which preserve a Monarchy must be considered separately. Let us first distinguish between Tyranny and Kingship. Tyranny combines the vices of Democracy and Oligarchy. Kingship is exposed to the same defects as Aristocracy. But both these kinds of Monarchy are especially endangered by the insolence of their representatives and by the fear or contempt which they inspire in others. Tyranny is weak against both external and domestic foes; Kingship is strong against invasion, weak against sedition (c. 10). Moderation is the best preservative of Kingship. Tyranny may rely on the traditional expedients of demoralizing and dividing its subjects, or it may imitate Kingship by showing moderation in expenditure, and courtesy and temperance in social relations, by the wise use of ministers, by holding the balance evenly between the rich and poor (c. 11). But the Tyrannies of the past have been short-lived.

Plato's discussion of revolutions in the *Republic* is inadequate; e.g. he does not explain the results of a revolution against a tyranny, and could not do so on his theory; nor is he correct about the cause of revolution in an Oligarchy; nor does he distinguish between the different varieties of Oligarchy and Democracy (c. 12).

BOOK VI (VII).

cc. 1–8. *Concerning the proper organization of Democracies and Oligarchies.*

(A) Democracies differ *inter se* (1) according to the character of the citizen body, (2) according to the mode in which the

characteristic features of democracy are combined (c. 1).
Liberty is the first principle of democracy. The results of
liberty are that the numerical majority is supreme, and that
each man lives as he likes. From these characteristics we
may easily infer the other features of democracy (c. 2). In
oligarchies it is not the numerical majority, but the wealthier
men, who are supreme. Both these principles are unjust if
the supreme authority is to be absolute and above the law.
Both numbers and wealth should have their share of
influence. But it is hard to find the true principles of political
justice, and harder still to make men act upon them (c. 3).
Democracy has four species (cf. Bk. IV, c. 4). The best
is (1) an Agricultural Democracy, in which the magistrates
are elected by, and responsible to, the citizen body, while
each office has a property qualification proportionate to its
importance. These democracies should encourage agriculture
by legislation. The next best is (2) the Pastoral Democracy.
Next comes (3) the Commercial Democracy. Worst of all is
(4) the Extreme Democracy with manhood suffrage (c. 4).

It is harder to preserve than to found a Democracy. To
preserve it we must prevent the poor from plundering the
rich; we must not exhaust the public revenues by giving pay
for the performance of public duties; we must prevent the
growth of a pauper class (c. 5).

(B) The modes of founding Oligarchies call for little explanation. Careful organization is the best way of preserving
these governments (c. 6). Much depends on the military
arrangements; oligarchs must not make their subjects too
powerful an element in the army. Admission to the governing
body should be granted on easy conditions. Office should be
made a burden, not a source of profit (c. 7).

Both in oligarchies and democracies the right arrangement of offices is important. Some kinds of office are necessary in every state; others are peculiar to special types of state (c. 8).

BOOK VII (IV).

cc. 1–3. *The Summum Bonum for individuals and states.*

Before constructing the ideal state we must know what is the most desirable life for states and individuals. True happiness flows from the possession of wisdom and virtue, and not from the possession of external goods. But a virtuous life must be equipped with external goods as instruments. These laws hold good of both states and individuals (c. 1). But does the highest virtue consist in contemplation or in action? The states of the past have lived for action in the shape of war and conquest. But war cannot be regarded as a reasonable object for a state (c. 2). A virtuous life implies activity, but activity may be speculative as well as practical. Those are wrong who regard the life of a practical politician as degrading. But again they are wrong who treat political power as the highest good (c. 3).

cc. 4–12. *A picture of the Ideal State.*

We must begin by considering the population and the territory. The former should be as small as we can make it without sacrificing independence and the capacity for a moral life. The smaller the population the more manageable it will be (c. 4). The territory must be large enough to supply the citizens with the means of living liberally and temperately, with an abundance of leisure.

The city should be in a central position (c. 5). Communica·
tion with the sea is desirable for economic and military
reasons; but the moral effects of sea-trade are bad. If the
state has a marine, the port town should be at some distance
from the city (c. 6).

The character of the citizens should be a mean between that
of Asiatics and that of the northern races; intelligence and
high spirit should be harmoniously blended as they are in
some Greek races (c. 7). We must distinguish the members
of the state from those who are necessary as its servants,
but no part of it. There must be men who are able to
provide food, to practise the arts, to bear arms, to carry
on the work of exchange, to supervise the state religion,
to exercise political and judicial functions (c. 8). But of
these classes we should exclude from the citizen body (1) the
mechanics, (2) the traders, (3) the husbandmen. Warriors,
rulers, priests remain as eligible for citizenship. The same
persons should exercise these three professions, but at
different periods of life. Ownership of land should be
confined to them (c. 9). Such a distinction between a ruling
and a subject class, based on a difference of occupation, is
nothing new. It still exists in Egypt, and the custom
of common meals in Crete and Italy proves that it formerly
existed there. Most of the valuable rules of politics have
been discovered over and over again in the course of history.

In dealing with the land of the state we must distinguish
between public demesnes and private estates. Both kinds
of land should be tilled by slaves or barbarians of a servile
disposition (c. 10). The site of the city should be chosen
with regard (1) to public health, (2) to political convenience,
(3) to strategic requirements. The ground-plan of the city

should be regular enough for beauty, not so regular as to make defensive warfare difficult. Walls are a practical necessity (c. 11). It is well that the arrangement of the buildings in the city should be carefully thought out (c. 12).

cc. 13–17. *The Educational System of the Ideal State, its aim, and early stages.*

The nature and character of the citizens must be determined with reference to the kind of happiness which we desire them to pursue. Happiness was defined in the *Ethics* as the perfect exercise of virtue, the latter term being understood not in the conditional, but in the absolute sense. Now a man acquires virtue of this kind by the help of nature, habit, and reason (c. 13). Habit and reason are the fruits of education, which must therefore be discussed.

The citizens should be educated to obey when young and to rule when they are older. Rule is their ultimate and highest function. Since the good ruler is the same as the good man, our education must be so framed as to produce the good man. It should develope all man's powers and fit him for all the activities of life; but the highest powers and the highest activities must be the supreme care of education. An education which is purely military, like the Laconian, neglects this principle (c. 14). The virtues of peace (intellectual culture, temperance, justice) are the most necessary for states and individuals; war is nothing but a means towards securing peace. But education must follow the natural order of human development, beginning with the body, dealing next with the appetites, and training the intellect last of all (c. 15).

To produce a healthy physique the legislator must fix

the age of marriage, regulate the physical condition of the parents, provide for the exposure of infants, and settle the duration of marriage (c. 16). He must also prescribe a physical training for infants and young children. For their moral education the very young should be committed to overseers; these should select the tales which they are told, their associates, the pictures, plays, and statues which they see. From five to seven years of age should be the period of preparation for intellectual training (c. 17).

BOOK VIII (V).

cc. 1–7. *The Ideal Education continued. Its Music and Gymnastic.*

Education should be under state-control and the same for all the citizens (c. 1). It should comprise those useful studies which every one must master, but none which degrade the mind or body (c. 2). Reading, writing, and drawing have always been taught on the score of their utility; gymnastic as producing valour. Music is taught as a recreation, but it serves a higher purpose. The noble employment of leisure is the highest aim which a man can pursue; and music is valuable for this purpose. The same may be said of drawing, and other subjects of education have the same kind of value (c. 3).

Gymnastic is the first stage of education; but we must not develope the valour and physique of our children at the expense of the mind, as they do in Sparta. Until puberty, and for three years after, bodily exercise should be light (c. 4). Music, if it were a mere amusement, should not be taught to children; they would do better by listening to professionals. But music is a moral discipline and a rational enjoyment (c. 5). By learning music children become better critics and are given a suitable occupation. When of riper age they should abandon music; professional skill is not for them; nor should they be taught difficult instruments (c. 6). The various musical harmonies should be used for different purposes. Some inspire virtue, others valour, others enthusiasm. The ethical harmonies are those which children should learn. The others may be left to professionals. The Dorian harmony is the best for education. The Phrygian is bad; but the Lydian may be beneficial to children.

Cetera desunt.

THE POLITICS

BOOK I

EVERY state is a community of some kind, and every I. 1
Ed.
Bekker,
1252 a community is established with a view to some good; for mankind always act in order to obtain that which they think good. But, if all communities aim at some good, the state or political community, which is the highest of all, and which embraces all the rest, aims, and in a greater degree than any other, at the highest good.

Now there is an erroneous opinion [1] that a statesman, king,   2 householder, and master are the same, and that they differ, not in kind, but only in the number of their subjects. For example, the ruler over a few is called a master; over more, the manager of a household; over a still larger number, a statesman or king, as if there were no difference between a great household and a small state. The distinction which is made between the king and the statesman is as follows: When the government is personal, the ruler is a king; when, according to the principles of the political science, the citizens rule and are ruled in turn, then he is called a statesman.

But all this is a mistake; for governments differ in kind, as will be evident to any one who considers the matter according to the method [2] which has hitherto guided us. As in other departments of science, so in politics, the compound should always be resolved into the simple elements or least parts of the whole. We must therefore look at the

---

[1] Cp. Plato, Politicus, 258 E foll.   [2] Cp. c. 8. § 1.

I. 1 elements of which the state is composed, in order that we may see [1] in what they differ from one another, and whether any scientific distinction can be drawn between the different kinds of rule [1].

2   He who thus considers things in their first growth and origin, whether a state or anything else, will obtain the clearest view of them.   In the first place (1) there must be a union of those who cannot exist without each other; for example, of male and female, that the race may continue; and this is a union which is formed, not of deliberate purpose, but because, in common with other animals and with plants, mankind have a natural desire to leave behind them an image of themselves.   And (2) there must be a union of natural ruler and subject, that both may be preserved.   For he who can foresee with his mind is by nature intended to be lord and master, and he who can work with his body is a subject,

3 and by nature a slave; hence master and slave have the same
1252 b interest.   Nature, however, has distinguished between the female and the slave.   For she is not niggardly, like the smith who fashions the Delphian knife for many uses; she makes each thing for a single use, and every instrument is best made when intended for one and not for many uses.

4 But among barbarians no distinction is made between women and slaves, because there is no natural ruler among them: they are a community of slaves, male and female.   Wherefore the poets say,—

'It is meet that Hellenes should rule over barbarians [2];'

[1] Or, with Bernays, 'how the different kinds of rule differ from one another, and generally whether any scientific result can be attained about each one of them.'

[2] Eurip. Iphig. in Aulid. 1400.

as if they thought that the barbarian and the slave were I. 2
by nature one.

Out of these two relationships between man and woman, 5
master and slave, the family first arises, and Hesiod is right
when he says,—

'First house and wife and an ox for the plough[1],'

for the ox is the poor man's slave. The family is the association established by nature for the supply of men's every-day
wants, and the members of it are called by Charondas 'companions of the cupboard' [ὁμοσιπύους], and by Epimenides
the Cretan, '[2]companions of the manger[2]' [ὁμοκάπους].
But when several families are united, and the association
aims at something more than the supply of daily needs,
then comes into existence the village.   And the most natural 6
form of the village appears to be that of a colony from the
family, composed of the children and grandchildren, who are
said to be 'suckled with the same milk.'   And this is the
reason why Hellenic states were originally governed by
kings; because the Hellenes were under royal rule before
they came together, as the barbarians still are.   Every family
is ruled by the eldest, and therefore in the colonies of
the family the kingly form of government prevailed because
they were of the same blood.   As Homer says [of the 7
Cyclopes] :—

'Each one gives law to his children and to his wives[3].'

For they lived dispersedly, as was the manner in ancient

---

[1] Op. et Di. 405.

[2] Or, reading with the old translator (William of Moerbek) ὁμο-
κάπνους, 'companions of the hearth.'

[3] Od. ix. 114, quoted by Plato, Laws, iii. 680, and in N. Eth. x. 9. § 13.

I. 2 times. Wherefore men say that the Gods have a king, because they themselves either are or were in ancient times under the rule of a king. For they imagine, not only the forms of the Gods, but their ways of life to be like their own.

8   When several villages are united in a single community, perfect and large enough to be nearly or quite self-sufficing, the state comes into existence, originating in the bare needs of life, and continuing in existence for the sake of a good life. And therefore, if the earlier forms of society are natural, so is the state, for it is the end of them, and the [completed] nature is the end. For what each thing is when fully developed, we call its nature, whether we are speaking 9 of a man, a horse, or a family. Besides, the final cause and end of a thing is the best, and to be self-sufficing is the end 1253 a and the best.

Hence it is evident that the state is a creation of nature, and that man is by nature a political animal. And he who by nature and not by mere accident is without a state, is either above humanity, or below it; he is the

‘Tribeless, lawless, hearthless one,’

10 whom Homer[1] denounces—the outcast who is a lover of war; he may be compared to an unprotected piece in the game of draughts.

Now the reason why man is more of a political animal than bees or any other gregarious animals is evident. Nature, as we often say, makes nothing in vain[2], and man is the only animal whom she has endowed with the gift of 11 speech[3]. And whereas mere sound is but an indication

---

[1] Il. ix. 63.   [2] Cp. c. 8. § 12.   [3] Cp. vii. 13. § 12.

of pleasure or pain, and is therefore found in other animals **I. 2**
(for their nature attains to the perception of pleasure and
pain and the intimation of them to one another, and no
further), the power of speech is intended to set forth the
expedient and inexpedient, and likewise the just and the
unjust. And it is a characteristic of man that he alone **12**
has any sense of good and evil, of just and unjust, and the
association of living beings who have this sense makes a
family and a state.

Thus the state is by nature clearly prior to the family
and to the individual, since the whole is of necessity **13**
prior to the part; for example, if the whole body be
destroyed, there will be no foot or hand, except in an
equivocal sense, as we might speak of a stone hand; for
when destroyed the hand will be no better. But things are
defined by their working and power; and we ought not
to say that they are the same when they are no longer
the same, but only that they have the same name. The **14**
proof that the state is a creation of nature and prior to the
individual is that the individual, when isolated, is not self-
sufficing; and therefore he is like a part in relation to the
whole. But he who is unable to live in society, or who has
no need because he is sufficient for himself, must be either a
beast or a god: he is no part of a state. A social instinct is **15**
implanted in all men by nature, and yet he who first founded
the state was the greatest of benefactors. For man, when
perfected, is the best of animals, but, when separated from
law and justice, he is the worst of all; since armed injustice **16**
is the more dangerous, and he is equipped at birth with the
arms of intelligence and with moral qualities which he may
use for the worst ends. Wherefore, if he have not virtue, he

I. 2 is the most unholy and the most savage of animals, and the most
full of lust and gluttony.   But justice is the bond of men in
states, and the administration of justice, which is the determina-
tion of what is just [1], is the principle of order in political society.

3   Seeing then that the state is made up of households, before
speaking of the state we must speak of the [2] management
1253 b of the household [2].   The parts of the household are the
persons who compose it, and a complete household consists
of slaves and freemen.   Now we should begin by examining
everything in its least elements ; and the first and least parts
of a family are master and slave, husband and wife, father
and children.   We have therefore to consider what each
2 of these three relations is and ought to be :—I mean the
relation of master and servant, of husband and wife, and
thirdly of parent and child.   [I say γαμική and τεκνοποιητική,
there being no words for the two latter notions which ade-
3 quately represent them.]   And there is another element
of a household, the so-called art of money-making, which,
according to some, is identical with household management,
according to others, a principal part of it ; the nature of
this art will also have to be considered by us.

Let us first speak of master and slave, looking to the
needs of practical life and also seeking to attain some better
4 theory of their relation than exists at present.   For some are
of opinion that the rule of a master is a science, and that the
management of a household, and the mastership of slaves,
and the political and royal rule, as I was saying at the out-
set [3], are all the same.   Others affirm that the rule of a master

[1] Cp. N. Eth. v. 6. § 4.
[2] Reading with the MSS. οἰκονομίας.
[3] Plato in Pol. 258 ε foll., referred to already in c. 1. § 2.

over slaves is contrary to nature, and that the distinction **I. 3**
between slave and freeman exists by law only, and not
by nature; and being an interference with nature is therefore
unjust.

Property is a part of the household, and therefore the art **4**
of acquiring property is a part of the art of managing the
household; for no man can live well, or indeed live at all,
unless he be provided with necessaries. And as in the arts
which have a definite sphere the workers must have their own
proper instruments for the accomplishment of their work, so
it is in the management of a household. Now, instruments **2**
are of various sorts; some are living, others lifeless; in the
rudder, the pilot of a ship has a lifeless, in the look-out man,
a living instrument; for in the arts the servant is a kind
of instrument. Thus, too, a possession is an instrument
for maintaining life. And so, in the arrangement of the
family, a slave is a living possession, and property a number
of such instruments; and the servant is himself an instrument,
which takes precedence of all other instruments. For if **3**
every instrument could accomplish its own work, obeying or
anticipating the will of others, like the statues of Daedalus,
or the tripods of Hephaestus, which, says the poet [1],

‘ of their own accord entered the assembly of the Gods’;

if, in like manner, the shuttle would weave and the plectrum
touch the lyre without a hand to guide them, chief workmen
would not want servants, nor masters slaves. Here, how- **1254 a**
ever, another distinction must be drawn : the instruments **4**
commonly so called are instruments of production, whilst
a possession is an instrument of action. The shuttle, for

---

[1] Hom. Il. xviii. 376.

I. 4 example, is not only of use, but something else is made by it, whereas of a garment or of a bed there is only the use. Further, as production and action are different in kind, and both require instruments, the instruments which they 5 employ must likewise differ in kind. But life is action and not production, and therefore the slave is the minister of action [for he ministers to his master's life]. Again, a possession is spoken of as a part is spoken of; for the part is not only a part of something else, but wholly belongs to it; and this is also true of a possession. The master is only the master of the slave; he does not belong to him, whereas the slave is not only the slave of his master, 6 but wholly belongs to him. Hence we see what is the nature and office of a slave; he who is by nature not his own but another's and yet a man, is by nature a slave; and he may be said to belong to another who, being a human being, is also a possession. And a possession may be defined as an instrument of action, separable from the possessor.

5   But is there any one thus intended by nature to be a slave, and for whom such a condition is expedient and right, or rather is not all slavery a violation of nature?

There is no difficulty in answering this question, on 2 grounds both of reason and of fact. For that some should rule and others be ruled is a thing, not only necessary, but expedient; from the hour of their birth, some are marked out for subjection, others for rule.

And whereas there are many kinds both of rulers and subjects, that rule is the better which is exercised over better subjects—for example, to rule over men is better than to rule over wild beasts. The work is better which is executed

by better workmen; and where one man rules and another is I. 5
ruled, they may be said to have a work. In all things
which form a composite whole and which are made up of
parts, whether continuous or discrete, a distinction between
the ruling and the subject element comes to light. Such a 4
duality exists in living creatures, but not in them only;
it originates in the constitution of the universe; even in
things which have no life, there is a ruling principle, as
[1] in musical harmony [1]. But we are wandering from the
subject. We will, therefore, restrict ourselves to the living
creature which, in the first place, consists of soul and body:
and of these two, the one is by nature the ruler, and the
other the subject. But then we must look for the intentions 5
of nature in things which retain their nature, and not in
things which are corrupted. And therefore we must study
the man who is in the most perfect state both of body and
soul, for in him we shall see the true relation of the two;
although in bad or corrupted natures the body will often 1254 b
appear to rule over the soul, because they are in an evil
and unnatural condition. First then we may observe in living 6
creatures both a despotical and a constitutional rule; for the
soul rules the body with a despotical rule, whereas the intellect rules the appetites with a constitutional and royal rule.
And it is clear that the rule of the soul over the body, and
of the mind and the rational element over the passionate is
natural and expedient; whereas the equality of the two or the
rule of the inferior is always hurtful. The same holds good 7
of animals as well as of men; for tame animals have a better
nature than wild, and all tame animals are better off when
they are ruled by man; for then they are preserved. Again,

---

[1] Or, ' of harmony [in music].'

I. 5 the male is by nature superior, and the female inferior; and the one rules, and the other is ruled; this principle, of 8 necessity, extends to all mankind. Where then there is such a difference as that between soul and body, or between men and animals (as in the case of those whose business is to use their body, and who can do nothing better), the lower sort are by nature slaves, and it is better for them as for all 9 inferiors that they should be under the rule of a master. For he who can be, and therefore is another's, and he who participates in reason enough to apprehend, but not to have, reason, is a slave by nature. Whereas the lower animals cannot even apprehend reason; they obey their instincts. And indeed the use made of slaves and of tame animals is not very different; for both with their bodies minister to 10 the needs of life. Nature would like to distinguish between the bodies of freemen and slaves, making the one strong for servile labour, the other upright, and although useless for such services, useful for political life in the arts both of war and peace. But this does not hold universally: for some slaves have the souls and others have the bodies of freemen. And doubtless if men differed from one another in the mere forms of their bodies as much as the statues of the Gods do from men, all would acknowledge that the inferior class 11 should be slaves of the superior. And if there is a difference in the body, how much more in the soul! But the beauty of the 1255 a body is seen, whereas the beauty of the soul is not seen. It is clear, then, that some men are by nature free, and others slaves, and that for these latter slavery is both expedient and right.

6 But that those who take the opposite view have in a certain way right on their side, may be easily seen. For the words slavery and slave are used in two senses. There is a slave

or slavery by law as well as by nature. The law of which **I. 6**
I speak is a sort of convention, according to which whatever
is taken in war is supposed to belong to the victors. But **2**
this right many jurists impeach, as they would an orator who
brought forward an unconstitutional measure : they detest the
notion that, because one man has the power of doing violence
and is superior in brute strength, another shall be his slave
and subject. Even among philosophers there is a difference
of opinion. The origin of the dispute, and the reason why **3**
the arguments cross, is as follows : Virtue, when furnished
with means, may be deemed to have the greatest power of
doing violence : and as superior power is only found where
there is superior excellence of some kind, power is thought to
imply virtue. But does it likewise imply justice ?—that is the
question. And, in order to make a distinction between them, **4**
some assert that justice is benevolence : to which others reply
that justice is nothing more than the rule of a superior. If
the two views are regarded as antagonistic and exclusive [i. e.
if the notion that justice is benevolence excludes the idea of
a just rule of a superior], the alternative [viz. that no one
should rule over others [1]] has no force or plausibility, because
it implies that not even the superior in virtue ought to rule, or
be master. Some, clinging, as they think, to a principle of **5**
justice (for law and custom are a sort of justice), assume that
slavery in war is justified by law, but they are not consistent.
For what if the cause of the war be unjust ? No one would
ever say that he is a slave who is unworthy to be a slave.
Were this the case, men of the highest rank would be slaves
and the children of slaves if they or their parents chance to
have been taken captive and sold. Wherefore Hellenes do **6**

[1] Cp. § 2.

I. 6 not like to call themselves slaves, but confine the term to barbarians. Yet, in using this language, they really mean the natural slave of whom we spoke at first; for it must be admitted that some are slaves everywhere, others nowhere.

7 The same principle applies to nobility. Hellenes regard themselves as noble everywhere, and not only in their own country, but they deem the barbarians noble only when at home, thereby implying that there are two sorts of nobility and freedom, the one absolute, the other relative. The Helen of Theodectes says :—

'Who would presume to call me servant who am on both sides sprung from the stem of the Gods?'

8 What does this mean but that they distinguish freedom and slavery, noble and humble birth, by the two principles of **1255 b** good and evil? They think that as men and animals beget men and animals, so from good men a good man springs. But this is what nature, though she may intend it, often fails to accomplish.

9 We see then that there is some foundation for this difference of opinion, and that some actual slaves and freemen are not so by nature, and also that there is in some cases a marked distinction between the two classes, rendering it expedient and right for the one to be slaves and the others to be masters: the one practising obedience, the others exercising the autho-**10** rity which nature intended them to have. The abuse of this authority is injurious to both; for the interests of part and whole[1], of body and soul, are the same, and the slave is a part of the master, a living but separated part of his bodily frame. Where the relation between them is natural they are friends

[1] Cp. c. 4. § 5.

and have a common interest, but where it rests merely on law **I. 6**
and force the reverse is true.

The previous remarks are quite enough to show that the **7**
rule of a master is not a constitutional rule, and therefore that
all the different kinds of rule are not, as some affirm, the
same with each other [1]. For there is one rule exercised over
subjects who are by nature free, another over subjects who
are by nature slaves. The rule of a household is a monarchy,
for every house is under one head : whereas constitutional rule
is a government of freemen and equals. The master is not **2**
called a master because he has science, but because he is of
a certain character, and the same remark applies to the slave
and the freeman. Still there may be a science for the master
and a science for the slave. The science of the slave would
be such as the man of Syracuse taught, who made money by
instructing slaves in their ordinary duties. And such a know- **3**
ledge may be carried further, so as to include cookery and
similar menial arts. For some duties are of the more necessary, others of the more honourable sort; as the proverb says,
'slave before slave, master before master.' But all such **4**
branches of knowledge are servile. There is likewise a science
of the master, which teaches the use of slaves ; for the master
as such is concerned, not with the acquisition, but with the use
of them. Yet this so-called science is not anything great or
wonderful; for the master need only know how to order that
which the slave must know how to execute. Hence those **5**
who are in a position which places them above toil, have
stewards who attend to their households while they occupy
themselves with philosophy or with politics. But the art of
acquiring slaves, I mean of justly acquiring them, differs both

---

[1] Plato Pol. 258 E foll., referred to already in c. I. § 2.

I. 7 from the art of the master and the art of the slave, being a species of hunting or war[1]. Enough of the distinction between master and slave.

1256 a
8 Let us now enquire into property generally, and into the art of money-making, in accordance with our usual method [of resolving a whole into its parts[2]], for a slave has been shown to be a part of property. The first question is whether the art of money-making is the same with the art of managing a household or a part of it, or instrumental to it; and if the last, whether in the way that the art of making shuttles is instrumental to the art of weaving, or in the way that the casting of bronze is instrumental to the art of the statuary, for they are not instrumental in the same way, but the one pro-
2 vides tools and the other material; and by material I mean the substratum out of which any work is made; thus wool is the material of the weaver, bronze of the statuary. Now it is easy to see that the art of household management is not identical with the art of money-making, for the one uses the material which the other provides. And the art which uses household stores can be no other than the art of household management. There is, however, a doubt whether the art of money-making is a part of household management or a distinct
3 art. [They appear to be connected]; for the money-maker has to consider whence money and property can be procured, but there are many sorts of property and wealth :—there is husbandry and the care and provision of food in general; are
4 these parts of the money-making art or distinct arts ? Again, there are many sorts of food, and therefore there are many kinds of lives both of animals and men; they must all have food, and the differences in their food have made differences

---

[1] Cp. vii. 14. § 21.   [2] Cp. c. 1. § 3.

in their ways of life. For of beasts, some are gregarious, I. 8
others are solitary; they live in the way which is best adapted 5
to sustain them, accordingly as they are carnivorous or herbivorous or omnivorous: and their habits are determined for
them by nature in such a manner that they may obtain with
greater facility the food of their choice. But, as different
individuals have different tastes, the same things are not
naturally pleasant to all of them; and therefore the lives of
carnivorous or herbivorous animals further differ among themselves. In the lives of men too there is a great difference. 6
The laziest are shepherds, who lead an idle life, and get
their subsistence without trouble from tame animals; their
flocks having to wander from place to place in search of pas-
ture, they are compelled to follow them, cultivating a sort of
living farm. Others support themselves by hunting, which is 7
of different kinds. Some, for example, are pirates, others,
who dwell near lakes or marshes or rivers or a sea in which
there are fish, are fishermen, and others live by the pursuit of
birds or wild beasts. The greater number obtain a living from
the fruits of the soil. Such are the modes of subsistence 8
which prevail among those [1] whose industry is employed
immediately upon the products of nature[1], and whose food is
not acquired by exchange and retail trade—there is the shep- 1256 b
herd, the husbandman, the pirate, the fisherman, the hunter.
Some gain a comfortable maintenance out of two employments, eking out the deficiencies of one of them by another:
thus the life of a shepherd may be combined with that of
a brigand, the life of a farmer with that of a hunter. Other 9
modes of life are similarly combined in any way which the
needs of men may require. Property, in the sense of a bare

[1] Or, 'whose labour is personal.'

T. 8 livelihood, seems to be given by nature herself to all, both
10 when they are first born, and when they are grown up.   For
some animals bring forth, together with their offspring, so
much food as will last until they are able to supply themselves;
of this the vermiparous or oviparous animals are an instance;
and the viviparous animals have up to a certain time a supply
of food for their young in themselves, which is called milk.
11 In like manner we may infer that, after the birth of animals,
plants exist for their sake, and that the other animals exist
for the sake of man, the tame for use and food, the wild, if
not all, at least the greater part of them, for food, and for the
12 provision of clothing and various instruments.   Now if nature
makes nothing incomplete, and nothing in vain, the inference
must be that she has made all animals and plants for the sake
of man.   And so, in one point of view, the art of war is
a natural art of acquisition, for it includes hunting, an art
which we ought to practise against wild beasts, and against
men who, though intended by nature to be governed, will not
submit; for war of such a kind is naturally just[1].

13   Of the art of acquisition then there is one kind [2] which is
natural and is a part of the management of a household[2].
Either we must suppose the necessaries of life to exist previously, or the art of household management must provide
a store of them for the common use of the family or state.
14 They are the elements of true wealth; for the amount of
property which is needed for a good life is not unlimited,
although Solon in one of his poems says that,

'No bound to riches has been fixed for man[3].'

---

[1] Cp. c. 7. § 5, and vii. 14. § 21.
[2] Or, with Bernays, 'which by nature is a part of the management
of a household.'   [3] Bergk, Poet. Lyr. Solon, 13. v. 71.

But there is a boundary fixed, just as there is in the arts; for I. 8 the instruments of any art are never unlimited, either in 15 number or size, and wealth may be defined as a number of instruments to be used in a household or in a state. And so we see that there is a natural art of acquisition which is prac- tised by managers of households and by statesmen, and what is the reason of this.

There is another variety of the art of acquisition which is 9 commonly and rightly called the art of making money, and 1257 a has in fact suggested the notion that wealth and property have no limit. Being nearly connected with the preceding, it is often identified with it. But though they are not very different, neither are they the same. The kind already described is given by nature, the other is gained by experience and art.

Let us begin our discussion of the question with the fol- 2 lowing considerations :—

Of everything which we possess there are two uses: both belong to the thing as such, but not in the same manner, for one is the proper, and the other the improper or secondary use of it. For example, a shoe is used for wear, and is used for exchange; both are uses of the shoe. He who gives 3 a shoe in exchange for money or food to him who wants one, does indeed use the shoe as a shoe, but this is not its proper or primary purpose, for a shoe is not made to be an object of barter. The same may be said of all possessions, for the art of exchange extends to all of them, and it 4 arises at first in a natural manner from the circumstance that some have too little, others too much. Hence we may infer that retail trade is not a natural part of the art of money- making; had it been so, men would have ceased to exchange when they had enough. And in the first community, which 5

I. 9 is the family, this art is obviously of no use, but only begins
to be useful when the society increases. For the members
of the family originally had all things in common; in a more
divided state of society they [1] still shared in many things, but
they were different things [1] which they had to give in exchange for what they wanted, a kind of barter which is still
6 practised among barbarous nations who exchange with one
another the necessaries of life and nothing more; giving and
receiving wine, for example, in exchange for corn and the
like. This sort of barter is not part of the money-making
art and is not contrary to nature, but is needed for the satis-
7 faction of men's natural wants. The other or more complex
form of exchange grew out of the simpler. When the inhabitants of one country became more dependent on those of
another, and they imported what they needed, and exported
8 the surplus, money necessarily came into use. For the various
necessaries of life are not easily carried about, and hence men
agreed to employ in their dealings with each other something
which was intrinsically useful and easily applicable to the
purposes of life, for example, iron, silver, and the like. Of
this the value was at first measured by size and weight, but in
process of time they put a stamp upon it, to save the trouble
of weighing and to mark the value.

1257 b   When the use of coin had once been discovered, out of the
9 barter of necessary articles arose the other art of money-
making, namely, retail trade; which was at first probably
a simple matter, but became more complicated as soon as men
learned by experience whence and by what exchanges the
10 greatest profit might be made. Originating in the use of coin,
the art of money-making is generally thought to be chiefly

[1] Or, more simply, 'shared in many more things.'

concerned with it, and to be the art which produces wealth **I. 9**
and money; having to consider how they may be accumulated.
Indeed, wealth is assumed by many to be only a quantity of
coin, because the art of money-making and retail trade are
concerned with coin. Others maintain that coined money is 11
a mere sham, a thing not natural, but conventional only,
which would have no value or use for any of the purposes of
daily life if another commodity were substituted by the users.
And, indeed, he who is rich in coin may often be in want of
necessary food. But how can that be wealth of which a man
may have a great abundance and yet perish with hunger, like
Midas in the fable, whose insatiable prayer turned everything
that was set before him into gold?

Men seek after a better notion of wealth and of the art of 12
making money than the mere acquisition of coin, and they
are right. For natural wealth and the natural art of money-
making are a different thing; in their true form they are part
of the management of a household; whereas retail trade is
the art of producing wealth, not in every way, but by
exchange. And it seems to be concerned with coin; for
coin is the starting-point and the goal of exchange. And 13
there is no bound to the wealth which springs from this art
of money-making[1]. As in the art of medicine there is no
limit to the pursuit of health, and as in the other arts there is
no limit to the pursuit of their several ends, for they aim
at accomplishing their ends to the uttermost; (but of the
means there is a limit, for the end is always the limit), so,
too, in this art of money-making there is no limit of the end,
which is wealth of the spurious kind, and the acquisition of
money. But the art of household management has a limit; 14

[1] Cp. c. 8. § 14.

I. 9 the unlimited acquisition of money is not its business. And, therefore, in one point of view, all wealth must have a limit; nevertheless, as a matter of fact, we find the opposite to be the case; for all money-makers increase their hoard of coin without limit. The source of the confusion is the near

15 connexion between the two kinds of money-making; in either, the instrument [i. e. wealth] is the same, although the use is different, and so they pass into one another; for each is a use of the same property [1], but with a difference: accumulation is the end in the one case, but there is a further end in the other. Hence some persons are led to believe that making money is the object of household management, and the whole idea of their lives is that they ought either to increase their money

16 without limit, or at any rate not to lose it. The origin of

1258 a this disposition in men is that they are intent upon living only, and not upon living well; and, as their desires are unlimited, they also desire that the means of gratifying them should be without limit. Even those who aim at a good life seek the means of obtaining bodily pleasures; and, since the enjoyment of these appears to depend on property, they are absorbed in making money: and so there arises the second species of

17 money-making. For, as their enjoyment is in excess, they seek an art which produces the excess of enjoyment; and, if they are not able to supply their pleasures by the art of money-making, they try other arts, using in turn every faculty in a manner contrary to nature. The quality of courage, for example, is not intended to make money, but to inspire confidence; neither is this the aim of the general's or of the physician's art; but the one aims at victory and the other at

18 health. Nevertheless, some men turn every quality or art

[1] Reading κτήσεως χρῆσις.

into a means of making money; this they conceive to be I. 9
the end, and to the promotion of the end all things must
contribute.

Thus, then, we have considered the art of money-making,
which is unnecessary, and why men want it; and also the
necessary art of money-making, which we have seen to be
different from the other, and to be a natural part of the art of
managing a household, concerned with the provision of food,
not, however, like the former kind, unlimited, but having
a limit.

And we have found the answer to our original question [1], 10
Whether the art of money-making is the business of the
manager of a household and of the statesman or not their
business?—viz. that it is an art which is presupposed by them.
For political science does not make men, but takes them from
nature and uses them; and nature provides them with food
from the element of earth, air, or sea.   At this stage begins
the duty of the manager of a household, who has to order the
things which nature supplies;—he may be compared to the 2
weaver who has not to make but to use wool, and to know
what sort of wool is good and serviceable or bad and un-
serviceable.   Were this otherwise, it would be difficult to see
why the art of money-making is a part of the management
of a household and the art of medicine not; for surely the
members of a household must have health just as they must
have life or any other necessary.   And as from one point 3
of view the master of the house and the ruler of the state
have to consider about health, from another point of view not
they but the physician; so in one way the art of household
management, in another way the subordinate art, has to

[1] Cp. c. 8. § I.

I. 10 consider about money. But, strictly speaking, as I have
already said, the means of life must be provided beforehand
by nature; for the business of nature is to furnish food to
that which is born, and the food of the offspring always
4 remains over in the parent[1]. Wherefore the art of making
money out of fruits and animals is always natural.

Of the two sorts of money-making one, as I have just
said, is a part of household management, the other is retail
trade: the former necessary and honourable, the latter a kind
1258 b of exchange which is justly censured; for it is unnatural,
and a mode by which men gain from one another. The most
hated sort, and with the greatest reason, is usury, which
makes a gain out of money itself, and not from the natural use
5 of it. For money was intended to be used in exchange, but
not to increase at interest. And this term usury [τόκος],
which means the birth of money from money, is applied
to the breeding of money because the offspring resembles the
parent. Wherefore of all modes of making money this is
the most unnatural.

11 Enough has been said about the theory of money-making;
we will now proceed to the practical part. [2] The discussion
of such matters is not unworthy of philosophy, but to be
engaged in them practically is illiberal and irksome[2]. The
useful parts of money-making are, first, the knowledge of
live-stock,—which are most profitable, and where, and
how,—as, for example, what sort of horses or sheep or
oxen or any other animals are most likely to give a return.
2 A man ought to know which of these pay better than others,

---

[1] Cp. c. 8. § 10.

[2] Or, ‘We are free to speculate about them, but in practice we are
limited by circumstances.’ (Bernays.)

and which pay best in particular places, for some do better in I. 11
one place and some in another.   Secondly, husbandry, which
may be either tillage or planting, and the keeping of bees and
of fish, or fowl, or of any animals which may be useful to
man.   These are the divisions of the true or proper art of 3
money-making and come first.   Of the other, which consists
in exchange, the first and most important division is commerce
(of which there are three kinds—commerce by sea, commerce
by land, selling in shops—these again differing as they are
safer or more profitable), the second is usury, the third,
service for hire—of this, one kind is employed in the 4
mechanical arts, the other in unskilled and bodily labour.
There is still a third sort of money-making intermediate
between this and the first or natural mode which is partly
natural, but is also concerned with exchange of the fruits and
other products of the earth.   Some of these latter, although
they bear no fruit, are nevertheless profitable ; for example,
wood and minerals.   The art of mining, by which minerals 5
are obtained, has many branches, for there are various kinds
of things dug out of the earth.   Of the several divisions of
money-making I now speak generally; a minute consideration of them might be useful in practice, but it would be
tiresome to dwell upon them at greater length now.

Those occupations are most truly arts in which there is 6
the least element of chance ; they are the meanest in which
the body is most deteriorated, the most servile in which there
is the greatest use of the body, and the illiberal in which
there is the least need of excellence.

Works have been written upon these subjects by various 7
persons; for example, by Chares the Parian, and Apollodorus
the Lemnian, who have treated of Tillage and Planting,

I. 11 while others have treated of other branches; any one who
1259 a cares for such matters may refer to their writings. It
would be well also to collect the scattered stories of the ways
in which individuals have succeeded in amassing a fortune;
8 for all this is useful to persons who value the art of making
money. There is the anecdote of Thales the Milesian and
his financial device, which involves a principle of universal
application, but is attributed to him on account of his reputa-
9 tion for wisdom. He was reproached for his poverty,
which was supposed to show that philosophy was of no use.
According to the story, he knew by his skill in the stars
while it was yet winter that there would be a great harvest of
olives in the coming year; so, having a little capital, he gave
earnest-money for the use of all the olive-presses in Chios and
Miletus, which he hired at a low price because no one bid
against him. When the harvest-time came, and many wanted
them all at once and of a sudden, he let them out at any rate
which he pleased, and made a quantity of money. Thus he
showed the world that philosophers can easily be rich if
10 they like, but that their ambition is of another sort. He is
supposed to have given a striking proof of his wisdom, but, as
I was saying, his device for getting money is of universal
application, and is nothing but the creation of a monopoly.
It is an art often practised by cities when they are in want of
money; they make a monopoly of provisions.
11   There was a man of Sicily, who, having money deposited
with him, bought up all the iron from the iron mines; afterwards, when the merchants from their various markets came
to buy, he was the only seller, and without much increasing
12 the price he gained 200 per cent. Which when Dionysius
heard, he told him that he might take away his money, but

that he must not remain at Syracuse, for he thought that the **I. 11**
man had discovered a way of making money which was
injurious to his own interests. He had the same idea[1] as
Thales; they both contrived to create a monopoly for themselves. And statesmen ought to know these things; for a **13**
state is often as much in want of money and of such devices
for obtaining it as a household, or even more so; hence some
public men devote themselves entirely to finance.

Of household management we have seen[2] that there are **12**
three parts—one is the rule of a master over slaves, which
has been discussed already[3], another of a father, and the
third of a husband. A husband and father rules over wife
and children, both free, but the rule differs, the rule over
his children being a royal, over his wife a constitutional rule. **1259 b**
For although there may be exceptions to the order of nature,
the male is by nature fitter for command than the female, just
as the elder and full-grown is superior to the younger and
more immature. But in most constitutional states the citizens **2**
rule and are ruled by turns, for the idea of a constitutional
state implies that the natures of the citizens are equal, and
do not differ at all[4]. Nevertheless, when one rules and the
other is ruled we endeavour to create a difference of outward
forms and modes of address and titles of respect, which may
be illustrated by the saying of Amasis about his foot-pan[5].
The relation of the male to the female is of this kind, but **3**
there the inequality is permanent. The rule of a father over
his children is royal, for he receives both love and the respect
due to age, exercising a kind of royal power. And therefore

---

[1] Reading εὕρημα with Bernays.　　　　[2] Cp. c. 3. § 1.
[3] Cp. c. 3–7.　　　　[4] Cp. ii. 2. § 6; iii. 17. § 4.
[5] Herod. ii. 172, and note on this passage.

I. 12 Homer has appropriately called Zeus 'father of Gods and men,' because he is the king of them all. For a king is the natural superior of his subjects, but he should be of the same kin or kind with them, and such is the relation of elder and younger, of father and son.

13   Thus it is clear that household management attends more to men than to the acquisition of inanimate things, and to human excellence more than to the excellence of property which we call wealth, and to the virtue of freemen more than 2 to the virtue of slaves. A question may indeed be raised, whether there is any excellence at all in a slave beyond merely instrumental and ministerial qualities—whether he can have the virtues of temperance, courage, justice, and the like; or whether slaves possess only bodily and ministerial qualities. And, whichever way we answer the question, a difficulty 3 arises; for, if they have virtue, in what will they differ from freemen? On the other hand, since they are men and share in reason, it seems absurd to say that they have no virtue. A similar question may be raised about women and children, whether they too have virtues: ought a woman to be temperate and brave and just, and is a child to be called temperate, 4 and intemperate, or not? So in general we may ask about the natural ruler, and the natural subject, whether they have the same or different virtues. For a noble nature is equally required in both, but if so, why should one of them always rule, and the other always be ruled? Nor can we say that this is a question of degree, for the difference between ruler and subject is a difference of kind, and therefore not of degree; yet how strange is the supposition that the one 5 ought, and that the other ought not, to have virtue! For if the ruler is intemperate and unjust, how can he rule well?

if the subject, how can he obey well? If he be licentious **I. 13**
and cowardly, he will certainly not do his duty. It is evident, ^{1260 a}
therefore, that both of them must have a share of virtue, but
varying according to their various natures. And this is at 6
once indicated by the soul, in which one part naturally rules,
and the other is subject, and the virtue of the ruler we maintain to be different from that of the subject;—the one being
the virtue of the rational, and the other of the irrational part.
Now, it is obvious that the same principle applies generally,
and therefore almost all things rule and are ruled according to
nature. But the kind of rule differs;—the freeman rules over 7
the slave after another manner from that in which the male
rules over the female, or the man over the child; although
the parts of the soul are present in all of them, they are present in different degrees. For the slave has no deliberative
faculty at all; the woman has, but it is [1] without authority[1],
and the child has, but it is immature. So it must necessarily 8
be with the moral virtues also; all may be supposed to partake
of them, but only in such manner and degree as is required by
each for the fulfilment of his duty. Hence the ruler ought
to have moral virtue in perfection, for his duty is entirely
that of a master artificer, and the master artificer is reason;
the subjects, on the other hand, require only that measure of
virtue which is proper to each of them. Clearly, then, moral 9
virtue belongs to all of them; but the temperance of a man
and of a woman, or the courage and justice of a man and of
a woman, are not, as Socrates maintained[2], the same; the
courage of a man is shown in commanding, of a woman in
obeying. And this holds of all other virtues, as will be more 10
clearly seen if we look at them in detail, for those who say

[1] Or, with Bernays, ' inconclusive.'   [2] Plato Meno, 71-73.

I. 13 generally that virtue consists in a good disposition of the
soul, or in doing rightly, or the like, only deceive themselves.
Far better than such definitions is their mode of speaking,
11 who, like Georgias[1], enumerate the virtues.   All classes
must be deemed to have their special attributes; as the poet
says of women,

'Silence is a woman's glory[2],'

but this is not equally the glory of man.   The child is imperfect, and therefore obviously his virtue is not relative to him-
12 self alone, but to the perfect man and to his teacher[3], and in
like manner the virtue of the slave is relative to a master.
Now we determined that a slave is useful for the wants of
life, and therefore he will obviously require only so much
virtue as will prevent him from failing in his duty through
cowardice and intemperance.   Some one will ask whether, if
what we are saying is true, virtue will not be required also in
the artisans, for they often fail in their work through miscon-
13 duct.   But is there not a great difference in the two cases?
For the slave shares in his master's life; the artisan is less
closely connected with him, and only attains excellence in
proportion as he becomes a slave, [i. e. is under the direction
of a master].   The meaner sort of mechanic has a special
1260 b and separate slavery; and whereas the slave exists by nature,
14 not so the shoemaker or other artisan.   It is manifest, then,
that the master ought to be the source of excellence in the
slave; but not merely because he possesses the art which trains
him in his duties[4].   Wherefore they are mistaken who forbid
us to converse with slaves and say that we should employ

[1] Plato Meno, 71–73.   [2] Soph. Aj. 293.
[3] 'His father who guides him' (Bernays).   [4] Cp. c. 7. § 4.

command only [1], for slaves stand even more in need of admoni- I. 13
tion than children.

The relations of husband and wife, parent and child, their 15
several virtues, what in their intercourse with one another is
good, and what is evil, and how we may pursue the good and
escape the evil, will have to be discussed when we speak of
the different forms of government. For, inasmuch as every
family is a part of a state, and these relationships are the
parts of a family, the virtue of the part must have regard to
the virtue of the whole. And therefore women and children
must be trained by education with an eye to the state [2], if the
virtues of either of them are supposed to make any difference
in the virtues of the state. And they must make a difference : 16
for the children grow up to be citizens, and half the free
persons in a state are women [3].

Of these matters, enough has been said ; of what remains, 14
let us speak at another time. Regarding, then, our present
enquiry as complete, we will make a new beginning. And,
first, let us examine the various theories of a perfect state.

---

[1] Plato Laws, vi. 777.   [2] Cp. v. 9. §§ 11–15 ; viii. 1. § 1.
[3] Plato Laws, vi. 781 B.

BOOK II

II. 1 OUR purpose is to consider what form of political community is best of all for those who are most able to realize their ideal of life. We must therefore examine not only this but other constitutions, both such as actually exist in well-governed states, and any theoretical forms which are held in esteem ; that what is good and useful may be brought to light. And let no one suppose that in seeking for something beyond them [1] we at all want to philosophize at the expense of truth [1]; we only undertake this enquiry because all the constitutions with which we are acquainted are faulty.

2 We will begin with the natural beginning of the subject. Three alternatives are conceivable : The members of a state must either have (1) all things or (2) nothing in common, or (3) some things in common and some not. That they should have nothing in common is clearly impossible, for the state is a community, and must at any rate have a common place— 1261 a one city will be in one place, and the citizens are those who **3** share in that one city. But should a well-ordered state have all things, as far as may be, in common, or some only and not others ? For the citizens might conceivably have wives and children and property in common, as Socrates proposes in the Republic of Plato [2]. Which is better, our present condition, or the proposed new order of society ?

---

[1] Or, as Bernays, taking πάντως with σοφίζεσθαι βουλομένων, ' we are anxious to make a sophistical display at any cost.'

[2] Rep. v. 457 c.

There are many difficulties in the community of women. II. 2
The principle on which Socrates rests the necessity of such
an institution does not appear to be established by his arguments; and then again as a means to the end which he ascribes
to the state, taken literally, it is impossible, and how we are to
limit and qualify it is nowhere precisely stated.   I am speak- 2
ing of the premiss from which the argument of Socrates proceeds, ' that the greater the unity of the state the better.'   Is
it not obvious that a state may at length attain such a degree
of unity as to be no longer a state?—since the nature of a
state is to be a plurality, and in tending to greater unity, from
being a state, it becomes a family, and from being a family,
an individual; for the family may be said to be more one
than the state, and the individual than the family.   So that
we ought not to attain this greatest unity even if we could, for
it would be the destruction of the state.   Again, a state is 3
not made up only of so many men, but of different kinds of
men; for similars do not constitute a state.   It is not like
a military alliance, of which the usefulness depends upon
its quantity even where there is no difference in quality.
For in that mutual protection is the end aimed at; and the
question is the same as about the scales of a balance: which
is the heavier?

In like manner, a state differs from a nation, whenever in
a nation the people are not dispersed in villages, but are in
the condition of the Arcadians; in a state the elements out of
which the unity is to be formed differ in kind.   Wherefore 4
the principle of reciprocity [1], as I have already remarked in
the Ethics [2], is the salvation of states.   And among freemen
and equals this is a principle which must be maintained, for

[1] Or, ' reciprocal proportion.'   [2] N. Eth. v. 8. § 6.

II. 2 they cannot all rule together, but must change at the end of
    a year or some other period of time or in some order of suc-
  5 cession.   The result is that upon this plan they all govern;
    [but the manner of government is] just as if shoemakers and
    carpenters were to exchange their occupations, and the same
    persons did not always continue shoemakers and carpenters.
  6 And it is clearly better that, as in business, so also in politics
    there should be continuance of the same persons where this
1261 b is possible.   But where this is not possible by reason of the
    natural equality of the citizens, and it would be unjust that
    any one should be excluded from the government (whether
    to govern be a good thing or a bad [1]), then it is better,
    instead of all holding power, to adopt a principle of rotation,
    equals giving place to equals, as the original rulers gave place
  7 to them [2].   Thus the one party rule and the others are ruled
    in turn, as if they were no longer the same persons.   In like
    manner there is a variety in the offices held by them.   Hence
    it is evident that a city is not by nature one in that sense
    which some persons affirm; and that what is said to be the
    greatest good of cities is in reality their destruction; but
    surely the good of things must be that which preserves them [3].
  8 Again, in another point of view, this extreme unification
    of the state is clearly not good; for a family is more self-
    sufficing than an individual, and a city than a family, and
    a city only comes into being when the community is large
    enough to be self-sufficing.   If then self-sufficiency is to be
    desired, the lesser degree of unity is more desirable than the
    greater.
  3   But, even supposing that it were best for the community to

---

[1] Cp. Pl. Rep. i. 345–6.   [2] Cp. i. 12. § 2; iii. 17. § 4.
[3] Cp. Pl. Rep. i. 352.

have the greatest degree of unity, this unity is by no means II. 3
indicated by the fact 'of all men saying "mine" and "not
mine" at the same instant of time,' which, according to
Socrates[1], is the sign of perfect unity in a state. For the 2
word 'all' is ambiguous. If the meaning be that every individual says 'mine' and ' not mine' at the same time, then
perhaps the result at which Socrates aims may be in some
degree accomplished; each man will call the same person his
own son and his own wife, and so of his property and of all
that belongs to him. This, however, is not the way in which
people would speak who had their wives and children in
common; they would say 'all' but not 'each.' In like man- 3
ner their property would be described as belonging to them,
not severally but collectively. There is an obvious fallacy in
the term 'all': like some other words, 'both,' 'odd,' 'even,'
it is ambiguous, and in argument becomes a source of logical
puzzles. That all persons call the same thing mine in the
sense in which each does so may be a fine thing, but it is
impracticable; or if the words are taken in the other sense
[i. e. the sense which distinguishes 'all' from 'each'], such
a unity in no way conduces to harmony. And there is 4
another objection to the proposal. For that which is common
to the greatest number has the least care bestowed upon it.
Every one thinks chiefly of his own, hardly at all of the
common interest; and only when he is himself concerned as
an individual. For besides other considerations, everybody is
more inclined to neglect the duty which he expects another to
fulfil; as in families many attendants are often less useful than
a few. Each citizen will have a thousand sons who will not 5
be his sons individually, but anybody will be equally the son

[1] Pl. Rep. v. 462 c.

II. 3 of anybody, and will therefore be neglected by all alike.
1262 a Further, upon this principle, every one will call another
'mine' or 'not mine' according as he is prosperous or the
reverse ;—however small a fraction he may be of the whole
number, he will say of every individual of the thousand, or
whatever be the number of the city, 'such a one is mine,'
'such a one his'; and even about this he will not be posi-
tive; for it is impossible to know who chanced to have a
child, or whether, if one came into existence, it has survived.
6 But which is better—to be able to say 'mine' about every
one of the two thousand or the ten thousand citizens, or to
use the word 'mine' in the ordinary and more restricted
7 sense ?   For usually the same person is called by one man
his son whom another calls his brother or cousin or kinsman
or blood-relation or connexion by marriage either of himself
or of some relation of his, and these relationships he distinguishes from the tie which binds him to his tribe or ward;
and how much better is it to be the real cousin of somebody
8 than to be a son after Plato's fashion !   Nor is there any
way of preventing brothers and children and fathers and
mothers from sometimes recognizing one another; for children are born like their parents, and they will necessarily be
9 finding indications of their relationship to one another.   Geo-
graphers declare such to be the fact; they say that in Upper
Libya, where the women are common, nevertheless the children who are born are assigned to their respective fathers on
the ground of their likeness [1].   And some women, like the
females of other animals—for example mares and cows—
have a strong tendency to produce offspring resembling their

[1] Cp. Herod. iv. 180.

parents, as was the case with the Pharsalian mare called **II. 3**
Dicaea (the Just)[1].

Other evils, against which it is not easy for the authors of **4**
such a community to guard, will be assaults and homicides,
voluntary as well as involuntary, quarrels and slanders, all
which are most unholy acts when committed against fathers
and mothers and near relations, but not equally unholy when
there is no relationship. Moreover, they are much more
likely to occur if the relationship is unknown, and, when they
have occurred, the customary expiations of them cannot
be made. Again, how strange it is that Socrates, after **2**
having made the children common, should hinder lovers
from carnal intercourse only, but should permit familiarities
between father and son or between brother and brother,
than which nothing can be more unseemly, since even
without them, love of this sort is improper. How strange, **3**
too, to forbid intercourse for no other reason than the violence
of the pleasure, as though the relationship of father and son
or of brothers with one another made no difference.

This community of wives and children seems better **4**
suited to the husbandmen than to the guardians, for if they
have wives and children in common, they will be bound **1262 b**
to one another by weaker ties, as a subject class should be,
and they will remain obedient and not rebel[2]. In a word, the **5**
result of such a law would be just the opposite of that which
good laws ought to have, and the intention of Socrates
in making these regulations about women and children would
defeat itself. For friendship we believe to be the greatest good
of states[3] and the preservative of them against revolutions;

---

[1] Cp. Hist. Anim. vii. 6, p. 586 a. 13.
[2] Cp. vii. 10. § 13.   [3] Cp. N. Eth. viii. 1. § 4.

II. 4 neither is there anything which Socrates so greatly lauds as the unity of the state which he and all the world declare to be created by friendship. But the unity which he commends [1] would be like that of the lovers in the Symposium [2], who, as Aristophanes says, desire to grow together in the excess of their affection, and from being two to 7 become one, in which case one or both would certainly perish. Whereas [the very opposite will really happen;] in a state having women and children common, love will be watery; and the father will certainly not say 'my son,' or 8 the son 'my father [3].' As a little sweet wine mingled with a great deal of water is imperceptible in the mixture, so, in this sort of community, the idea of relationship which is based upon these names will be lost; there is no reason why the so-called father should care about the son, or the son about the father, or brothers about one another. 9 Of the two qualities which chiefly inspire regard and affection —that a thing is your own and that you love it—neither can exist in such a state as this.

Again, the transfer of children as soon as they are born from the rank of husbandmen or of artisans to that of guardians, and from the rank of guardians into a lower rank [4], will be very difficult to arrange; the givers or transferrers cannot but know whom they are giving and transferring, and 10 to whom. And the previously mentioned evils, such as assaults, unlawful loves, homicides, will happen more often amongst those who are transferred to the lower classes, or who have a place assigned to them among the guardians; for they will no longer call the members of any other class

[1] Cp. c. 2.   [2] Symp. 189-193.   [3] Cp. c. 3.
[4] Rep. iii. 415.

brothers, and children, and fathers, and mothers, and will **II. 4**
not, therefore, be afraid of committing any crimes by reason
of consanguinity. Touching the community of wives and
children, let this be our conclusion.

Next let us consider what should be our arrangements **5**
about property : should the citizens of the perfect state have
their possessions in common or not ? This question may **2**
be discussed separately from the enactments about women
and children. Even supposing that the women and children **1268 a**
belong to individuals, according to the custom which is at
present universal, may there not be an advantage in having and
using possessions in common? Three cases are possible :
(1) the soil may be appropriated, but the produce may be
thrown for consumption into the common stock; and this is
the practice of some nations. Or (2), the soil may be
common, and may be cultivated in common, but the produce
divided among individuals for their private use ; this is a form
of common property which is said to exist among certain
barbarians. Or (3), the soil and the produce may be alike
common.

When the husbandmen are not the citizens, the case will **3**
be different and easier to deal with ; but when the citizens till
the ground themselves the question of ownership will give a
world of trouble. If they do not share equally in enjoyments
and toils, those who labour much and get little will necessarily
complain of those who labour little and receive or consume
much. There is always a difficulty in men living together and **4**
having things in common, but especially in their having
common property. The partnerships of fellow-travellers are
an example to the point ; for they generally fall out by
the way and quarrel about any trifle which turns up. So

II. 5 with servants : we are most liable to take offence at those
with whom we most frequently come into contact in daily
life.

5   These are only some of the disadvantages which attend
the community of property; the present arrangement, if im-
proved as it might be by good customs and laws, would be
far better, and would have the advantages of both systems.
Property should be in a certain sense common, but, as a
6 general rule, private; for, when every one has a distinct
interest [1], men will not complain of one another, and they
will make more progress, because every one will be attending
to his own business. And yet among the good, and in
respect of use, ' Friends,' as the proverb says, ' will have all
things common [2].' Even now there are traces of such a
principle, showing that it is not impracticable, but, in well-
ordered states, exists already to a certain extent and may
7 be carried further. For, although every man has his own
property, some things he will place at the disposal of his
friends, while of others he shares the use with them. The
Lacedaemonians, for example, use one another's slaves, and
horses and dogs, as if they were their own; and when they
happen to be in the country, they appropriate in the fields
8 whatever provisions they want. It is clearly better that property
should be private, but the use of it common; and the special
business of the legislator is to create in men this benevolent
disposition. Again, how immeasurably greater is the pleasure,
1263 b when a man feels a thing to be his own; for the love of self [3]
is a feeling implanted by nature and not given in vain,
9 although selfishness is rightly censured; this, however, is not

---

[1] Cp. Rep. ii. 374.   [2] Cp. Rep. iv. 424 A.
[3] Cp. N. Eth. ix. 8. § 6.

the mere love of self, but the love of self in excess, like **II. 5**
the miser's love of money; for all, or almost all, men love
money, and other such objects in a measure. And further,
there is the greatest pleasure in doing a kindness or service to
friends or guests or companions, which can only be rendered
when a man has private property. The advantage is lost by 10
the excessive unification of the state. Two virtues are
annihilated in such a state : first, temperance towards women
(for it is an honourable action to abstain from another's wife
for temperance sake); secondly, liberality in the matter of
property. No one, when men have all things in common,
will any longer set an example of liberality or do any
liberal action ; for liberality consists in the use which is made
of property[1].

Such legislation may have a specious appearance of 11
benevolence; men readily listen to it, and are easily induced
to believe that in some wonderful manner everybody will
become everybody's friend, especially when some one[2] is
heard denouncing the evils now existing in states, suits
about contracts, convictions for perjury, flatteries of rich men
and the like, which are said to arise out of the possession of
private property. These evils, however, are due to a very 12
different cause—the wickedness of human nature. Indeed,
we see that there is much more quarrelling among those
who have all things in common, though there are not many
of them when compared with the vast numbers who have
private property.

Again, we ought to reckon, not only the evils from 13
which the citizens will be saved, but also the advantages
which they will lose. The life which they are to lead appears

[1] Cp. N. Eth. iv. 1. § 1.   [2] Rep. v. 464, 465.

II. 5 to be quite impracticable. The error of Socrates must be attributed to the false notion of unity from which he starts.

14 Unity there should be, both of the family and of the state, but in some respects only. For there is a point at which a state may attain such a degree of unity as to be no longer a state, or at which, without actually ceasing to exist, it will become an inferior state, like harmony passing into unison,

15 or rhythm which has been reduced to a single foot. The state, as I was saying, is a plurality[1], which should be united and made into a community by education; and it is strange that the author of a system of education, which he thinks will make the state virtuous, should expect to improve his citizens by regulations of this sort, and not by philosophy or by customs and laws, like those which prevail at Sparta and Crete respecting common meals, where-

1264 a by the legislator has [to a certain degree] made property

16 common. Let us remember that we should not disregard the experience of ages; in the multitude of years these things, if they were good, would certainly not have been unknown; for almost everything has been found out, although sometimes they are not put together; in other cases men do not use the

17 knowledge which they have. Great light would be thrown on this subject if we could see such a form of government in the actual process of construction; for the legislator could not form a state at all without distributing and dividing the citizens into associations for common meals, and into phratries and tribes. But all this legislation ends only in forbidding agriculture to the guardians, a prohibition which the Lace-daemonians try to enforce already.

18   Again, Socrates has not said, nor is it easy to decide,

[1] Cp. c. 2. § 2.

what in such a community will be the general form of the II. 5
state.   The citizens who are not guardians are the majority,
and about them nothing has been determined: are the
husbandmen, too, to have their property in common?   Or,
besides the common land which he tills, is each individual
to have his own? and are their wives and children to
be individual or common?   If, like the guardians, they are to 19
have all things in common, in what do they differ from them,
or what will they gain by submitting to their government?
Or, upon what principle would they submit, unless indeed
the governing class adopt the ingenious policy of the Cretans,
who give their slaves the same institutions as their own,
but forbid them gymnastic exercises and the possession of
arms.   If, on the other hand, the inferior classes are too 20
like other cities in respect of marriage and property, what will
be the form of the community?   Must it not contain two
states in one [1], each hostile to the other?   [2] One class will
consist of the guardians, who are a sort of watchmen;
another, of the husbandmen, and there will be the artisans and
the other citizens [2].   But [if so] the suits and quarrels, and all 21
the evils which Socrates affirms [3] to exist in other states, will
exist equally among them.   He says indeed that, having so
good an education, the citizens will not need many laws, for
example, laws about the city or about the markets [4]; but then
he confines his education to the guardians.   Again, he makes 22
the husbandmen owners of the land upon condition of their
paying a tribute [5].   But in that case they are likely to be much

[1] Cp. Rep. iv. 422 E.

[2] Or (with Bernays), ' He makes the guardians into a mere occupying
garrison, while the husbandmen and artisans and the rest are the real
citizens;' see note.

[3] Rep. v. 464, 465.   [4] Rep. iv. 425 D.   [5] Rep. v. 464 C.

II. 5 more unmanageable and conceited than the Helots, or
23 Penestae, or slaves in general[1]. And whether community
of wives and property be necessary for the lower equally
with the higher class or not, and the questions akin to this,
what will be the education, form of government, laws of
the lower class, Socrates has nowhere determined: neither
is it easy, though very important, to discover what should
be the character of the inferior classes, if the common life of
the guardians is to be maintained.

1264 b Again, if Socrates makes the women common, and retains
24 private property, the men will see to the fields, but who
will see to the house? [2] And what will happen if the
agricultural class have both their property and their wives
in common[2]? Once more; it is absurd to argue, from
the analogy of the animals, that men and women should
follow the same pursuits[3]; for animals have not to manage
25 a household. The government, too, as constituted by
Socrates, contains elements of danger; for he makes the same
persons always rule. And if this is often a cause of disturbance among the meaner sort, how much more among high-
26 spirited warriors? But that the persons whom he makes
rulers must be the same is evident; for the gold which the
God mingles in the souls of men is not at one time given to
one, at another time to another, but always to the same: as
he says, ' God mingles gold in some, and silver in others,
from their very birth; but brass and iron in those who are
27 meant to be artisans and husbandmen[4].' Again, he deprives
the guardians of happiness, and says that the legislator ought
to make the whole state happy[5]. But the whole cannot

---

[1] Cp. c. 9. § 2.   [2] These words are bracketed by Bekker.
[3] Cp. Rep. v. 451 D.   [4] Cp. Rep. iii. 415 A.   [5] Rep. iv. 419, 420.

be happy unless most, or all, or some of its parts enjoy II. 5
happiness[1]. In this respect happiness is not like the even
principle in numbers, which may exist only in the whole,
but in none of the parts; not so happiness. And if the 28
guardians are not happy, who are? Surely not the artisans,
or the common people. The Republic of which Socrates
discourses has all these difficulties, and others quite as
great.

The same, or nearly the same, objections apply to Plato's 6
later work, the Laws, and therefore we had better examine
briefly the constitution which is therein described. In the
Republic, Socrates has definitely settled in all a few questions
only; such as the community of women and children, the
community of property, and the constitution of the state.
The population is divided into two classes—one of husband- 2
men, and the other of warriors; from this latter is taken
a third class of counsellors and rulers of the state. But 3
Socrates has not determined whether the husbandmen and
artisans are to have a share in the government, and whether
they, too, are to carry arms and share in military service,
or not. He certainly thinks that the women ought to share
in the education of the guardians, and to fight by their side.
The remainder of the work is filled up with digressions
foreign to the main subject, and with discussions about the
education of the guardians. In the Laws there is hardly 1265 a
anything but laws; not much is said about the constitution. 4
This, which he had intended to make more of the ordinary
type, he gradually brings round to the other or ideal form.
For with the exception of the community of women and 5
property, he supposes everything to be the same in both

[1] Cp. vii. 9. § 7.

II. 6 states; there is to be the same education; the citizens of
both are to live free from servile occupations, and there are to
be common meals in both.   The only difference is that in the
Laws, the common meals are extended to women[1], and
the warriors number about 5000[2], but in the Republic only
1000[3].

6   The discourses of Socrates are never commonplace; they
always exhibit grace and originality and thought; but perfection in everything can hardly be expected.   We must not
overlook the fact that the number of 5000 citizens, just now
mentioned, will require a territory as large as Babylonia, or
some other huge country, if so many persons are to be supported in idleness, together with their women and attendants,
7 who will be a multitude many times as great.   [In framing
an ideal] we may assume what we wish, but should avoid
impossibilities[4].

It is said [in the Laws] that the legislator ought to have
his eye directed to two points,—the people and the country[5].
But neighbouring countries also must not be forgotten by
him[6], if the state for which he legislates is to have a true
political life[7].   For a state must have such a military force
as will be serviceable against her neighbours, and not merely
8 useful at home.   Even if the life of action is not admitted to
be the best, either for individuals or states[8], still a city should
be formidable to enemies, whether invading or retreating.

There is another point: Should not the amount of property be defined in some clearer way?   For Socrates says

---

[1] Laws, vi. 781.   [2] Laws, v. 737 E.
[3] Rep. iv. 423 A (but see note on this passage).
[4] Cp. vii. 4. § 2.   [5] Perhaps Laws, 703–707 and 747 D (?).
[6] Cp. c. 7. § 14.   [7] Cp. vii. 6. § 7.   [8] Cp. vii. c. 2 and 3.

that a man should have so much property as will enable him II. 6
to live temperately[1], which is only a way of saying ' to live
well '; this would be the higher or more general conception.
But a man may live temperately and yet miserably.   A better 9
definition would be that a man must have so much property
as will enable him to live not only temperately but liberally[2];
if the two are parted, liberality will combine with luxury; toil
will be associated with temperance.   For liberality and temperance are the only virtues[3] which have to do with the use
of property.   A man cannot use property with mildness or
courage, but temperately and liberally he may; and therefore
the practice of these virtues is inseparable from property.
There is an inconsistency, too, in equalizing the property and 10
not regulating the number of the citizens[4]; the population is
to remain unlimited, and he thinks that it will be sufficiently
equalized by a certain number of marriages being unfruitful,
however many are born to others, because he finds this to be 1265 b
the case in existing states.   But [in Plato's imaginary state] 11
greater care will be required than now; for among ourselves,
whatever may be the number of citizens, the property is always
distributed among them, and therefore no one is in want; but,
if the property were incapable of division [as in the Laws],
the supernumeraries, whether few or many, would get nothing.
One would have thought that it was even more necessary to 12
limit population than property; and that the limit should be
fixed by calculating the chances of mortality in the children,
and of sterility in married persons.   The neglect of this sub- 13
ject, which in existing states is so common, is a never-failing

---

[1] Laws, v. 737 D.   [2] Cp. vii. 5. § 1.
[3] Omitting ἕξεις and reading ἀρεταί with the MSS., or, reading with
Bekk. ἕξεις αἱρεταί, ' eligible qualities.'   [4] But see Laws, v. 740.

II. 6 cause of poverty among the citizens; and poverty is the parent
of revolution and crime. Pheidon the Corinthian, who was
one of the most ancient legislators, thought that the families
and the number of citizens ought to remain the same, although
originally all the lots may have been of different sizes; but in
14 the Laws, the opposite principle is maintained. What in our
opinion is the right arrangement will have to be explained
hereafter [1].

There is another omission in the Laws; Socrates does not
tell us how the rulers differ from their subjects; he only says
that they should be related as the warp and the woof, which
15 are made out of different wools [2]. He allows that a man's
whole property may be increased fivefold [3], but why should not
his land also increase to a certain extent? Again, will the
good management of a household be promoted by his arrangement of homesteads? for he assigns to each individual two
16 homesteads in separate places [4], and it is difficult to live in two
houses.

The whole system of government tends to be neither democracy nor oligarchy, but something in a mean between them,
which is usually called a polity, and is composed of the heavy
armed soldiers. Now, if he intended to frame a constitution
which would suit the greatest number of states, he was very
likely right, but not if he meant to say that this constitutional
form came nearest to his first or ideal state; for many would
17 prefer the Lacedaemonian, or, possibly, some other more aris-
tocratic government. Some, indeed, say that the best consti-

[1] Cp. vii. 5. § 1; 10. § 11; 16. § 15; but the promise is hardly
fulfilled.
[2] Laws, v. 734 E, 735 A.   [3] Laws, v. 744 E.
[4] Laws, v. 745, but cp. infra, vii. 10. § 11.

tution is a combination of all existing forms, and they praise the **II.**
Lacedaemonian [1] because it is made up of oligarchy, monarchy,
democracy, the king forming the monarchy, and the council
of elders the oligarchy, while the democratic element is
represented by the Ephors; for the Ephors are selected from
the people. Others, however, declare the Ephoralty to be
a tyranny, and find the element of democracy in the common
meals and in the habits of daily life. In the Law [2], it is

1266 a

18
maintained that the best state is made up of democracy and
tyranny, which are either not constitutions at all, or are the
worst of all. But they are nearer the truth who combine
many forms; for the state is better which is made up of
more numerous elements. The constitution proposed in the
Laws has no element of monarchy at all; it is nothing but
oligarchy and democracy, leaning rather to oligarchy. This 19
is seen in the mode of appointing magistrates [3]; for although
the appointment of them by lot from among those who have
been already selected combines both elements, the way in
which the rich are compelled by law to attend the assembly [4]
and vote for magistrates or discharge other political duties,
while the rest may do as they like, and the endeavour to have
the greater number of the magistrates appointed out of the
richest classes and the highest officers selected from those
who have the greatest incomes, both these are oligarchical 20
features. The oligarchical principle prevails also in the
choice of the council [5]; for all are compelled to choose, but
the compulsion extends only to the choice out of the first

[1] Cp. iv. § 7; 7. § 4; 9. §§ 7-9.   [2] vi. 756 E; cp. iv. 710.
[3] Laws, vi. 755, 763 E, 765.
[4] Laws, vi. 764 A; and Pol. iv. 9. § 2; 14. § 12.
[5] Laws, vi. 756 B-E.

II. 6 class, and of an equal number out of the second class and out
of the third class, but not in this latter case to all the voters
of the third and forth class; and the selection of candidates
out of the fourth class [1] is only compulsory on the first and
21 second.   Then, he says that there ought to be an equal
number of each class selected.   Thus a preponderance will
be given to the better sort of people, who have the larger
incomes, because many of the lower classes, not being com-
22 pelled, will not vote.   These considerations, and others which
will be adduced when the time comes for examining similar
polities, tend to show that states like Plato's should not be
composed of democracy and monarchy.   There is also a
danger in electing the magistrates out of a body who are
themselves elected; for, if but a small number choose to combine, the elections will always go as they desire.   Such is the
constitution which is described in the Laws.

7   Other constitutions have been proposed; some by private
persons, others by philosophers and statesmen, which all
come nearer to established or existing ones than either of
Plato's.   No one else has introduced such novelties as the
community of women and children, or public tables for women:
2 other legislators begin with what is necessary.   In the
opinion of some, the regulation of property is the chief point
of all, that being the question upon which all revolutions turn.
This danger was recognized by Phaleas of Chalcedon, who
was the first to affirm that the citizens of a state ought to have
3 equal possessions.   He thought that in a new colony the
1266 b equalization might be accomplished without difficulty, not so
easily when a state was already established; and that then
the shortest way of compassing the desired end would be for

---

[1] Omitting either τοῦ τετάρτου or τῶν τετάρτων.

the rich to give and not to receive marriage portions, and for **II. 7**
the poor not to give but to receive them.

Plato in the Laws was of opinion that, to a certain extent, 4
accumulation should be allowed, forbidding, as I have already
observed [1], any citizen to possess more than five times the
minimum qualification. But those who make such laws should 5
remember what they are apt to forget—that the legislator
who fixes the amount of property should also fix the number
of children; for, if the children are too many for the property,
the law must be broken. And, besides the violation of the
law, it is a bad thing that many from being rich should
become poor; for men of ruined fortunes are sure to stir up
revolutions. That the equalization of property exercises an 6
influence on political society was clearly understood even by
some of the old legislators. Laws were made by Solon and
others prohibiting an individual from possessing as much land
as he pleased; and there are other laws in states which forbid
the sale of property: among the Locrians, for example, there
is a law that a man is not to sell his property unless he can
prove unmistakably that some misfortune has befallen him. 7
Again, there have been laws which enjoin the preservation of
the original lots. Such a law existed in the island of Leucas,
and the abrogation of it made the constitution too democratic,
for the rulers no longer had the prescribed qualification.
Again, where there is equality of property, the amount may
be either too large or too small, and the possessor may be
living either in luxury or penury. Clearly, then, the legislator ought not only to aim at the equalization of properties, 8
but at moderation in their amount. And yet, if he prescribe
this moderate amount equally to all, he will be no nearer the

[1] c. 6. § 15.

II. 7 mark; for it is not the possessions but the desires of mankind
which require to be equalized[1], and this is impossible, unless
a sufficient education is provided by the state.   But Phaleas
will probably reply that this is precisely what he means; and
that, in his opinion, there ought to be in states, not only equal
9 property, but equal education.   Still he should tell us what
will be the character of his education; there is no use in
having one and the same for all, if it is of a sort that predis-
10 poses men to avarice, or ambition, or both.   Moreover, civil
troubles arise, not only out of the inequality of property, but
out of the inequality of honour, though in opposite ways.   For
1267 a the common people quarrel about the inequality of property, the
higher class about the equality of honour; as the poet says—

'The bad and good alike in honour share[2].'

11   There are crimes of which the motive is want; and for
these Phaleas expects to find a cure in the equalization of
property, which will take away from a man the temptation to
12 be a highwayman, because he is hungry or cold.   But want
is not the sole incentive to crime; men desire to gratify some
passion which preys upon them, or they are eager to enjoy the
pleasures which are unaccompanied with the pain of desire,
and therefore they commit crimes.

Now what is the cure of these three disorders?   Of the first,
moderate possessions and occupation; of the second, habits
of temperance; as to the third, if any desire pleasures which
depend on themselves, they will find the satisfaction of their
desires nowhere but in philosophy; for all other pleasures
13 we are dependent on others.   The fact is that the greatest
crimes are caused by excess and not by necessity.   Men do

---

[1] Cp. c. 5. § 12.   [2] Il. ix. 319.

not become tyrants in order that they may not suffer cold ; **II. 7**
and hence great is the honour bestowed, not on him who kills
a thief, but on him who kills a tyrant. Thus we see that the
institutions of Phaleas avail only against petty crimes.

There is another objection to them. They are chiefly 14
designed to promote the internal welfare of the state. But
the legislator should consider also its relation to neighbouring
nations, and to all who are outside of it [1]. The government
must be organized with a view to military strength; and of
this he has said not a word. And so with respect to pro- 15
perty : there should not only be enough to supply the internal
wants of the state, but also to meet dangers coming from
without. The property of the state should not be so large
that more powerful neighbours may be tempted by it, while
the owners are unable to repel the invaders ; nor yet so small
that the state is unable to maintain a war even against states
of equal power, and of the same character. Phaleas has not 16
laid down any rule; and we should bear in mind [2] that a certain amount of wealth [2] is an advantage. The best limit will
probably be, not so much as will tempt a more powerful neighbour, or make it his interest to go to war with you. There 17
is a story that Eubulus, when Autophradates was going to
besiege Atarneus, told him to consider how long the opera-
tion would take, and then reckon up the cost which would
be incurred in the time. 'For,' said he, 'I am willing for
a smaller sum than that to leave Atarneus at once.' These
words of Eubulus made an impression on Autophradates, and
he desisted from the siege.

One advantage gained by the equalization of property is 18
that it prevents the citizens from quarrelling. Not that the

---

[1] Cp. ∴ 6. § 7.   [2] Or reading ὅ τι, 'what amount of wealth.'

II. 7 gain in this direction is very great.   For the nobles will be dissatisfied because they do not receive the honours which they think their due; and this is often found to be a cause

1267 b of sedition and revolution [1].   And the avarice of mankind

19 is insatiable; at one time two obols was pay enough, but now, when this sum has become customary, men always want more and more without end; for it is of the nature of desire not to be satisfied, and most men live only for the gratification of it.   [2] The beginning of reform [2] is not so

20 much to equalize property as to train the nobler sort of natures not to desire more, and to prevent the lower from getting more; that is to say, they must be kept down, but not

21 illtreated.   Besides, the equalization proposed by Phaleas is imperfect; for he only equalizes land, whereas a man may be rich also in slaves, and cattle, and money, and in the abundance of what are called his movables.   Now either all these things must be equalized, or some limit must be imposed on

22 them, or they must all be let alone.   It would appear that Phaleas is legislating for a small city only, if, as he supposes, all the artisans are to be public slaves and not to form a part

23 of the population of the city.   But if there is a law that artisans are to be public slaves, it should only apply to those engaged on public works [3], as at Epidamnus, or at Athens on the plan which Diophantus once introduced.

From these observations any one may judge how far Phaleas was wrong or right in his ideas.

8   Hippodamus, the son of Euryphon, a native of Miletus, the

---

[1] Cp. § 10.

[2] Or, reading with Bernays ἄκη, ' the remedy for such evils.'

[3] Putting a comma after εἶναι and removing the comma after ἐργαζομένοις.

same who invented the art of planning cities, and who also **II. 8**
laid out the Piraeus—a strange man, whose fondness for distinction led him into a general eccentricity of life, which
made some think him affected (for he would wear flowing hair
and expensive ornaments ; and yet he dressed himself in the
same cheap warm garment both in winter and summer); he,
besides aspiring to be an adept in the knowledge of nature,
was the first person not a statesman who made enquiries about
the best form of government.

The city of Hippodamus was composed of 10,000 citizens **2**
divided into three parts—one of artisans, one of husbandmen,
and a third of armed defenders of the state. He also divided **3**
the land into three parts, one sacred, one public, the third
private : the first was set apart to maintain the customary
worship of the gods, the second was to support the warriors,
the third was the property of the husbandmen. He also **4**
divided his laws into three classes, and no more, for he maintained that there are three subjects of lawsuits—insult,
injury, and homicide. He likewise instituted a single final
court of appeal, to which all causes seeming to have been
improperly decided might be referred ; this court he formed
of elders chosen for the purpose. He was further of opinion **1268 a**
that the decisions of the courts ought not to be given by the **5**
use of a voting pebble, but that every one should have a tablet
on which he might not only write a simple condemnation, or
leave the tablet blank for a simple acquittal ; but, if he partly
acquitted and partly condemned, he was to distinguish accordingly. To the existing law he objected that it obliged the
judges to be guilty of perjury, whichever way they voted.
He also enacted that those who discovered anything for the **6**
good of the state should be rewarded ; and he provided that

II. 8 the children of citizens who died in battle should be maintained at the public expense, as if such an enactment had never been heard of before, yet it actually exists at Athens [1]
7 and in other places.   As to the magistrates, he would have them all elected by the people, that is, by the three classes already mentioned, and those who were elected were to watch over the interests of the public, of strangers and of orphans. These are the most striking points in the constitution of Hippodamus.   There is not much else.

The first of these proposals to which objection may be
8 taken, is the threefold division of the citizens.   The artisans, and the husbandmen, and the warriors, all have a share in the government.   But the husbandmen have no arms, and the artisans neither arms nor land, and therefore they become all
9 but slaves of the warrior class.   That they should share in all the offices is an impossibility; for generals and guardians of the citizens, and nearly all the principal magistrates, must be taken from the class of those who carry arms.   Yet, if the two other classes have no share in the government, how can they be loyal citizens?   It may be said that those who have arms must necessarily be masters of both the other classes, but this is not so easily accomplished unless they are numer-
10 ous; and if they are, why should the other classes share in the government at all, or have power to appoint magistrates? Artisans there must be, for these are wanted in every city, and they can live by their craft, as elsewhere; and the husbandmen, too, if they really provided the warriors with food, might fairly have a share in the government.   But in the republic of Hippodamus they are supposed to have land of their own, which they cultivate for their private benefit.

[1] Cp. Thuc. ii. c. 46.

Again, as to this common land out of which the soldiers are **II. 8**
maintained, if they are themselves to be the cultivators of it, **11**
the warrior class will be identical with the husbandmen,
although the legislator intended to make a distinction between
them. If, again, there are to be other cultivators distinct
both from the husbandmen, who have land of their own, and
from the warriors, they will make a fourth class, which has
no place in the state and no share in anything. Or, if the **12**
same persons are to cultivate their own lands and those of the
public as well, they will have a difficulty in supplying the
quantity of produce which will maintain two households: and **1268 b**
why, in this case, should there be any division, for they
might find food themselves and give to the warriors from the
same lots? There is surely a great confusion in all this.

Neither is the law to be commended which says that the **13**
judges, when a simple issue is laid before them, should distinguish in their judgment; for the judge is thus converted
into an arbitrator. Now, in an arbitration, although the
arbitrators are many, they confer with one another about the
decision, and therefore they can distinguish; but in courts of
law this is impossible, and, indeed, most legislators take pains
to prevent the judges from holding any communication with
one another. Again, will there not be confusion if the judge **14**
thinks that damages should be given, but not so much as the
suitor demands? He asks, say, for twenty minae, and the
judge allows him ten minae, or one judge more and another
less; one five, another four minae. In this way they will go
on apportioning the damages, and some will grant the whole
and others nothing: how is the final reckoning to be taken? **15**
Again, no one who votes for a simple acquittal or condemnation is compelled to perjure himself, if the indictment is quite

II. 8 simple and in right form; for the judge who acquits does not
decide that the defendant owes nothing, but that he does not
owe the twenty minae.   He only is guilty of perjury who
thinks that the defendant ought not to pay twenty minae, and
yet condemns him.

16   To reward those who discover anything which is useful to
the state is a proposal which has a specious sound, but cannot
safely be enacted by law, for it may encourage informers, and
perhaps even lead to political commotions.   This question
involves another.   It has been doubted whether it is or is not
expedient to make any changes in the laws of a country, even
17 if another law be better.   Now, if all changes are inexpedient,
we can hardly assent to the proposal of Hippodamus; for,
under pretence of doing a public service, a man may introduce
measures which are really destructive to the laws or to the
constitution.   But, since we have touched upon this subject,
18 perhaps we had better go a little into detail, for, as I was
saying, there is a difference of opinion, and it may sometimes
seem desirable to make changes.   Such changes in the other
arts and sciences have certainly been beneficial; medicine, for
example, and gymnastic, and every other art and science have
departed from traditional usage.   And, if politics be an art,
19 change must be necessary in this as in any other art.   The
need of improvement is shown by the fact that old customs
are exceedingly simple and barbarous.   For the ancient
Hellenes went about armed[1] and bought their wives of each
20 other.   The remains of ancient laws which have come down
1269 a to us are quite absurd; for example, at Cumae there is a law
about murder, to the effect that if the accuser produce a certain
number of witnesses from among his own kinsmen, the accused

----

[1] Cp. Thucyd. i. c. 5 and 6.

shall be held guilty. Again, men in general desire the good, II. 8 and not merely what their fathers had. But the primaeval 21 inhabitants[1], whether they were born of the earth, or were the survivors of some destruction, may be supposed to have been no better than ordinary foolish people among ourselves[1] (such is certainly the tradition[2] concerning the earth-born men); and it would be ridiculous to rest contented with their notions. Even when laws have been written down, they ought not always to remain unaltered. As in other arts, so in 22 making a constitution, it is impossible that all things should be precisely set down in writing; for enactments must be universal, but actions are concerned with particulars[3]. Hence we infer that sometimes and in certain cases laws may be changed; but when we look at the matter from another point of view, great caution would seem to be required. For the habit of 23 lightly changing the laws is an evil, and, when the advantage is small, some errors both of lawgivers and rulers had better be left; the citizen will not gain so much by the change as he will lose by the habit of disobedience. The analogy of the 24 arts is false; a change in a law is a very different thing from a change in an art. For the law has no power to command obedience except that of habit, which can only be given by time, so that a readiness to change from old to new laws enfeebles the power of the law. Even if we admit that the 25 laws are to be changed, are they all to be changed, and in every state? And are they to be changed by anybody who

[1] Or, referring ὁμοίους to γηγενεῖς, 'whether they were born of the earth or were the survivors of some destruction, who were no better (ὁμοίους) than earth-born men, may be supposed to have been ordinary foolish people.'

[2] Cp. Plato, Laws, iii. 677 A; Polit. 271 A; Tim. 22 C.

[3] Cp. Plato, Polit. 295 A.

II. 8 likes, or only by certain persons? These are very important
questions; and therefore we had better reserve the discussion
of them to a more suitable occasion.

9   In the governments of Lacedaemon and Crete, and indeed
in all governments, two points have to be considered; first,
whether any particular law is good or bad, when compared
with the perfect state; secondly, whether it is or is not consistent with the idea and character which the lawgiver has set

2 before his citizens [1]. That in a well-ordered state the citizens
should have leisure and not have to provide for their daily
wants is generally acknowledged, but there is a difficulty in
seeing how this leisure is to be attained. [For, if you employ
slaves, they are liable to rebel.] The Thessalian Penestae
have often risen against their masters, and the Helots in like
manner against the Lacedaemonians, for whose misfortunes

3 they are always lying in wait. Nothing, however, of this
1269 b kind has as yet happened to the Cretans; the reason probably
is that the neighbouring cities, even when at war with one
another, never form an alliance with rebellious serfs, rebellions
not being for their interest, since they themselves have a dependent population [2]. Whereas all the neighbours of the
Lacedaemonians, whether Argives, Messenians, or Arcadians,
are their enemies [and the Helots are always revolting to
them]. In Thessaly, again, the original revolt of the slaves
occurred at a time when the Thessalians were still at war with
the neighbouring Achaeans, Perrhaebians, and Magnesians.

4 Besides, if there were no other difficulty, the treatment or
management of slaves is a troublesome affair; for, if not kept
in hand, they are insolent, and think that they are as good as
their masters, and, if harshly treated, they hate and conspire

[1] Or 'himself' (Bernays).   [2] Cp. c. 10. § 5.

against them.   Now it is clear that when these are the re- **II. 9**
sults the citizens of a state have not found out the secret of
managing their subject population.

Again, the licence of the Lacedaemonian women defeats **5**
the intention of the Spartan constitution, and is adverse to the
good order of the state.   For a husband and a wife, being
each a part of every family, the state may be considered as
about equally divided into men and women; and, therefore, in
those states in which the condition of the women is bad, half
the city[1] may be regarded as having no laws.   And this is **6**
what has actually happened at Sparta; the legislator wanted to
make the whole state hardy and temperate, and he has carried
out his intention in the case of the men, but he has neglected
the women, who live in every sort of intemperance and luxury.
The consequence is that in such a state wealth is too highly **7**
valued, especially if the citizens fall under the dominion of
their wives, after the manner of all warlike races, except the
Celts and a few others who openly approve of male loves.
The old mythologer would seem to have been right in uniting **8**
Ares and Aphrodite, for all warlike races are prone to the
love either of men or of women.   This was exemplified among
the Spartans in the days of their greatness; many things were
managed by their women.   But what difference does it make **9**
whether women rule, or the rulers are ruled by women?   The
result is the same.   Even in regard to courage, which is of no
use in daily life, and is needed only in war, the influence of
the Lacedaemonian women has been most mischievous.   The **10**
evil showed itself in the Theban invasion, when, unlike the
women in other cities, they were utterly useless and caused
more confusion than the enemy.   This licence of the Lacedae-

[1] Cp. i. 13. §. 16.

II. 9 monian women existed from the earliest times, and was only
1270 a what might be expected.   For, during the wars of the Lace-
11 daemonians, first against the Argives, and afterwards against
the Arcadians and Messenians, the men were long away from
home, and, on the return of peace, they gave themselves into
the legislator's hand, already prepared by the discipline of
a soldier's life (in which there are many elements of virtue),
to receive his enactments.   But, when Lycurgus, as tradition
says, wanted to bring the women under his laws, they resisted,
12 and he gave up the attempt.   They, and not he, are to blame
for what then happened, and this defect in the constitution is
clearly to be attributed to them.   We are not, however, considering what is or is not to be excused, but what is right or
13 wrong ; and the disorder of the women, as I have already said,
not only of itself gives an air of indecorum to the state, but
tends in a measure to foster avarice.

The mention of avarice naturally suggests a criticism on the
14 inequality of property.   While some of the Spartan citizens
have quite small properties, others have very large ones ; hence
the land has passed into the hands of a few.   And here is
another fault in their laws ; for, although the legislator rightly
holds up to shame the sale or purchase of an inheritance, he
15 allows anybody who likes to give and bequeath it.   Yet both
practices lead to the same result.   And nearly two-fifths of
the whole country are held by women ; this is owing to the
number of heiresses and to the large dowries which are customary.   It would surely have been better to have given no
dowries at all, or, if any, but small or moderate ones.   As the
law now stands, a man may bestow his heiress on any one
whom he pleases, and, if he die intestate, the privilege of
16 giving her away descends to his heir.   Hence, although the

country is able to maintain 1500 cavalry and 30,000 hoplites, **II. 9**
the whole number of Spartan citizens [at the time of the
Theban invasion] fell below 1000. The result proves the
faulty nature of their laws respecting property; for the city
sank under a single defeat; the want of men was their ruin.
There is a tradition that, in the days of their ancient kings, 17
they were in the habit of giving the rights of citizenship to
strangers, and therefore, in spite of their long wars, no lack of
population was experienced by them; indeed, at one time
Sparta is said to have numbered not less than 10,000 citizens.
Whether this statement is true or not, it would certainly have
been better to have maintained their numbers by the equalization of property. Again, the law which relates to the pro- 18
creation of children is adverse to the correction of this
inequality. For the legislator, wanting to have as many 1270 b
Spartans as he could, encouraged the citizens to have large
families; and there is a law at Sparta that the father of three
sons shall be exempt from military service, and he who has
four from all the burdens of the state. Yet it is obvious that, 19
if there were many children, the land being distributed as it is,
many of them must necessarily fall into poverty.

The Lacedaemonian constitution is defective in another
point; I mean the Ephoralty. This magistracy has authority
in the highest matters, but the Ephors are all chosen from the
people, and sô the office is apt to fall into the hands of very
poor men, who, being badly off, are open to bribes. There 20
have been many examples at Sparta of this evil in former
times; and quite recently, in the matter of the Andrians,
certain of the Ephors who were bribed did their best to ruin
the state. And so great and tyrannical is their power, that
even the kings have been compelled to court them; through

II. 9 their influence the constitution has deteriorated, and from
21 being an aristocracy has turned into a democracy. The
Ephoralty certainly does keep the state together; for the
people are contented when they have a share in the highest
office, and the result, whether due to the legislator or to
22 chance, has been advantageous. For if a constitution is to be
permanent, all the parts of the state must wish that it should
exist and be maintained[1]. This is the case at Sparta, where
the kings desire permanence because they have due honour in
their own persons; the nobles are represented in the council
of elders (for the office of elder is a reward of virtue); and
23 the people in the Ephoralty, for all are eligible to it. The
election of Ephors out of the whole people is perfectly right,
but ought not to be carried on in the present fashion, which is
too childish. Again, they have the decision of great causes,
although they are quite ordinary men, and therefore they should
not determine them merely on their own judgment, but accord-
24 ing to written rules, and to the laws. Their way of life, too,
is not in accordance with the spirit of the constitution—they
have a deal too much licence; whereas, in the case of the
other citizens, the excess of strictness is so intolerable that
they run away from the law into the secret indulgence of
sensual pleasures.

25 Again, the council of elders is not free from defects. It
may be said that the elders are good men and well trained in
manly virtue; and that, therefore, there is an advantage to the
state in having them. But that judges of important causes
should hold office for life is not a good thing, for the mind
1271 a grows old as well as the body. And when men have been
educated in such a manner that even the legislator himself

[1] Cp. iv. 9. § 10; v. 9. § 5.

cannot trust them, there is real danger.   Many of the elders **II. 9**
are well known to have taken bribes and to have been guilty of 26
partiality in public affairs.   And therefore they ought not to
be irresponsible; yet at Sparta they are so.   But (it may be
replied), 'All magistracies are accountable to the Ephors.'
Yes, but this prerogative is too great for them, and we maintain that the control should be exercised in some other manner.
Further, the mode in which the Spartans elect their elders is 27
childish; and it is improper that[1] the person to be elected
should canvass for the office; the worthiest should be appointed, whether he chooses or not.   And here the legislator 28
clearly indicates the same intention which appears in other
parts of his constitution; he would have his citizens ambitious,
and he has reckoned upon this quality in the election of the
elders; for no one would ask to be elected if he were not.
Yet ambition and avarice, almost more than any other passions,
are the motives of crime.

Whether kings are or are not an advantage to states, I will 29
consider at another time[2]; they should at any rate be chosen,
not as they are now, but with regard to their personal life and
conduct.   The legislator himself obviously did not suppose 30
that he could make them really good men; at least he shows
a great distrust of their virtue.   For this reason the Spartans
used to join enemies in the same embassy, and the quarrels
between the kings were held to be conservative of the state.

Neither did the first introducer of the common meals, called
'phiditia,' regulate them well.   The entertainment ought to 31
have been provided at the public cost, as in Crete[3]; but

---

[1] Reading τὸ αὐτόν, not τόν, as Bekker, 2nd edit., apparently by
a misprint.

[2] Cp. iii. 14 foll.   [3] Cp. c. 10. §§ 7, 8.

II. 9 among the Lacedaemonians every one is expected to contribute, and some of them are too poor to afford the expense;
32 thus the intention of the legislator is frustrated. The common
meals were meant to be a popular institution, but the existing
manner of regulating them is the reverse of popular. For the
very poor can scarcely take part in them; and, according to
ancient custom, those who cannot contribute are not allowed
to retain their rights of citizenship.

33 The law about the Spartan admirals has often been censured,
and with justice; it is a source of dissension, for the kings are
perpetual generals [1], and this office of admiral is but the setting
up of another king.

1271 b The charge which Plato brings, in the Laws [2], against the
34 intention of the legislator, is likewise justified; the whole constitution has regard to one part of virtue only—the virtue of
the soldier, which gives victory in war. And so long as they
were at war, their power was preserved, but when they had
attained empire they fell [3], for of the arts of peace they knew
nothing, and had never engaged in any employment higher
35 than war. There is another error, equally great, into which
they have fallen. Although they truly think that the goods
for which they contend are to be acquired by virtue rather than
by vice, they err in supposing that these goods are to be preferred to the virtue which gains them.

36 Once more: the revenues of the state are ill-managed;
there is no money in the treasury, although they are obliged
to carry on great wars, and they are unwilling to pay taxes.
The greater part of the land being in the hands of the Spartans, they do not look closely into one another's contributions.

---

[1] Reading διδίοις.   [2] Laws, i. 630.
[3] Cp. vii. 14. § 22.

The result which the legislator has produced is the reverse of II. 9
beneficial; for he has made his city poor, and his citizens 37
greedy.

Enough respecting the Spartan constitution, of which these
are the principal defects.

The constitutions of the Cretan cities nearly resemble the 10
Spartan, and in some few points are quite as good; but for the
most part less perfect in form. The older constitutions are
generally less elaborate than the later, and the Lacedaemonian
is said to be, and probably is, in a very great measure, a copy 2
of those in Crete. According to tradition, Lycurgus, when
he ceased to be the guardian of King Charilaus, went abroad
and spent a long time in Crete. For the two countries are
nearly connected; the Lyctians are a colony of the Lacedaemonians, and the colonists, when they came to Crete, adopted
the constitution which they found existing among the inhabi- 3
tants. Even to this day the Perioeci, or subject population of
Crete, are governed by the original laws which Minos enacted.
The island seems to be intended by nature for dominion in
Hellas, and to be well situated; it extends right across the
sea, around which nearly all the Hellenes are settled; and
while one end is not far from the Peloponnese, the other
almost reaches to the region of Asia about Triopium and 4
Rhodes. Hence Minos acquired the empire of the sea, sub-
duing some of the islands and colonizing others; at last he
invaded Sicily, where he died near Camicus.
                                                              5
The Cretan institutions resemble the Lacedaemonian. The
Helots are the husbandmen of the one, the Perioeci of the 1272 a
other, and both Cretans and Lacedaemonians have common
meals, which were anciently called by the Lacedaemonians not
' phiditia ' but ' andria '; and the Cretans have the same word,

II. 10 the use of which proves that the common meals [or syssitia]
6 originally came from Crete. Further, the two constitutions
are similar [in many particulars]; for the office of the Ephors
is the same as that of the Cretan Cosmi, the only difference
being that whereas the Ephors are five, the Cosmi are ten in
number. The elders, too, answer to the elders in Crete, who
are termed by the Cretans the council. And the kingly office
once existed in Crete, but was abolished, and the Cosmi have
7 now the duty of leading them in war. All classes share in
the ecclesia, but it can only ratify the decrees of the elders
and the Cosmi.

The common meals of Crete are certainly better managed
than the Lacedaemonian; for in Lacedaemon every one pays
so much per head, or, if he fails, the law, as I have already
explained, forbids him to exercise the rights of citizenship.
8 But in Crete they are of a more popular character. There, of
all the fruits of the earth, of cattle, of the public revenues, and
of the tribute which is paid by the Perioeci, one portion is
assigned to the gods and to the service of the state, and
another to the common meals, so that men, women, and
9 children are all supported out of a common stock[1]. The
legislator has many ingenious ways of securing moderation in
eating which he conceives to be a gain; he likewise encourages
the separation of men from women, lest they should have too
many children, and the companionship of men with one another
—whether this is a good or bad thing I shall have an opportunity of considering at another time[2]. But that the Cretan
common meals are better ordered than the Lacedaemonian
there can be no doubt.

On the other hand, the Cosmi are even a worse institution

[1] Cp. vii. 10. § 10.   [2] vii. 16 (?).

than the Ephors, of which they have all the evils without the **II. 10** good. Like the Ephors, they are any chance persons, but in 10 Crete this is not counterbalanced by a corresponding political advantage. At Sparta every one is eligible, and the body of the people, having a share in the highest office, want the state to be permanent[1]. But in Crete the Cosmi are elected out of certain families, and not out of the whole people, and the elders out of those who have been Cosmi.

The same criticism may be made about the Cretan, which 11 has been already made about the Lacedaemonian elders. Their irresponsibility and life tenure is too great a privilege, and their arbitrary power of acting upon their own judgment, and dispensing with written law, is dangerous. It is no proof 12 of the goodness of the institution that the people are not discontented at being excluded from it. For there is no profit to be made out of the office; and, unlike the Ephors, 1272 b the Cosmi, being in an island, are removed from temptation.

The remedy by which they correct the evil of this institu- 13 tion is an extraordinary one, suited rather to a close oligarchy than to a constitutional state. For the Cosmi are often expelled by a conspiracy of their own colleagues, or of private individuals; and they are allowed also to resign before their term of office has expired. Surely all matters of this kind are better regulated by law than by the will of man, which is a very unsafe rule. Worst of all is the suspension of the 14 office of Cosmi, a device to which the nobles often have recourse when they will not submit to justice. This shows that the Cretan government, although possessing some of the characteristics of a constitutional state, is really a close oligarchy.

[1] Cp. supra, c. 9. § 21.

II. 10   The Cretans have a habit, too, of setting up a chief; they
get together a party among the common people and gather
their friends and then quarrel and fight with one another.
15 What is this but the temporary destruction of the state and
dissolution of society?   A city is in a dangerous condition
when those who are willing are also able to attack her.   But,
as I have already said, the island of Crete is saved by her
situation; distance has the same effect as the Lacedaemonian
16 prohibition of strangers; and the Cretans have no foreign
dominions.   This is the reason why the Perioeci are contented
in Crete, whereas the Helots are perpetually revolting.   But
when lately foreign invaders found their way into the island,
the weakness of the Cretan constitution was revealed.   Enough
of the government of Crete.

11   The Carthaginians are also considered to have an excellent
form of government, which differs from that of any other
state in several respects, though it is in some very like the
Lacedaemonian.   Indeed, all three states—the Lacedaemonian,
the Cretan, and the Carthaginian—nearly resemble one another,
and are very different from any others.   Many of the Cartha-
2 ginian institutions are excellent.   The superiority of their
constitution is proved by the fact that, although containing an
element of democracy, it has been lasting; the Carthaginians
have never had any rebellion worth speaking of, and have
never been under the rule of a tyrant.

3   Among the points in which the Carthaginian constitution
resembles the Lacedaemonian are the following:—The common tables of the clubs answer to the Spartan phiditia, and
their magistracy of the 104 to the Ephors; but, whereas the
Ephors are any chance persons, the magistrates of the Carthaginians are elected according to merit—this is an improvement.

They have also their kings and their gerusia, or council of **II. 11**
elders, who correspond to the kings and elders of Sparta.
Their kings, unlike the Spartan, are not always of the same **4**
family, and this an ordinary one, but if there is some distinguished family they are selected out of it and not appointed
by seniority—this is far better.   Such officers have great
power, and therefore, if they are persons of little worth, do
a great deal of harm, and they have already done harm at **1273 a**
Lacedaemon.

Most of the defects or deviations from the perfect state, for **5**
which the Carthaginian constitution would be censured, apply
equally to all the forms of government which we have mentioned.   But of the deflections from aristocracy and constitutional government, some incline more to democracy and some to
oligarchy. The kings and elders, if unanimous, may determine
whether they will or will not bring a matter before the people,
but when they are not unanimous, the people may decide
whether or not the matter shall be brought forward.   And **6**
whatever the kings and elders bring before the people is not
only heard but also determined by them, and any one who likes
may oppose it; now this is not permitted in Sparta and Crete.
That the magistracies of five who have under them many **7**
important matters should be co-opted, that they should choose
the supreme council of 100, and should hold office longer than
other magistrates (for they are virtually rulers both before and
after they hold office)—these are oligarchical features; their
being without salary and not elected by lot, and any similar
points, such as the practice of having all suits tried by the
magistrates[1], and not some by one class of judges or jurors
and some by another, as at Lacedaemon, are characteristic of

---

[1] Cp. iii. 1. §§ 10, 11; and see note at end.

II. 11 aristocracy. The Carthaginian constitution deviates from
8 aristocracy and inclines to oligarchy, chiefly on a point where
popular opinion is on their side. For men in general think
that magistrates should be chosen not only for their merit, but
for their wealth : a man, they say, who is poor cannot rule well
9 —he has not the leisure. If, then, election of magistrates for
their wealth be characteristic of oligarchy, and election for
merit of aristocracy, there will be a third form under which the
constitution of Carthage is comprehended ; for the Carthaginians choose their magistrates, and particularly the highest
of them—their kings and generals—with an eye both to merit
and to wealth.

10   But we must acknowledge that, in thus deviating from
aristocracy, the legislator has committed an error. Nothing is
more absolutely necessary than to provide that the highest class,
not only when in office, but when out of office, should have leisure
and not demean themselves in any way ; and to this his attention should be first directed. Even if you must have regard to
wealth, in order to secure leisure, yet it is surely a bad thing
that the greatest offices, such as those of kings and generals,
11 should be bought. The law which allows this abuse makes
wealth of more account than virtue, and the whole state
becomes avaricious. For, whenever the chiefs of the state
deem anything honourable, the other citizens are sure to follow
1273 b their example ; and, where virtue has not the first place, there
12 aristocracy cannot be firmly established. Those who have
been at the expense of purchasing their places will be in the
habit of repaying themselves ; and it is absurd to suppose that
a poor and honest man will be wanting to make gains, and that
a lower stamp of man who has incurred a great expense will
not. Wherefore they should rule who are able to rule best

[ἀρισταρχεῖν].   And even if the legislator does not care to **II. 11** protect the good from poverty, he should at any rate secure leisure for those in office[1].

It would seem also to be a bad principle that the same 13 person should hold many offices, which is a favourite practice among the Carthaginians, for one business is better done by one man[2].   The legislator should see to this and should not appoint the same person to be a flute-player and a shoemaker. Hence, where the state is large, it is more in accordance both 14 with constitutional and with democratic principles that the offices of state should be distributed among many persons. For, as I was saying, this arrangement is more popular, and any action familiarized by repetition is better and sooner performed.   We have a proof in military and naval matters; the duties of command and of obedience in both these services extend to all.

The government of the Carthaginians is oligarchical, but 15 they successfully escape the evils of oligarchy by their wealth, which enables them from time to time to send out some portion of the people[3] to their colonies.   This is their panacea and the means by which they give stability to the state.   Accident favours them, but the legislator should be able to provide against revolution without trusting to accidents. As things are, if any misfortune occurred, and the people 16 revolted from their rulers, there would be no way of restoring peace by legal methods.

---

[1] Cp. c. 9. § 2.   [2] Cp. Plato, Rep. ii. 374 A.

[3] Or, removing the comma after πλουτεῖν, and adding one after μέρος, 'by enriching one portion of the people after another whom they send to their colonies.'   Cp. vi. 5. § 9, which tends to confirm this way of taking the words.

II. 11   Such is the character of the Lacedaemonian, Cretan, and Carthaginian constitutions, which are justly celebrated.

12   Of those who have treated of governments, some have never taken any part at all in public affairs, but have passed their lives in a private station; about most of them, what was worth telling has been already told.   Others have been law-givers, either in their own or in foreign cities, whose affairs they have administered; and of these some have only made laws, others have framed constitutions; for example, Lycurgus 2 and Solon did both.   Of the Lacedaemonian constitution I have already spoken.   As to Solon, he is thought by some to have been a good legislator, who put an end to the ex-clusiveness of the oligarchy, emancipated the people, established the ancient Athenian democracy, and harmonized the different elements of the state.   According to their view, the council of Areopagus was an oligarchical element, the elected magis-1274 a tracy, aristocratical, and the courts of law, democratical.   The truth seems to be that the council and the elected magistracy 3 existed before the time of Solon, and were retained by him, but that he formed the courts of law out of all the citizens, thus creating the democracy, which is the very reason why he is sometimes blamed.   For in giving the supreme power to the law courts, which are elected by lot, he is thought to have 4 destroyed the non-democratic element.   When the law courts grew powerful, to please the people, who were now playing the tyrant, the old constitution was changed into the existing democracy.   Ephialtes and Pericles curtailed the power of the Areopagus; they also instituted the payment of the juries, and thus every demagogue in turn increased the power of the 5 democracy until it became what we now see.   All this is true; it seems however to be the result of circumstances, and not to

have been intended by Solon. For the people having been **II. 12**
instrumental in gaining the empire of the sea in the Persian
War[1], began to get a notion of itself, and followed worthless
demagogues, whom the better class opposed. Solon himself
appears to have given the Athenians only that power of electing
to offices and calling to account the magistrates, which was
absolutely necessary[2]; for without it they would have been
in a state of slavery and enmity to the government. All the **6**
magistrates he appointed from the notables and the men of
wealth, that is to say, from the pentacosio-medimni, or from
the class called zeugitae (because they kept a yoke of oxen), or
from a third class of so-called knights or cavalry. The fourth
class were labourers who had no share in any magistracy.

Mere legislators were Zaleucus, who gave laws to the Epi-
zephyrian, Locrians, and Charondas, who legislated for his
own city of Catana, and for the other Chalcidian cities in
Italy and Sicily. Some persons attempt [3] to make out that **7**
Onomacritus was the first person who had any special skill in
legislation[3], and that he, although a Locrian by birth, was
trained in Crete, where he lived in the exercise of his prophetic
art; that Thales was his companion, and that Lycurgus and
Zaleucus were disciples of Thales, as Charondas was of
Zaleucus. But their account is quite inconsistent with **8**
chronology.

There was also a Theban legislator, whose name was
Philolaus, the Corinthian. This Philolaus was one of the
family of the Bacchiadae, and a lover of Diocles, the Olympic
victor, who left Corinth in horror of the incestuous passion

---

[1] Cp. v. 4. § 8; viii. 6. § 11.   [2] Cp. iii. 11. § 8.
[3] Or (with Bernays), 'to make out an unbroken series of great legislators, Onomacritus being considered the first.'

II. 12 which his mother Halcyone had conceived for him, and retired
to Thebes, where the two friends together ended their days.
9 The inhabitants still point out their tombs, which are in full
view of one another, but one looks towards Corinth, the other
not. Tradition says that the two friends arranged them in
this way, Diocles out of horror at his misfortunes, so that the
land of Corinth might not be visible from his tomb; Philolaus
1274 b that it might. This is the reason why they settled at Thebes,
10 and so Philolaus legislated for the Thebans, and, besides some
other enactments, gave them laws about the procreation of
children, which they call the 'Laws of Adoption.' These
laws were peculiar to him, and were intended to preserve the
number of the lots.

11   In the legislation of Charondas there is nothing remarkable,
except the laws about false witnesses. He is the first who
instituted actions for perjury. His laws are more exact and
more precisely expressed than even those of our modern
legislators.

12   Characteristic of Phaleas is the equalization of property; of
Plato, the community of women, children, and property, the
common meals of women, and the law about drinking, that
the sober shall be masters of the feast[1]; also the training of
soldiers to acquire by practice equal skill with both hands, so
that one should be as useful as the other[2].

13   Draco has left laws, but he adapted them to a constitution
which already existed, and there is no peculiarity in them
which is worth mentioning, except the greatness and severity
of the punishments.

   Pittacus, too, was only a lawgiver, and not the author of
a constitution; he has a law which is peculiar to him, that, if

[1] Cp. Laws, ii. 671 D–672 A.   [2] Cp. Laws, vii. 794 D.

a drunken man strike another, he shall be more heavily II. 12
punished than if he were sober[1]; he looked not to the excuse
which might be offered for the drunkard, but only to expediency, for drunken more often than sober people commit acts
of violence.

Androdamas of Rhegium gave laws to the Chalcidians of 14
Thrace. Some of them relate to homicide, and to heiresses;
but there is nothing remarkable in them.

And here let us conclude our enquiry into the various constitutions which either actually exist, or have been devised by
theorists.

[1] Cp. N. Eth. iii. 5. § 8.

BOOK III

III. 1 HE who would enquire into the nature and various kinds of government must first of all determine 'What is a state?' At present this is a disputed question. Some say that the state has done a certain act; others, no, not the state [1], but the oligarchy or the tyrant. And the legislator or statesman is concerned entirely with the state; a constitution or government being an **2** arrangement of the inhabitants of a state. But a state is composite, and, like any other whole, made up of many parts;— these are the citizens, who compose it. It is evident, there- **1275 a** fore, that we must begin by asking, Who is the citizen, and what is the meaning of the term? For here again there may be a difference of opinion. He who is a citizen in a demo- **3** cracy will often not be a citizen in an oligarchy. Leaving out of consideration those who have been made citizens, or who have obtained the name of citizen in any other accidental manner, we may say, first, that a citizen is not a citizen **4** because he lives in a certain place, for resident aliens and slaves share in the place; nor is he a citizen who has no legal right except that of suing and being sued; for this right may be enjoyed under the provisions of a treaty. Even resident aliens in many places possess such rights, although in an imperfect form; for they are obliged to have a patron. **5** Hence they do but imperfectly participate in citizenship, and we call them citizens only in a qualified sense, as we might apply the term to children who are too young to be on the

[1] Cp. c. 3. § 1.

register, or to old men who have been relieved from state III. 1
duties. Of these we do not say simply that they are citizens,
but add in the one case tnat they are not of age, and in the
other, that they are past the age, or something of that sort;
the precise expression is immaterial, for our meaning is clear.
Similar difficulties to those which I have mentioned may be
raised and answered about deprived citizens and about exiles.
But the citizen, whom we are seeking to define, is a citizen in
the strictest sense, against whom no such exception can be
taken, and his special characteristic is that he shares in the
administration of justice, and in offices. Now of offices some 6
have a limit of time, and the same persons are not allowed to
hold them twice, or can only hold them after a fixed interval;
others have no limit of time—for example, the office of dicast
or ecclesiast [1]. It may, indeed, be argued that these are not 7
magistrates at all, and that their functions give them no share
in the government. But surely it is ridiculous to say that
those who have the supreme power do not govern. Not to
dwell further upon this, which is a purely verbal question,
what we want is a common term including both dicast and
ecclesiast. Let us, for the sake of distinction, call it 'indeterminate office,' and we will assume that those who share in
such office are citizens. This is the most comprehensive 8
definition of a citizen, and best suits all those who are generally
so called.

But we must not forget that things of which the underlying
notions differ in kind, one of them being first, another second,
another third, have, when regarded in this relation, nothing,
or hardly anything, worth mentioning in common. Now we 9

[1] 'Dicast' = juryman and judge in one: 'ecclesiast' = member of the
ecclesia or assembly of the citizens.

III. 1 see that governments differ in kind, and that some of them
1275 b are prior and that others are posterior; those which are faulty
or perverted are necessarily posterior to those which are
perfect. (What we mean by perversion will be hereafter
explained [1].) The citizen then of necessity differs under each
10 form of government; and our definition is best adapted to the
citizen of a democracy; but not necessarily to other states.
For in some states the people are not acknowledged, nor have
they any regular assembly, but only extraordinary ones; and
suits are distributed in turn among the magistrates. At Lacedaemon, for instance, the Ephors determine suits about contracts, which they distribute among themselves, while the
elders are judges of homicide, and other causes are decided
11 by other magistrates. A similar principle prevails at Carthage [2]; there certain magistrates decide all causes. We may,
indeed, modify our definition of the citizen so as to include
these states. [But strictly taken it only applies in democracies.]
In other states it is the holder of a determinate, not of an
indeterminate, office who legislates and judges, and to some
or all such holders of determinate offices is reserved the right
of deliberating or judging about some things or about all
32 things. The conception of the citizen now begins to clear up.

He who has the power to take part in the deliberative or
judicial administration of any state is said by us to be a citizen
of that state; and speaking generally, a state is a body of
citizens sufficing for the purposes of life.

2 But in practice a citizen is defined to be one of whom both
the parents are citizens; others insist on going further back;
say to two or three or more grandparents. This is a short
and practical definition; but there are some who raise the

---

[1] Cp. c. 6. § 11.   [2] Cp. ii. 11. § 7.

further question : How this third or fourth ancestor came to III. 2
be a citizen?   Gorgias of Leontini, partly because he was in
a difficulty, partly in irony, said—'Mortars are made by the
mortar-makers, and the citizens of Larissa are also a manufactured article, made, like the kettles which bear their name
[λαρισαῖοι], by the magistrates[1].'   Yet the question is really 3
simple, for if, according to the definition just given, they
shared in the government[2], they were citizens.   [This is a
better definition than the other.]   For the words, 'born of
a father or mother, who is a citizen,' cannot possibly apply to
the first inhabitants or founders of a state.

There is a greater difficulty in the case of those who have
been made citizens after a revolution, as by Cleisthenes at
Athens after the expulsion of the tyrants, for he enrolled in
tribes a number of strangers and slaves and[3] resident aliens.
The doubt in these cases is, not who is, but whether he, who 4
is, ought to be a citizen; and there will still be a further 1276 a
doubt, whether he who ought not to be a citizen is one in
fact, for what ought not to be is what is false and is not.
Now, there are some who hold office, and yet ought not to 5
hold office, whom we call rulers, although they rule unjustly.
And the citizen was defined by the fact of his holding some
kind of rule or office—he who holds a judicial or legislative
office fulfils our definition of a citizen.   It is evident, therefore, that the citizens about whom the doubt has arisen must

[1] An untranslatable play upon the word δημιουργοί, which means
either 'a magistrate' or 'an artisan.'

[2] Cp. c. 1. § 12.

[3] Inserting καί before μετοίκους with Bekker in his second edition. If
καί is omitted, as in all the MSS., we must translate—'he enrolled in
tribes many metics, both strangers and slaves': or, 'he enrolled in tribes
many strangers, and metics who had been slaves.'

III. 2 be called citizens; whether they ought to be so or not is
a question which is bound up with the previous enquiry[1].

3 A parallel question is raised respecting the state whether
a certain act is or is not an act of the state; for example, in
the transition from an oligarchy or a tyranny to a democracy.

2 In such cases persons refuse to fulfil their contracts or any
other obligations on the ground that the tyrant, and not the
state, contracted them; they argue that some constitutions are
established by force, and not for the sake of the common
good. But this would apply equally to democracies, for they
too may be founded on violence, and then the acts of the
democracy will be neither more nor less legitimate than those

3 of an oligarchy or of a tyranny. This question runs up into
another—When shall we say that the state is the same, and
when different? It would be a very superficial view which
considered only the place and the inhabitants; for the soil and
the population may be separated, and some of the inhabitants

4 may live in one place and some in another. This, however,
is not a very serious difficulty; we need only remark that the
word 'state' is ambiguous, meaning both state and city.

It is further asked: When are men, living in the same
place, to be regarded as a single city—what is the limit?

5 Certainly not the wall of the city, for you might surround all
Peloponnesus with a wall. But a city, having such vast
circuit, would contain a nation rather than a state, like Baby-
lon[2], which, as they say, had been taken for three days before

6 some part of the inhabitants became aware of the fact. This
difficulty may, however, with advantage be deferred[3] to
another occasion; the statesman has to consider the size of

----

[1] Cp. c. i. § i.   [2] Cp. ii. 6. § 6.
                [3] Cp. vii. c. 4 and c. 5.

the state, and whether it should consist of more than one III. **3**
nation or not.

Again, shall we say that while the race of inhabitants, as
well as their place of abode, remain the same, the city is also
the same, although the citizens are always dying and being
born, as we call rivers and fountains the same, although the
water is always flowing away and coming again? Or shall
we say that the generations of men, like the rivers, are the
same, but that the state changes? For, since the state is 1276 b
a community of citizens united by sharing in one form of **7**
government, when the form of the government changes and
becomes different, then it may be supposed that the state is
no longer the same, just as a tragic differs from a comic
chorus, although the members of both may be identical. And **8**
in this manner we speak of every union or composition of
elements, when the form of their composition alters; for
example, harmony of the same sounds is said to be different,
accordingly as the Dorian or the Phrygian mode is employed.
And if this is true it is evident that the sameness of the state **9**
consists chiefly in the sameness of the constitution, and may
be called or not called by the same name, whether the inhabitants are the same or entirely different. It is quite another
question, whether a state ought or ought not to fulfil engagements when the form of government changes.

There is a point nearly allied to the preceding: Whether **4**
the virtue of a good man and a good citizen is the same or
not[1]. But, before entering on this discussion, we must first
obtain some general notion of the virtue of the citizen. Like
the sailor, the citizen is a member of a community. Now, **2**
sailors have different functions, for one of them is a rower,

[1] Cp. N. Eth. v. 2. § 11.

III. 4 another a pilot, a third a look-out man, and a fourth is described by some similar term; and while the precise definition of each individual's virtue applies exclusively to him, there is, at the same time, a common definition applicable to them all. For they have all of them a common object, which **3** is safety in navigation. Similarly, one citizen differs from another, but the salvation of the community is the common business of them all. This community is the state; the virtue of the citizen must therefore be relative to the constitution of which he is a member. If, then, there are many forms of government, it is evident that the virtue of the good citizen cannot be the one perfect virtue. But we say that the good **4** man is he who has perfect virtue. Hence it is evident that the good citizen need not of necessity possess the virtue which makes a good man.

The same question may also be approached by another road, **5** from a consideration of the perfect state. If the state cannot be entirely composed of good men, and each citizen is expected to do his own business well, and must therefore have virtue, **1277 a** inasmuch as all the citizens cannot be alike, the virtue of the citizen and of the good man cannot coincide. All must have the virtue of the good citizen—thus, and thus only, can the state be perfect; but they will not have the virtue of a good man, unless we assume that in the good state all the citizens must be good.

6 Again, the state may be compared to the living being: as the first elements into which the living being is resolved are soul and body, as the soul is made up of reason and appetite, the family of husband and wife, property of master and slave, so out of all these, as well as other dissimilar elements, the state is composed; and, therefore, the virtue of all the

citizens cannot possibly be the same, any more than the III. 4
excellence of the leader of a chorus is the same as that of the
performer who stands by his side. I have said enough to 7
show why the two kinds of virtue cannot be absolutely and
always the same.

But will there then be no case in which the virtue of the
good citizen and the virtue of the good man coincide? To
this we answer [not that the good citizen, but] that the good
ruler is a good and wise man, and that he who would be
a statesman must be a wise man. And some persons say that 8
even the education of the ruler should be of a special kind;
for are not the children of kings instructed in riding and
military exercises? As Euripides says:

'No subtle arts for me, but what the state requires[1].'
As though there were a special education needed by a ruler.
If then the virtue of a good ruler is the same as that of a good 9
man, and we assume further that the subject is a citizen as
well as the ruler, the virtue of the good citizen and the virtue
of the good man cannot be always the same, although in some
cases [i.e. in the perfect state] they may; for the virtue of
a ruler differs from that of a citizen. It was the sense of this
difference which made Jason say that 'he felt hungry when he
was not a tyrant,' meaning that he could not endure to live in
a private station. But, on the other hand, it may be argued 10
that men are praised for knowing both how to rule and how
to obey, and he is said to be a citizen of approved virtue who
is able to do both. Now if we suppose the virtue of a good
man to be that which rules, and the virtue of the citizen to
include ruling and obeying, it cannot be said that they are

---

[1] Fragment from the Aeolus, quoted in Stobaeus, 45. 13.

III. 4 equally worthy of praise.   Since, then, it is occasionally held
   11 that the ruler and the ruled should learn different things and
not the same things, and that the citizen must know and share
in both; the inference is obvious[1].   There is, indeed, the
rule of a master which is concerned with menial offices[2],—the
master need not know how to perform these, but may employ
others in the execution of them: anything else would be
12 degrading; and by anything else I mean the menial duties
which vary much in character and are executed by various
classes of slaves, such, for example, as handicraftsmen, who,
as their name signifies, live by the labour of their hands:—
1277 b under these the mechanic is included.   Hence in ancient
times, and among some nations, the working classes had no
share in the government—a privilege which they only acquired
13 under the extreme democracy.   Certainly the good man and
the statesman and the good citizen ought not to learn the
crafts of inferiors except for their own occasional use[3]; if
they habitually practise them, there will cease to be a distinction between master and slave.

14   This is not the rule of which we are speaking; but there
is a rule of another kind, which is exercised over freemen and
equals by birth—a constitutional rule, which the ruler must
learn by obeying, as he would learn the duties of a general of
cavalry by being under the orders of a general of cavalry, or
the duties of a general of infantry by being under the orders
of a general of infantry, or by having had the command of
a company or brigade.   It has been well said that 'he who
15 has never learned to obey cannot be a good commander.'   The

---

[1] Viz. that some kind of previous subjection is an advantage to the
ruler.   Cp. infra, § 14.

[2] Cp. i. 7. §§ 2–5.   [3] Cp. viii. 2. § 5.

two are not the same, but the good citizen ought to be capable **III. 4**
of both; he should know how to govern like a freeman, and
how to obey like a freeman—these are the virtues of a citizen.
And, although the temperance and justice of a ruler are dis- 16
tinct from those of a subject, the virtue of a good man will
include both; for the good man, who is free and also a subject,
will not have one virtue only, say justice, but he will have
distinct kinds of virtue, the one qualifying him to rule, the
other to obey, and differing as the temperance and courage of
men and women differ[1]. For a man would be thought a 17
coward if he had no more courage than a courageous woman,
and a woman would be thought loquacious if she imposed no
more restraint on her conversation than the good man; and
indeed their part in the management of the household is
different, for the duty of the one is to acquire, and of the
other to preserve. Practical wisdom only is characteristic of
the ruler[2]: it would seem that all other virtues must equally
belong to ruler and subject. The virtue of the subject is 18
certainly not wisdom, but only true opinion; he may be compared to the maker of the flute, while his master is like the
flute-player or user of the flute[3].

From these considerations may be gathered the answer to
the question, whether the virtue of the good man is the same
as that of the good citizen, or different, and how far the same,
and how far different[4].

There still remains one more question about the citizen: **5**
Is he only a true citizen who has a share of office, or is the
mechanic to be included? If they who hold no office are to
be deemed citizens, not every citizen can have this virtue of

---

[1] Cp. i. 13. § 9.   [2] Cp. Rep. iv. 428.   [3] Cp. Rep. x. 601 D, E.
[4] Cp. c. 5. § 10; c. 18. § 1; iv. 7. § 2; vii. 14. § 8.

III. 5 ruling and obeying [1] which makes a citizen [1].   And if none of
the lower class are citizens, in which part of the state are
they to be placed ?   For they are not resident aliens, and they
1278 a are not foreigners.   To this objection may we not reply, that
[2] there is no more absurdity in excluding them than in excluding
slaves and freedmen from any of the above-mentioned classes ?
It must be admitted that we cannot consider all those to be
citizens who are necessary to the existence of the state; for
example, children are not citizens equally with grown up men,
who are citizens absolutely, but children, not being grown up,
3 are only citizens in a qualified sense.   Doubtless in ancient
times, and among some nations, the artisan class were slaves
or foreigners, and therefore the majority of them are so now.
The best form of state will not admit them to citizenship;
but if they are admitted, then our definition of the virtue of
a citizen will apply to some citizens and freemen only, and
4 not to those who work for their living.   The latter class, to
whom toil is a necessity, are either slaves who minister to the
wants of individuals, or mechanics and labourers who are the
servants of the community.   These reflections carried a little
further will explain their position; and indeed what has been
said already is of itself explanation enough.

5   Since there are many forms of government there must be
many varieties of citizens, and especially of citizens who are
subjects; so that under some governments the mechanic and
the labourer will be citizens, but not in others, as, for example,

---

[1] Or, ' for this man (i.e. the meaner sort of man) is a citizen and does
not exercise rule' (see below, § 3, εἰ δὲ καὶ οὗτος πολίτης).   According
to the way of taking the passage which is followed in the text, οὗτος =
ὁ ἔχων τὴν τοιαύτην ἀρετήν: according to the second way, it refers to
βάναυσος

in aristocracy or the so-called government of the best (if there **III.** be such an one), in which honours are given according to virtue and merit; for no man can practise virtue who is living the life of a mechanic or labourer.   In oligarchies the qualifi- **6** cation for office is high, and therefore no labourer can ever be a citizen; but a mechanic may, for many of them are rich. At Thebes [1] there was a law that no man could hold office **7** who had not retired from business for ten years.   In many states the law goes to the length of admitting aliens; for in some democracies a man is a citizen though his mother only be a citizen [and his father an alien]; and a similar principle is applied to illegitimate children; the law is relaxed when **8** there is a dearth of population.   But when the number of citizens increases, first the children of a male or a female slave are excluded; then those whose mothers only are citizens; and at last the right of citizenship is confined to those whose fathers and mothers are both citizens.

Hence, as is evident, there are different kinds of citizens; **9** and he is a citizen in the highest sense who shares in the honours of the state.   In the poems of Homer [Achilles complains of Agamemnon treating him] 'like some dishonoured stranger [2];' for he who is excluded from the honours of the state is no better than an alien.   But when this exclusion is concealed, then the object is to deceive one's fellow-country-men.

As to the question whether the virtue of the good man is the 1278 b same as that of the good citizen, the considerations already **10** adduced prove that in some states the two are the same, and in others different.   When they are the same it is not the virtue of every citizen which is the same as that of the good

---

[1] Cp. vi. 7. § 4.   [2] Il. ix. 648.

III. 5 man, but only the virtue of the statesman and of those who have or may have, alone or in conjunction with others, the conduct of public affairs.

6   Having determined these questions, we have next to consider whether there is only one form of government or many, and if many, what they are, and how many, and what are the differences between them.

A constitution is the arrangement of magistracies in a state[1], especially of the highest of all. The government is everywhere sovereign in the state, and the constitution is in fact the **2** government. For example, in democracies the people are supreme, but in oligarchies, the few; and, therefore, we say that these two forms of government are different: and so in other cases.

First, let us consider what is the purpose of a state, and how many forms of government there are by which human **3** society is regulated. We have already said, in the former part of this treatise[2], when drawing a distinction between household-management and the rule of a master, that man is by nature a political animal. And therefore, men, even when they do not require one another's help, desire to live together all the same, and are in fact brought together by their common interests in proportion as they severally attain to any measure **4** of well-being. This is certainly the chief end, both of individuals and of states. And also for the sake of mere life (in which there is possibly some noble element) mankind meet together and maintain the political community, so long as the **5** evils of existence do not greatly overbalance the good[3]. And we all see that men cling to life even in the midst of

---

[1] Cp. c. i. § 1; iv. 1. § 10.   [2] Cp. i. 2. §§ 9, 10.
[3] Cp. Plato, Polit. 302 A.

misfortune, seeming to find in it a natural sweetness and III. 6
happiness.

There is no difficulty in distinguishing the various kinds of
authority; they have been often defined already in popular
works[1]. The rule of a master, although the slave by nature 6
and the master by nature have in reality the same interests, is
nevertheless exercised primarily with a view to the interest of
the master, but accidentally considers the slave, since, if the
slave perish, the rule of the master perishes with him. On 7
the other hand, the government of a wife and children and of
a household, which we have called household-management, is
exercised in the first instance for the good of the governed or
for the common good of both parties, but essentially for the
good of the governed, as we see to be the case in medicine, 1279 a
gymnastics, and the arts in general, which are only accidentally
concerned with the good of the artists themselves[2]. (For
there is no reason why the trainer may not sometimes practise
gymnastics, and the pilot is always one of the crew.) The 8
trainer or the pilot considers the good of those committed to
his care. But, when he is one of the persons taken care of,
he accidentally participates in the advantage, for the pilot is
also a sailor, and the trainer becomes one of those in training.
And so in politics: when the state is framed upon the prin- 9
ciple of equality and likeness, the citizens think that they
ought to hold office by turns. In the order of nature every
one would take his turn of service; and then again, somebody
else would look after his interest, just as he, while in office,
had looked after theirs[3]. [That was originally the way.]
But nowadays, for the sake of the advantage which is to be 10

[1] Or, 'in our popular works.'   [2] Cp. Plato, Rep. i. 341 D.
[3] Cp. ii. 2. §§ 6, 7.

III. 6 gained from the public revenues and from office, men want to be always in office. One might imagine that the rulers, being sickly, were only kept in health while they continued in office; in that case we may be sure that they would be hunting
11 after places. The conclusion is evident: that governments, which have a regard to the common interest, are constituted in accordance with strict principles of justice, and are therefore true forms; but those which regard only the interest of the rulers are all defective and perverted forms, for they are despotic, whereas a state is a community of freemen.

7 Having determined these points, we have next to consider how many forms of government there are, and what they are; and in the first place what are the true forms, for when they are determined the perversions of them will at once be
2 apparent. The words constitution and government have the same meaning, and the government, which is the supreme authority in states, must be in the hands of one, or of a few, or of many. The true forms of government, therefore, are those in which the one, or the few, or the many, govern with a view to the common interest; but governments which rule with a view to the private interest, whether of the one, or of the few, or of the many, are perversions [1]. For citizens, if they are truly citizens, ought to participate in the advantages of a state. Of forms of government in which one rules, we
3 call that which regards the common interests, kingship or royalty; that in which more than one, but not many, rule, aristocracy [the rule of the best]; and it is so called, either because the rulers are the best men, or because they have at heart the best interests of the state and of the citizens. But when the citizens at large administer the state for the common

[1] Cp. Eth. viii. 10

interest, the government is called by the generic name—a III. 7
constitution [πολιτεία]. And there is a reason for this use of
language. One man or a few may excel in virtue; but of 4
virtue there are many kinds: and as the number increases it
becomes more difficult for them to attain perfection in every 1279 b
kind, though they may in military virtue, for this is found in
the masses. Hence, in a constitutional government the
fighting-men have the supreme power, and those who possess
arms are the citizens.

Of the above-mentioned forms, the perversions are as 5
follows:—of royalty, tyranny; of aristocracy, oligarchy; of
constitutional government, democracy. For tyranny is a kind
of monarchy which has in view the interest of the monarch
only; oligarchy has in view the interest of the wealthy;
democracy, of the needy: none of them the common good
of all.

But there are difficulties about these forms of government, 8
and it will therefore be necessary to state a little more at
length the nature of each of them. For he who would make
a philosophical study of the various sciences, and does not
regard practice only, ought not to overlook or omit anything,
but to set forth the truth in every particular. Tyranny, as 2
I was saying, is monarchy exercising the rule of a master
over political society; oligarchy is when men of property have
the government in their hands; democracy, the opposite,
when the indigent, and not the men of property, are the
rulers. And here arises the first of our difficulties, and it 3
relates to the definition just given. For democracy is said to
be the government of the many. But what if the many are
men of property and have the power in their hands? In like
manner oligarchy is said to be the government of the few; but

III. 8 what if the poor are fewer than the rich, and have the power in their hands because they are stronger? In these cases the distinction which we have drawn between these different forms of government would no longer hold good.

4 Suppose, once more, that we add wealth to the few and poverty to the many, and name the governments accordingly— an oligarchy is said to be that in which the few and the wealthy, and a democracy that in which the many and the 5 poor are the rulers—there will still be a difficulty. For, if the only forms of government are the ones already mentioned, how shall we describe those other governments also just mentioned by us, in which the rich are the more numerous and the poor are the fewer, and both govern in their respective states?

6 The argument seems to show that, whether in oligarchies or in democracies, the number of the governing body, whether the greater number, as in a democracy, or the smaller number, as in an oligarchy, is an accident due to the fact that the rich everywhere are few, and the poor numerous. But if so, there is a misapprehension of the causes of the difference 7 between them. For the real difference between democracy 1280 a and oligarchy is poverty and wealth. Wherever men rule by reason of their wealth, whether they be few or many, that is an oligarchy, and where the poor rule, that is a democracy. But as a fact the rich are few and the poor many: for few are well-to-do, whereas freedom is enjoyed by all, and wealth and freedom are the grounds on which the oligarchical and democratical parties respectively claim power in the state.

9 Let us begin by considering the common definitions of oligarchy and democracy, and what is justice oligarchical and

democratical. For all men cling to justice of some kind, but **III. 9**
their conceptions are imperfect and they do not express the
whole idea. For example, justice is thought by them to be,
and is, equality, not, however, for all, but only for equals.
And inequality is thought to be, and is, justice; neither is **2**
this for all, but only for unequals. When the persons are
omitted, then men judge erroneously. The reason is that
they are passing judgment on themselves, and most people
are bad judges in their own case. And whereas justice **3**
implies a relation to persons as well as to things, and a just
distribution, as I have already said in the Ethics[1], embraces
alike persons and things, they acknowledge the equality of the
things, but dispute about the merit of the persons, chiefly for
the reason which I have just given—because they are bad
judges in their own affairs; and secondly, because both the
parties to the argument are speaking of a limited and partial
justice, but imagine themselves to be speaking of absolute
justice. For those who are unequal in one respect, for **4**
example wealth, consider themselves to be unequal in all;
and any who are equal in one respect, for example freedom,
consider themselves to be equal in all. But they leave out
the capital point. For if men met and associated out of **5**
regard to wealth only, their share in the state would be
proportioned to their property, and the oligarchical doctrine
would then seem to carry the day. It would not be just
that he who paid one mina should have the same share of
a hundred minae, [2] whether of the principal or of the profits[2],
as he who paid the remaining ninety-nine. But a state **6**

[1] N. Eth. v. 3. § 4.
[2] Or, with Bernays, 'either in the case of the original contributors
or their successors.'

III. 9 exists for the sake of a good life, and not for the sake of life only: if life only were the object, slaves and brute animals might form a state, but they cannot, for they have no share in happiness or in a life of free choice.   Nor does a state exist for the sake of alliance and security from injustice [1], nor yet for the sake of exchange and mutual intercourse; for then the Tyrrhenians and the Carthaginians, and all who have commercial treaties with one another, would be the citizens of

7 one state.   True, they have agreements about imports, and engagements that they will do no wrong to one another, and

1280 b written articles of alliance.   But there are no magistracies common to the contracting parties who will enforce their engagements; different states have each their own magistracies. Nor does one state take care that the citizens of the other are such as they ought to be, nor see that those who come under the terms of the treaty do no wrong or wickedness at all, but only that they do no injustice to one another.

8 Whereas, those who care for good government take into consideration [the larger question of] virtue and vice in states. Whence it may be further inferred that [2] virtue must be the serious care of a state which truly deserves the name [2]: for [without this ethical end] the community becomes a mere alliance which differs only in place from alliances of which the members live apart; and law is only a convention, 'a surety to one another of justice,' as the sophist Lycophron says, and has no real power to make the citizens good and just.

9   This is obvious; for suppose distinct places, such as

[1] Cp. c. 1. § 4.

[2] Or, 'virtue must be the care of a state which is truly so called, and not merely in name.'

Corinth and Megara, to be united by a wall, still they would **III. 9**
not be one city, not even if the citizens had the right to 10
intermarry, which is one of the rights peculiarly characteristic
of states. Again, if men dwelt at a distance from one
another, but not so far off as to have no intercourse, and
there were laws among them that they should not wrong
each other in their exchanges, neither would this be a state.
Let us suppose that one man is a carpenter, another a
husbandman, another a shoemaker, and so on, and that their
number is ten thousand : nevertheless, if they have nothing in
common but exchange, alliance, and the like, that would not
constitute a state. Why is this? Surely not because they 11
are at a distance from one another : for even supposing that
such a community were to meet in one place, and that each
man had a house of his own, which was in a manner his
state, and that they made alliance with one another, but only
against evil-doers ; still an accurate thinker would not deem
this to be a state, if their intercourse with one another was of
the same character after as before their union. It is clear 12
then that a state is not a mere society, having a common
place, established for the prevention of crime and for the sake
of exchange. These are conditions without which a state
cannot exist; but all of them together do not constitute
a state, which is a community of well-being in families and
aggregations of families, for the sake of a perfect and self-
sufficing life. Such a community can only be established 13
among those who live in the same place and intermarry.
Hence arise in cities family connexions, brotherhoods,
common sacrifices, amusements which draw men together.
They are created by friendship, for friendship is the motive
of society. The end is the good life, and these are the

III. 9 means towards it. And the state is the union of families and
14 villages having for an end a perfect and self-sufficing life, by
1281 a which we mean a happy and honourable life[1].

Our conclusion, then, is that political society exists for the
15 sake of noble actions, and not of mere companionship. And
they who contribute most to such a society have a greater
share in it than those who have the same or a greater freedom
or nobility of birth but are inferior to them in political virtue;
or than those who exceed them in wealth but are surpassed
by them in virtue.

From what has been said it will be clearly seen that all the
partisans of different forms of government speak of a part of
justice only.

10 There is also a doubt as to what is to be the supreme
power in the state :—Is it the multitude? Or the wealthy?
Or the good? Or the one best man? Or a tyrant? Any
of these alternatives seems to involve disagreeable conse-
quences. If the poor, for example, because they are more in
number, divide among themselves the property of the rich,
is not this unjust? No, by heaven (will be the reply), for
2 the lawful authority [i. e. the people] willed it. But if this is
not injustice, pray what is? Again, when [in the first
division] all has been taken, and the majority divide anew the
property of the minority, is it not evident, if this goes on,
that they will ruin the state? Yet surely, virtue is not the
ruin of those who possess her, nor is justice destructive of
a state[2]; and therefore this law of confiscation clearly cannot
3 be just. If it were, all the acts of a tyrant must of necessity
be just; for he only coerces other men by superior power,
just as the multitude coerce the rich. But is it just, then,

---

[1] Cp. i. 2. § 8; N. Eth. i. 7. § 6.   [2] Cp. Plato, Rep. i. 351, 352.

that the few and the wealthy should be the rulers? And **III. 10**
what if they, in like manner, rob and plunder the people—is
this just? If so, the other case [i. e. the case of the
majority plundering the minority] will likewise be just. But **4**
there can be no doubt that all these things are wrong and
unjust.

Then ought the good to rule and have supreme power?
But in that case everybody else, being excluded from power,
will be dishonoured. For the offices of a state are posts of
honour; and if one set of men always hold them, the rest
must be deprived of them. Then will it be well that the one **5**
best man should rule? Nay, that is still more oligarchical,
for the number of those who are dishonoured is thereby
increased. Some one may say that it is bad for a man,
subject as he is to all the accidents of human passion, to
have the supreme power, rather than the law. But what if the
law itself be democratical or oligarchical, how will that help
us out of our difficulties[1]? Not at all; the same conse-
quences will follow.

Most of these questions may be reserved for another **11**
occasion. The principle that the multitude ought to be
supreme rather than the few best is capable of a satisfactory
explanation, and, though not free from difficulty, yet seems to
contain an element of truth. For the many, of whom each **2**
individual is but an ordinary person, when they meet together **1281 b**
may very likely be better than the few good, if regarded not
individually but collectively, just as a feast to which many
contribute is better than a dinner provided out of a single
purse. For each individual among the many has a share
of virtue and prudence, and when they meet together they

[1] Cp. c. 11. § 20.

III. 11 become in a manner one man, who has many feet, and hands, and senses; that is a figure of their mind and disposition.

3 Hence the many are better judges than a single man of music and poetry; for some understand one part, and some another,

4 and among them, they understand the whole. There is a similar combination of qualities in good men, who differ from any individual of the many, as the beautiful are said to differ from those who are not beautiful, and works of art from realities, because in them the scattered elements are combined, although, if taken separately, the eye of one person or some other feature in another person would be fairer than

5 in the picture. Whether this principle can apply to every democracy, and to all bodies of men, is not clear. Or rather, by heaven, in some cases it is impossible of application; for the argument would equally hold about brutes; and wherein, it will be asked, do some men differ from brutes? But there may be bodies of men about whom our statement is neverthe-

6 less true. And if so, the difficulty which has been already raised, and also another which is akin to it—viz. what power should be assigned to the mass of freemen and citizens, who are not rich and have no personal merit—are both solved.

7 There is still a danger in allowing them to share the great offices of state, for their folly will lead them into error, and their dishonesty into crime. But there is a danger also in not letting them share, for a state in which many poor men are

8 excluded from office will necessarily be full of enemies. The only way of escape is to assign to them some deliberative and judicial functions. For this reason Solon [1] and certain other legislators give them the power of electing to offices, and of calling the magistrates to account, but they do not allow

[1] Cp. ii. 12. § 5.

them to hold office singly.   When they meet together their **III. 11**
perceptions are quite good enough, and combined with the 9
better class they are useful to the state (just as impure
food when mixed with what is pure sometimes makes the
entire mass more wholesome than a small quantity of the
pure would be), but each individual, left to himself, forms
an imperfect judgment.   On the other hand, the popular 10
form of government involves certain difficulties.   In the first
place, it might be objected that he who can judge of the
healing of a sick man would be one who could himself
heal his disease, and make him whole—that is, in other
words, the physician; and so in all professions and arts. 1282 a.
As, then, the physician ought to be called to account by
physicians, so ought men in general to be called to account
by their peers.   But physicians are of three kinds:—there 11
is the apothecary, and there is the physician of the higher
class, and thirdly the intelligent man who has studied the
art: in all arts there is such a class; and we attribute
the power of judging to them quite as much as to professors
of the art.   Now, does not the same principle apply to 12
elections?   For a right election can only be made by those
who have knowledge; a geometrician, for example, will
choose rightly in matters of geometry, or a pilot in matters
of steering; and, even if there be some occupations and
arts with which private persons are familiar, they certainly
cannot judge better than those who know.   So that, according 13
to this argument, neither the election of magistrates, nor the
calling of them to account, should be entrusted to the many. 14
Yet possibly these objections are to a great extent met by
our old answer, that if the people are not utterly degraded,
although individually they may be worse judges than those

III. 11 who have special knowledge—as a body they are as good or better. Moreover, there are some artists whose works are judged of solely, or in the best manner, not by themselves, but by those who do not possess the art; for example, the knowledge of the house is not limited to the builder only; the user, or, in other words, the master, of the house will even be a better judge than the builder, just as the pilot will judge better of a rudder than the carpenter, and the guest will judge better of a feast than the cook.

15   This difficulty seems now to be sufficiently answered, but there is another akin to it. That inferior persons should have authority in greater matters than the good would appear to be a strange thing, yet the election and calling to account of the magistrates is the greatest of all. And these, as I was saying, are functions which in some states are assigned to the people, for the assembly is supreme in all such matters.

16 Yet persons of any age, and having but a small property qualification, sit in the assembly and deliberate and judge, although for the great officers of state, such as controllers and generals, a high qualification is required. This difficulty may be solved in the same manner as the preceding, and the present practice of democracies may be really defensible.

17 For the power does not reside in the dicast, or senator, or ecclesiast, but in the court and the senate, and the assembly, of which individual senators, or ecclesiasts, or

18 dicasts, are only parts or members. And for this reason the many may claim to have a higher authority than the few; for the people, and the senate, and the courts consist of many persons, and their property collectively is greater than the property of one or of a few individuals holding great offices. But enough of this.

The discussion of the first question[1] shows nothing so **III. 11**
clearly as that laws, when good, should be supreme; and [19]
that the magistrate or magistrates should regulate those [1282 b]
matters only on which the laws are unable to speak with
precision owing to the difficulty of any general principle
embracing all particulars[2]. But what are good laws has **20**
not yet been clearly explained; the old difficulty remains[3].
The goodness or badness, justice or injustice, of laws is
of necessity relative to the constitutions of states. But if **21**
so, true forms of government will of necessity have just laws,
and perverted forms of government will have unjust laws.

In all sciences and arts the end is a good, and especially and **12**
above all in the highest of all[4]—this is the political science
of which the good is justice, in other words, the common
interest. All men think justice to be a sort of equality; and
to a certain extent[5] they agree in the philosophical distinctions
which have been laid down by us about Ethics[6]. For
they admit that justice is a thing having relation to persons,
and that equals ought to have equality. But there still re- **2**
mains a question—equality or inequality of what? Here is a
difficulty which the political philosopher has to resolve. For
very likely some persons will say that offices of state ought
to be unequally distributed according to superior excellence,
in whatever respect, of the citizen, although there is no other
difference between him and the rest of the community; for
that those who differ in any one respect have different rights
and claims. But, surely, if this is true, the complexion or **3**
height of a man, or any other advantage, will be a reason

[1] Cp. c. 10. § 1.   [2] Cp. N. Eth. v. 10. § 4.
[3] Cp. c. 10. § 5.   [4] Cp. i. 1. § 1; N. Eth. i. 1. § 1.
[5] Cp. c. 9. § 1.   [6] Cp. N. Eth. v. 3.

III. 12 for his obtaining a greater share of political rights. The
4 error here lies upon the surface, and may be illustrated from
the other arts and sciences. When a number of flute-players
are equal in their art, there is no reason why those of them
who are better born should have better flutes given to them;
for they will not play any better on the flute, and the superior
instrument should be reserved for him who is the superior
artist. If what I am saying is still obscure, it will be made
5 clearer as we proceed. For if there were a superior flute-
player who was far inferior in birth and beauty, although
either of these may be a greater good than the art of flute-
playing, and persons gifted with these qualities may excel the
flute-player in a greater ratio than he excels them in his art,
1283 a still he ought to have the best flutes given to him, unless
the advantages of wealth and birth contribute to excellence
6 in flute-playing, which they do not. Moreover upon this
principle any good may be compared with any other. For
if a given height, then height in general may be measured
either against height or against freedom. Thus if A excels in
height more than B in virtue, and height in general is more
excellent than virtue, all things will be commensurable
[which is absurd]; for if a certain magnitude is greater
than some other, it is clear that some other will be equal.
7 But since no such comparison can be made, it is evident that
there is good reason why in politics men do not ground their
claim to office on every sort of inequality any more than
in the arts. For if some be slow, and others swift, that
is no reason why the one should have little and the others
much; it is in gymnastic contests that such excellence is
8 rewarded. Whereas the rival claims of candidates for office
can only be based on the possession of elements which enter

into the composition of a state, [such as wealth, virtue, etc.]. III. 12 And therefore the noble, or freeborn, or rich, may with good reason claim office; for holders of offices must be freemen and tax-payers : a state can be no more composed entirely of poor men than entirely of slaves. But if wealth 9 and freedom are necessary elements, justice and valour are equally so [1]; for without the former a state cannot exist at all, without the latter not well.

If the existence of the state is alone to be considered, then 13 it would seem that all, or some at least, of these claims are just; but, if we take into account a good life, as I have already said [2], education and virtue have superior claims. As, however, those who are equal in one thing ought not to be equal in all, nor those who are unequal in one thing to be unequal in all, it is certain that all forms of government which rest on either of these principles are perversions. All men have a claim in a certain sense, as I have already 2 admitted, but they have not an absolute claim. The rich claim because they have a greater share in the land, and land is the common element of the state; also they are generally more trustworthy in contracts. The free claim under the same title as the noble; for they are nearly akin. And the noble are citizens in a truer sense than the ignoble, since good birth is always valued in a man's own home and country [3]. Another reason is, that those who are sprung from better 3 ancestors are likely to be better men, for nobility is excellence of race. Virtue, too, may be truly said to have a claim, for justice has been acknowledged by us to be a social [4] virtue, and it implies all others [5]. Again, the many may urge their 4

---

[1] Cp. iv. 4. §§ 12–16. [2] Cp. c. 9. §§ 14, 15.
[3] Cp. i. 6. § 7. [4] Cp. i. 2. § 16. [5] Cp. N. Eth. v. 1. § 15.

III. 13 claim against the few; for, when taken collectively, and
compared with the few, they are stronger and richer and
1283 b better.   But, what if the good, the rich, the noble, and the
other classes who make up a state, are all living together in
the same city; will there, or will there not, be any doubt
5 who shall rule ?—No doubt at all in determining who ought
to rule in each of the above-mentioned forms of government.
For states are characterized by differences in their governing
bodies—one of them has a government of the rich, another
of the virtuous, and so on.   But a difficulty arises when all
6 these elements coexist.   How are we to decide?   Suppose
the virtuous to be very few in number: may we consider
their numbers in relation to their duties, and ask whether they
are enough to administer the state, or must they be so many as
will make up a state?   Objections may be urged against all
7 the aspirants to political power.   For those who found their
claims on wealth or family have no basis of justice; on this
principle, if any one person were richer than all the rest, it is
clear that he ought to be the ruler of them.   In like manner
he who is very distinguished by his birth ought to have the
superiority over all those who claim on the ground that they are
8 freeborn.   In an aristocracy, or government of the best, a like
difficulty occurs about virtue; for if one citizen be better than
the other members of the government, however good they
may be, he too, upon the same principle of justice, should rule
over them.   And if the people are to be supreme because they
are stronger than the few, then if one man, or more than one,
but not a majority, is stronger than the many, they ought to
rule, and not the many.
9   All these considerations appear to show that none of
the principles on which men claim to rule, and hold all

other men in subjection to them, are strictly right. To **III. 13** those who claim to be the masters of state on the ground 10 of their virtue or their wealth, the many might fairly answer that they themselves are often better and richer than the few—I do not say individually, but collectively. And 11 another ingenious objection which is sometimes put forward may be met in a similar manner. Some persons doubt whether the legislator who desires to make the justest laws ought to legislate with a view to the good of the higher classes or of the many, when the case which we have mentioned occurs [i. e. when all the elements coexist [1]]. Now what is just or right is to be interpreted in the sense 12 of 'what is equal'; and that which is right in the sense of being equal is to be considered with reference to the advantage of the state, and the common good of the citizens. And a citizen is one who shares in governing and being governed. He differs under different forms of government, **1284 a** but in the best state he is one who is able and willing to be governed and to govern with a view to the life of virtue.

If, however, there be some one person, or more than one, 13 although not enough to make up the full complement of a state, whose virtue is so pre-eminent that the virtues or the political capacity of all the rest admit of no comparison with his or theirs, he or they can be no longer regarded as part of a state; for justice will not be done to the superior, if he is reckoned only as the equal of those who are so far inferior to him in virtue and in political capacity. Such an one may truly be deemed a God among men. Hence we see that 14 legislation is necessarily concerned only with those who are equal in birth and in power; and that for men of pre-eminent

[1] Cp. § 4.

III. 13 virtue there is no law—they are themselves a law.   Any one
would be ridiculous who attempted to make laws for them :
they would probably retort what, in the fable of Antisthenes,
the lions said to the hares ['where are your claws?'],
when in the council of the beasts the latter began haranguing
15 and claiming equality for all.   And for this reason democratic
states have instituted ostracism ; equality is above all things
their aim, and therefore they ostracise and banish from
the city for a time those who seem to predominate too much
through their wealth, or the number of their friends, or
16 through any other political influence.   Mythology tells us that
the Argonauts left Heracles behind for a similar reason ; the
ship Argo would not take him because she feared that he would
have been too much for the rest of the crew.   Wherefore
those who denounce tyranny and blame the counsel which
Periander gave to Thrasybulus cannot be held altogether just in
17 their censure.   The story is that Periander, when the herald
was sent to ask counsel of him, said nothing, but only cut off
the tallest ears of corn till he had brought the field to a level.
The herald did not know the meaning of the action, but
came and reported what he had seen to Thrasybulus, who
understood that he was to cut off the principal men in the
18 state [1]; and this is a policy not only expedient for tyrants
or in practice confined to them, but equally necessary in
oligarchies and democracies.   Ostracism [2] is a measure of the
same kind, which acts by disabling and banishing the most
19 prominent citizens.   Great powers do the same to whole
cities and nations, as the Athenians did to the Samians,
Chians, and Lesbians ; no sooner had they obtained a firm
grasp of the empire, than they humbled their allies contrary

[1] Cp. v. 10. § 13.   [2] Cp. v. 3. § 3.

to treaty; and the Persian king has repeatedly crushed the **III. 13**
Medes, Babylonians, and other nations, when their spirit has 1284 b
been stirred by the recollection of their former greatness.

The problem is a universal one, and equally concerns all 20
forms of government, true as well as false; for, although
perverted forms with a view to their own interests may
adopt this policy, those which seek the common interest do
so likewise. The same thing may be observed in the arts 21
and sciences [1]; for the painter will not allow the figure to
have a foot which, however beautiful, is not in proportion,
nor will the ship-builder allow the stern or any other part
of the vessel to be unduly large, any more than the chorus-
master will allow any one who sings louder or better than all
the rest to sing in the choir. [2] Monarchs, too, may practise 22
compulsion and still live in harmony with their cities, if
their government is for the interest of the state [2]. Hence
where there is an acknowledged superiority the argument in
favour of ostracism is based upon a kind of political justice.
It would certainly be better that the legislator should from the 23
first so order his state as to have no need of such a remedy.
But if the need arises, the next best thing is that he should
endeavour to correct the evil by this or some similar measure.
The principle, however, has not been fairly applied in states;
for, instead of looking to the public good, they have used
ostracism for factious purposes. It is true that under perverted 24
forms of government, and from their special point of view,
such a measure is just and expedient, but it is also clear that
it is not absolutely just. In the perfect state there would be

[1] Cp. v. 3. § 6; 9. § 7; vii. 4. § 10; Rep. iv. 420.
[2] Or, 'Monarchies do not differ in this respect (i. e. the employment
of compulsion) from free states, but their government must be,' etc.

III. 13 great doubts about the use of it, not when applied to excess in strength, wealth, popularity, or the like, but when used against some one who is pre-eminent in virtue,—what is to **25** be done with him? Mankind will not say that such an one is to be expelled and exiled; on the other hand, he ought not to be a subject—that would be as if men should claim to rule over Zeus on the principle of rotation of office. The only alternative is that all should joyfully obey such a ruler, according to what seems to be the order of nature, and that men like him should be kings in their state for life.

14   The preceding discussion, by a natural transition, leads to the consideration of royalty, which we admit to be one of the true forms of government[1]. Let us see whether in order to be well governed a state or country should be under the rule of a king or under some other form of government; and whether monarchy, although good for some, may not be **2** bad for others. But first we must determine whether there is **1285 a** one species of royalty or many. It is not easy to see that there are many, and that the manner of government is not the same in all of them.

3   (1) Of royalties according to law, the Lacedaemonian is thought to answer best to the true pattern; but there the royal power is not absolute, except when the kings go on an expedition, and then they take the command. Matters of **4** religion are likewise committed to them. The kingly office is in truth a kind of generalship, irresponsible and perpetual. The king has not the power of life and death, except[2]

---

[1] ii. 9. § 29.

[2] Omitting ἔν τινι βασιλείᾳ, which is bracketed by Bekker in his 2nd edit.

when upon a campaign and in the field ; after the manner of **III. 14**
the ancients which is described in Homer. For Agamemnon
is patient when he is attacked in the assembly, but when the
army goes out to battle he has the power even of life and
death.   Does he not say ?—   5

'When I find a man skulking apart from the battle, nothing
shall save him from the dogs and vultures, for in my hands is
death [1].'

This, then, is one form of royalty—a generalship for life :
and of such royalties some are hereditary and others elective.

(2) There is another sort of monarchy not uncommon 6
among the barbarians, which nearly resembles tyranny.   But
even this is legal and hereditary.   For barbarians, being more
servile in character than Hellenes, and Asiatics than
Europeans, do not rebel against a despotic government.   Such 7
royalties have the nature of tyrannies because the people are
by nature slaves [2]; but there is no danger of their being
overthrown, for they are hereditary and legal.   Wherefore
also their guards are such as a king and not such as a tyrant
would employ, that is to say, they are composed of
citizens, whereas the guards of tyrants are mercenaries [3].   For
kings rule according to law over voluntary subjects, but
tyrants over involuntary ; and the one are guarded by their
fellow-citizens, the others are guarded against them.

These are two forms of monarchy, and there was a 8
third (3) which existed in ancient Hellas, called an Aesym-
netia or dictatorship.   This may be defined generally as an
elective tyranny, which, like the barbarian monarchy, is legal,

---

[1] Il. ii. 391–393.   The last clause is not found in our Homer.
[2] Cp. i. 2. § 4.   [3] Cp. v. 10. § 10.

III. 14 but differs from it in not being hereditary. Sometimes the
9 office is held for life, sometimes for a term of years, or until
certain duties have been performed. For example, the
Mitylenaeans elected Pittacus leader against the exiles, who
10 were headed by Antimenides and Alcaeus the poet. And
Alcaeus himself says in one of his [1]irregular songs[1], 'They
chose Pittacus tyrant,' and he reproaches his fellow-citizens
for

'having made the low-born Pittacus tyrant of the spiritless
1285 b and ill-fated city, with one voice shouting his praises.'

11   These forms of government have always had the character
of despotism, because they possess tyrannical power; but
inasmuch as they are elective and acquiesced in by their
subjects, they are kingly.

(4) There is a fourth species of kingly rule—that of the
heroic times—which was hereditary and legal, and was exer-
12 cised over willing subjects. For the first chiefs were benefactors of the people [2] in arts or arms; they either gathered
them into a community, or procured land for them; and thus
they became kings of voluntary subjects, and their power was
inherited by their descendants. They took the command in
war and presided over the sacrifices, except those which
required a priest. They also decided causes either with or
without an oath; and when they swore, the form of the oath
13 was the stretching out of their sceptre. In ancient times their
power extended to all things whatsoever, in city and country,
as well as in foreign parts; but at a later date they relin-
quished several of these privileges, and others the people took
from them, until in some states nothing was left to them

[1] Or. 'banquet-odes,' σκόλια.   [2] Cp. v. c. 10. § 3.

but the sacrifices; and where they retained more of the III. 14
reality they had only the right of leadership in war beyond
the border.

These, then, are the four kinds of royalty. First the 14
monarchy of the heroic ages; this was exercised over voluntary subjects, but limited to certain functions; the king was
a general and a judge, and had the control of religion. The
second is that of the barbarians, which is an hereditary
despotic government in accordance with law. A third is the
power of the so-called Aesymnete or Dictator; this is an
elective tyranny. The fourth is the Lacedaemonian, which
is in fact a generalship, hereditary and perpetual. These 15
four forms differ from one another in the manner which
I have described.

There is a fifth form of kingly rule in which one has the
disposal of all, just as each tribe or each state has the disposal
of the public property; this form corresponds to the control
of a household. For as household management is the kingly
rule of a house, so kingly rule is the household management
of a city, or of a nation, or of many nations.

Of these forms we need only consider two, the Lacedae- 15
monian and the absolute royalty; for most of the others lie in
a region between them, having less power than the last, and
more than the first. Thus the enquiry is reduced to two 2
points: first, is it advantageous to the state that there should
be a perpetual general, and if so, should the office be confined
to one family, or open to the citizens in turn? Secondly, is 1286 a
it well that a single man should have the supreme power in all
things? The first question falls under the head of laws
rather than of constitutions; for perpetual generalship might
equally exist under any form of government, so that this 3

III. 15 matter may be dismissed for the present. The other kind of
royalty is a sort of constitution; this we have now to consider, and briefly to run over the difficulties involved in it.
We will begin by enquiring whether it is more advantageous
to be ruled by the best man or by the best laws [1].

4   The advocates of royalty maintain that the laws speak only
in general terms, and cannot provide for circumstances; and
that for any science to abide by written rules is absurd. Even
in Egypt the physician is allowed to alter his treatment after
the fourth day, but if sooner, he takes the risk.   Hence it is
argued that a government acting according to written laws is
5 plainly not the best.   Yet surely the ruler cannot dispense with
the general principle which exists in law; and he is a better
ruler who is free from passion than he who is passionate.
Whereas the law is passionless, passion must ever sway the
heart of man.

6   Yes, some one will answer, but then on the other hand an
individual will be better able to advise in particular cases. [To
whom we in turn make reply:] A king must legislate, and
laws must be passed, but these laws will have no authority
when they miss the mark, though in all other cases retaining
their authority.   [Yet a further question remains behind:]
When the law cannot determine a point at all, or not well,
7 should the one best man or should all decide?   According to
our present practice assemblies meet, sit in judgment, deliberate
and decide, and their judgments all relate to individual cases.
Now any member of the assembly, taken separately, is certainly inferior to the wise man.   But the state is made up of
many individuals.   And as a feast to which all the guests
contribute is better than a banquet furnished by a single man [2],

---

[1] Cp. Plato, Polit. pp. 293–295.   [2] Cp. supra, c. 11. § 2.

so a multitude **is** a better judge of many things than any III. 15
individual.

Again, the many are more incorruptible than the few; they 8
are like the greater quantity of water which is less easily corrupted than a little. The individual is liable to be overcome
by anger or by some other passion, and then his judgment is
necessarily perverted; but it is hardly to be supposed that a
great number of persons would all get into a passion and go
wrong at the same moment. Let us assume that they are 9
freemen, never acting in violation of the law, but filling up the
gaps which the law is obliged to leave. Or, if such virtue is
scarcely attainable by the multitude, we need only suppose
that the majority are good men and good citizens, and ask
which will be the more incorruptible, the one good ruler, or
the many who are all good? Will not the many? But, you 1286 b
will say, there may be parties among them, whereas the one
man is not divided against himself. To which we may 10
answer that their character is as good as his. If we call the
rule of many men, who are all of them good, aristocracy, and
the rule of one man royalty, then aristocracy will be better for
states than royalty, whether the government is supported by
force or not[1], provided only that a number of men equal in
virtue can be found.

The first governments were kingships, probably for this 11
reason, because of old, when cities were small, men of eminent
virtue were few. They were made kings because they were
benefactors[2], and benefits can only be bestowed by good
men. But when many persons equal in merit arose, no longer
enduring the pre-eminence of one, they desired to have a
commonwealth, and set up a constitution. The ruling class 12

[1] Cp. infra, § 15.   [2] Cp. c. 14. § 12.

III. 15 soon deteriorated and enriched themselves out of the public treasury; riches became the path to honour, and so oligarchies naturally grew up. These passed into tyrannies and tyrannies into democracies; for love of gain in the ruling classes was always tending to diminish their number, and so to strengthen the masses, who in the end set upon their masters and established democracies. Since cities have 13 increased in size, no other form of government appears to be any longer possible [1].

Even supposing the principle to be maintained that kingly power is the best thing for states, how about the family of the king? Are his children to succeed him? If they are no 14 better than anybody else, that will be mischievous. But [says the lover of royalty] the king, though he might, will not hand on his power to his children. That, however, is hardly to be expected, and is too much to ask of human nature. There is also a difficulty about the force which he is to employ; should a king have guards about him by whose 15 aid he may be able to coerce the refractory? but if not, how will he administer his kingdom? Even if he be the lawful sovereign who does nothing arbitrarily or contrary to law, still he must have some force wherewith to maintain the law. 16 In the case of a limited monarchy there is not much difficulty in answering this question; the king must have such force as will be more than a match for one or more individuals, but not so great as that of the people. The ancients observed this principle when they gave the guards to any one whom they appointed dictator or tyrant. Thus, when Dionysius asked the Syracusans to allow him guards, somebody advised that they should give him only a certain number.

[1] Cp. iv. 6. § 5; 13. § 10.

At this place in the discussion naturally follows the enquiry **III. 16** respecting the king who acts solely according to his own 1287 a will; he has now to be considered. The so-called limited monarchy, or kingship according to law, as I have already remarked [1], is not a distinct form of government, for under all governments, as, for example, in a democracy or aristocracy, there may be a general holding office for life, and one person is often made supreme over the internal administration of a state. A magistracy of this kind exists at Epidamnus [2], and also at Opus, but in the latter city has a more limited power. Now, absolute monarchy, or the arbitrary rule of **2** a sovereign over all the citizens, in a city which consists of equals, is thought by some to be quite contrary to nature; it is argued that those who are by nature equals must have the same natural right and worth, and that for unequals to have an equal share, or for equals to have an unequal share, in the offices of state, is as bad as for different bodily constitutions to have the same food and clothing or the same different. Wherefore it is thought to be just that among equals every **3** one be ruled as well as rule, and that all should have their turn. We thus arrive at law; for an order of succession implies law. And the rule of the law is preferable to that of any individual. On the same principle, even if it be better **4** for certain individuals to govern, they should be made only guardians and ministers of the law. For magistrates there must be,—this is admitted; but then men say that to give authority to any one man when all are equal is unjust. There may indeed be cases which the law seems unable to determine, but in such cases can a man? Nay, it will be replied, the **5** law trains officers for this express purpose, and appoints them

---

[1] Cp. c. 15. § 2.   [2] Cp. v. 1. §§ 10, 11; 4. § 7.

III. 16 to determine matters which are left undecided by it to the best of their judgment.   Further it permits them to make any amendment of the existing laws which experience suggests. [But still they are only the ministers of the law.]   He who bids the law rule, may be deemed to bid God and Reason alone rule, but he who bids man rule adds an element of the beast; for desire is a wild beast, and passion perverts the minds of rulers, even when they are the best of men.   The **6** law is reason unaffected by desire.   We are told that a patient should call in a physician; he will not get better if he is **7** doctored out of a book.   But the parallel of the arts is clearly not in point; for the physician does nothing contrary to reason from motives of friendship; he only cures a patient and takes a fee; whereas magistrates do many things from spite and partiality.   And, indeed, if a man suspected the physician of being in league with his enemies to destroy him **8** for a bribe, he would rather have recourse to the book.   Even **1287 b** physicians when they are sick, call in other physicians, and training-masters when they are in training, other training-masters, as if they could not judge truly about their own case and might be influenced by their feelings.   Hence it is evident that in seeking for justice men seek for the mean or **9** neutral[1], and the law is the mean.   Again, customary laws have more weight, and relate to more important matters, than written laws, and a man may be a safer ruler than the written law, but not safer than the customary law.

Again, it is by no means easy for one man to superintend many things; he will have to appoint a number of subordinates; and what difference does it make whether these subordinates always existed or were appointed by him because he

[1] Cp. N. Eth. v. 4. § 7.

needed them ?   If, as I said before [1], the good man has **III. 16**
a right to rule because he is better, then two good men are [10]
better than one : this is the old saying,—

'two going together [2] ; '

and the prayer of Agamemnon,—

'would that I had ten such counsellors [3] ! '

And at this day there are some magistrates, for example
judges [4], who have authority to decide matters which the law
is unable to determine, since no one doubts that the law would
command and decide in the best manner whatever it could.
But some things can, and other things cannot, be com- [11]
prehended under the law, and this is the origin of the vexed
question whether the best law or the best man should rule.
For matters of detail about which men deliberate cannot be
included in legislation.   Nor does any one deny that the
decision of such matters must be left to man, but it
is argued that there should be many judges, and not one
only.   For every ruler [5] who has been trained by the law [12]
judges well; and it would surely seem strange that a person
should see better with two eyes, or hear better with two ears,
or act better with two hands or feet, than many with many ;
indeed, it is already the practice of kings to make to themselves many eyes and ears and hands and feet.   For they
make colleagues of those who are the friends of themselves
and their governments. They must be friends of the monarch [13]
and of his government; if not his friends, they will not
do what he wants; but friendship implies likeness and
equality; and, therefore, if he thinks that friends ought to

[1] Cp. c. 13. § 25.   [2] Il. x. 224.   [3] Il. ii. 372.   [4] ὁ δικαστής.
[5] Cp. for similar arguments c. 15. § 9.

III. 16 rule, he must think that those who are equal to himself and like himself ought to rule. These are the principal controversies relating to monarchy.

17 But may not all this be true in some cases and not in others? [1] for there is a natural justice and expediency in the relation of a master to his servants, or, again, of a king to his subjects, as also in the relation of free citizens to one another; whereas there is no such justice or expediency in a tyranny[1], or in any other perverted form of government, which comes 1288 a into being contrary to nature. Now, from what has been said, **2** it is manifest that, where men are alike and equal, it is neither expedient nor just that one man should be lord of all, whether there are laws, or whether there are no laws, but he himself is in the place of law. Neither should a good man be lord over good men, or a bad man over bad; nor, even if he excels in virtue, should he have a right to rule, unless in a particular case, which I have already mentioned, and to which I will **3** once more recur[2]. But first of all, I must determine what natures are suited for royalties, and what for an aristocracy, and what for a constitutional government.

4 A people who are by nature capable of producing a race superior in virtue and political talent are fitted for kingly government; and a people [3] submitting to be ruled as freemen by men whose virtue renders them capable of political

---

[1] Or, 'for there are men who are by nature fitted to be ruled by a master, others to be ruled by a king, others to live under a constitutional government, and for whom these several relations are just and expedient; but there are no men naturally fitted to be ruled by a tyrant,' etc.

[2] c. 13. § 25, and § 5, infra.

[3] Omitting the words πλῆθος δ πέφυκε φέρειν, which appear to be a repetition from the previous clause.

command are adapted for an aristocracy: while the people **III. 17**
who are suited for constitutional freedom are those among
whom there naturally exists[1] a warlike multitude[2] able to
rule and to obey in turn by a law which gives office to the
well-to-do according to their desert. But when a whole **5**
family, or some individual, happens to be so pre-eminent in
virtue as to surpass all others, then it is just that they
should be the royal family and supreme over all, or that this
one citizen should be king of the whole nation. For, as **6**
I said before[3], to give them authority is not only agreeable to
that ground of right which the founders of all states, whether
aristocratical, or oligarchical, or again democratical, are
accustomed to put forward (for these all recognize the claim
of excellence, although not the same excellence), but accords
with the principle already laid down[4]. For it would not **7**
be right to kill, or ostracize, or exile such a person, or
require that he should take his turn in being governed. The
whole is naturally superior to the part, and he who has this
pre-eminence is in the relation of a whole to a part. But **8**
if so, the only alternative is that he should have the supreme
power, and that mankind should obey him, not in turn, but
always. These are the conclusions at which we arrive respecting royalty and its various forms, and this is the answer to the
question, whether it is or is not advantageous to states, and to
whom, and how.

We maintain that the true forms of government are three, **18**
and that the best must be that which is administered by the
best, and in which there is one man, or a whole family,

---

[1] Omitting καὶ ἕν.   [2] Cp. c. 7. § 4.
[3] Cp. c. 9. § 15.
[4] Or, 'but differing in the manner already laid down.

III. 18 or many persons, excelling in virtue, and both rulers and subjects are fitted, the one to rule, the others to be ruled [1], in such a manner as to attain the most eligible life. We showed at the commencement of our enquiry [2] that the virtue of the good man is necessarily the same as the virtue of the citizen of the perfect state. Clearly then in the same manner, and by the same means through which a man becomes truly good, he will frame a state [which will be truly good] whether

1288 b aristocratical, or under kingly rule, and the same education and the same habits will be found to make a good man and a good statesman and king.

2 Having arrived at these conclusions, we must proceed to speak of the perfect state, and describe how it comes into being and is established. He who would proceed with the enquiry in due manner. . . .[3]

[1] Omitting καὶ ἄρχειν, which is inserted, without MS. authority, in Bekker's 2nd edit.

[2] Cp. c. 4.

[3] Retaining the words of the MSS., Ἀνάγκη δὴ τὸν μέλλοντα περὶ αὐτῆς ποιήσασθαι τὴν προσήκουσαν σκέψιν, which are omitted by Bekker in his 2nd edit.

BOOK IV

In all arts and sciences which embrace the whole of any subject, and are not restricted to a part only, it is the province of a single art or science to consider all that appertains to a single subject. For example, the art of gymnastic considers not only the suitableness of different modes of training to different bodies (2), but what sort is absolutely the best (1) (for the absolutely best must suit that which is by nature best and best furnished with the means of life), and also what common form of training is adapted to the great majority of men (4). And if a man **2** does not desire the best habit of body or the greatest skill in gymnastics, which might be attained by him, still the trainer or the teacher of gymnastic should be able to impart any lower degree of either (3). The same principle equally holds in medicine and ship-building, and the making of clothes, and in the arts generally [1].

Hence it is obvious that government too is the subject **3** of a single science, which has to consider what kind of government would be best and most in accordance with our aspirations, if there were no external impediment, and also what kind of government is adapted to particular states. For the best is often unattainable, and therefore the true legislator and statesman ought to be acquainted, not only with (1) that which is best in the abstract, but also with

---

[1] The numbers in this paragraph are made to correspond with the numbers in the next.

IV. 1 (2) that which is best relatively to circumstances. We
4 should be able further to say how a state may be constituted
under any given conditions (3); both how it is originally
formed and, when formed, how it may be longest preserved;
the supposed state being so far from the very best that it
is unprovided even with the conditions necessary for the very
best; neither is it the best under the circumstances, but of an
inferior type.

5 He ought, moreover, to know (4) the form of government which is best suited to states in general; for political
writers, although they have excellent ideas, are often un-
6 practical. We should consider, not only what form of
government is best, but also what is possible and what is
easily attainable by all. There are some who would have
none but the most perfect; for this many natural advantages
1289 a are required. Others, again, speak of a more attainable form,
and, although they reject the constitution under which they
are living, they extol some one in particular, for example
7 the Lacedaemonian[1]. Any change of government which
has to be introduced should be one which men will be both
willing and able to adopt, since there is quite as much trouble
in the reformation of an old constitution as in the establishment of a new one, just as to unlearn is as hard as to learn.
And therefore, in addition to the qualifications of the statesman already mentioned, he should be able to find remedies
8 for the defects of existing constitutions[2]. This he cannot
do unless he knows how many forms of government there
are. It is often supposed that there is only one kind of
democracy and one of oligarchy. But this is a mistake;
and, in order to avoid such mistakes, we must ascertain what

[1] Cp. ii. 6. § 16.   [2] Cp. § 4.

differences there are in the constitutions of states, and in **IV. 1**
how many ways they are combined. The same political **9**
insight will enable a man to know which laws are the best,
and which are suited to different constitutions; for the laws
are, and ought to be, relative to the constitution, and not the
constitution to the laws. A constitution is the organization of **10**
offices in a state, and determines what is to be the governing
body, and what is the end of each community. But [1] laws
are not to be confounded with the principles of the constitution [1] : they are the rules according to which the magistrates
should administer the state, and proceed against offenders.
So that we must know the number and varieties of the **11**
several forms of government, if only with a view to making
laws. For the same laws cannot be equally suited to all
oligarchies and to all democracies, and there is certainly more
than one form both of democracy and of oligarchy.

In our original discussion [2] about governments we divided **2**
them into three true forms: kingly rule, aristocracy, and
constitutional government, and three corresponding perversions—tyranny, oligarchy, and democracy. Of kingly
rule and of aristocracy we have already spoken, for the
enquiry into the perfect state is the same thing with the
discussion of the two forms thus named, since both imply
a principle of virtue provided with external means. We
have already determined in what aristocracy and kingly rule
differ from one another, and when the latter should be
established [3]. In what follows we have to describe the
so-called constitutional government, which bears the common

---

[1] Or, 'laws, though in themselves distinct, show the character of
the constitution.'
[2] Book iii. 7 ; N. Eth. viii 10.   [3] Cp. iii. 17. § 8.

IV. 2 name of all constitutions, and the other forms, tyranny, oligarchy, and democracy.

2 It is obvious which of the three perversions is the worst, and which is the next in badness. That which is the perversion of the first and most divine is necessarily the

1289 b worst. And just as a royal rule, if not a mere name, must exist by virtue of some great personal superiority in the king, so tyranny, which is the worst of governments, is necessarily the farthest removed from a well-constituted form; oligarchy is a little better, but a long way from aristocracy, and democracy is the most tolerable of the three.

3 A writer[1] who preceded me has already made these distinctions, but his point of view is not the same as mine. For he lays down the principle that of all good constitutions (under which he would include a virtuous oligarchy and the like) democracy is the worst, but the best of bad ones. Whereas we maintain that they are all defective, and that one oligarchy is not to be accounted better than another, but only less bad.

4 Not to pursue this question further at present, let us begin by determining (1)[2] how many varieties of states there are (since of democracy and oligarchy there are several); (2)[3] what constitution is the most generally acceptable, and what is eligible in the next degree [4]after the perfect or any other aristocratical and well-constituted form of government—if any other there be—which is at the same time adapted to states in general[4]; (3)[5] of the other forms of

---

[1] Plato, Polit. 303 A.,   [2] c. 4-6.   [3] c. 7-9 and 11.

[4] Or, 'after the perfect state; and besides this what other there is which is aristocratical and well constituted, and at the same time adapted to states in general.'   [5] c. 12.

government to whom each is suited. For democracy may **IV. 2** meet the needs of some better than oligarchy, and conversely. **5** In the next place (4)[1] we have to consider in what manner a man ought to proceed who desires to establish some one among these various forms, whether of democracy or of oligarchy; and lastly, (5)[2] having briefly discussed these **6** subjects to the best of our power, we will endeavour to ascertain whence arise the ruin and preservation of states, both generally and in individual cases, and to what causes they are to be attributed.

The reason why there are many forms of government **3** is that every state contains many elements. In the first place we see that all states are made up of families, and in the multitude of citizens there must be some rich and some poor, and some in a middle condition; [3] the rich are heavy-armed, and the poor not[3]. Of the common people, some **2** are husbandmen, and some traders, and some artisans. There are also among the notables differences of wealth and property—for example, in the number of horses which they keep, for they cannot afford to keep them unless they are rich. And therefore in old times the cities whose strength **3** lay in the cavalry were oligarchies, and they used cavalry[4] in wars against their neighbours; as was the practice of the Eretrians and Chalcidians, and also of the Magnesians on the river Maeander, and of other peoples in Asia. Besides **4** differences of wealth there are differences of rank and merit,

---

[1] Book vi.   [2] Book v.

[3] Or, 'and again both of rich and poor some are armed and some are unarmed.'

[4] Reading either πολέμους with v. tr. (Moerbek) and Bekk. 2nd edit., or πολεμίους with the Greek MSS.; cp. c. 13. § 10; vi. c. 7. § 1.

IV. 3 and there are some other elements which were mentioned
1290 a by us when in treating of aristocracy we enumerated the
essentials of a state[1]. Of these elements, sometimes all,
sometimes the lesser and sometimes the greater number,
5 have a share in the government. It is evident then that
there must be many forms of government, differing in kind,
since the parts of which they are composed differ from
each other in kind. For a constitution is an organization
of offices which all the citizens distribute among themselves,
according to the power which different classes possess, for
example the rich or the poor, or according to some common
equality subsisting among them or some power common to
6 both. There must therefore be as many forms of government
as there are modes of arranging the offices, according to the
superiorities and other inequalities of the different parts of
the state.

There are generally thought to be two principal forms:
as men say of the winds that there are but two—north
and south—and that the rest of them are only variations
of these, so of governments there are said to be only two
7 forms—democracy and oligarchy. For aristocracy is considered to be a kind of oligarchy, as being the rule of
a few, and the so-called constitutional government to be
really a democracy, just as among the winds we make the
west a variation of the north, and the east of the south
wind. Similarly of harmonies there are said to be two
kinds, the Dorian and the Phrygian; the other arrangements
of the scale are comprehended under one of these two.
8 About forms of government this is a very favourite notion.
But in either case the better and more exact way is to

[1] Not in what has preceded, but cp. vii. 8.

distinguish, as I have done, the one or two which are **IV. 3**
true forms, and to regard the others as perversions, whether
of the most perfectly attempered harmony or of the best form
of government; we may compare the oligarchical forms to
the severer and more overpowering modes, and the democratic to the more relaxed and gentler ones.

It must not be assumed, as some are fond of saying, that **4**
democracy is simply that form of government in which
the greater number are sovereign[1], for in oligarchies, and
indeed in every government, the majority rules; nor again
is oligarchy that form of government in which a few are
sovereign. Suppose the whole population of a city to be **2**
1300, and that of these 1000 are rich, and do not allow
the remaining 300 who are poor, but free, and in all other
respects their equals, a share of the government—no one
will say that this is a democracy. In like manner, if the **3**
poor were few and the masters of the rich, who outnumber
them, no one would ever call such a government, in which
the rich majority have no share of office, an oligarchy.
Therefore we should rather say that democracy is the **1290 b**
form of government in which the free are rulers, and
oligarchy in which the rich; it is only an accident that **4**
the free are the many and the rich are the few. Otherwise
a government in which the offices were given according to
stature, as is said to be the case in Ethiopia, or according to
beauty, would be an oligarchy; for the number of tall or good-
looking men is small. And yet oligarchy and democracy **5**
are not sufficiently distinguished merely by these two characteristics of wealth and freedom. Both of them contain
many other elements, and therefore we must carry our

[1] Cp. iii. 8. §§ 3-7.

IV. 4 analysis further, and say that the government is not a democracy in which the freemen, being few in number, rule over the many who art not free, as at Apollonia, on the Ionian Gulf, and at Thera (for in each of these states the nobles, who were also the earliest settlers, were held in chief honour, although they were but a few out of many). Neither is it a democracy when the rich have the government, because they exceed in number; as was the case formerly at Colophon, where the bulk of the inhabitants were possessed **6** of large property before the Lydian War. But the form of government is a democracy when the free, who are also poor and the majority, govern, and oligarchy when the rich and the noble govern, they being at the same time few in number.

7   I have said that there are many forms of government, and have explained to what causes the variety is due. Why there are more than those already mentioned, and what they are, and whence they arise, I will now proceed to consider, starting from the principle already admitted [1], which is that **8** every state consists, not of one, but of many parts. If we were going to speak of the different species of animals, we should first of all determine the organs which are indispensable to every animal, as for example some organs of sense and instruments of receiving and digesting food, such as the mouth and the stomach, besides organs of locomotion. Assuming now that there are only so many kinds of organs, but that there may be differences in them—I mean different kinds of mouths, and stomachs, and perceptive and locomotive organs—the possible combinations of these differences will necessarily furnish many varieties of animals. (For animals

[1] Cp. c. 3. § 1.

cannot be the same which have different kinds of mouths or **IV. 4**
of ears.) And when all the combinations are exhausted,
there will be as many sorts of animals as there are combinations of the necessary organs. In like manner the forms of 9
government which have been described, as I have repeatedly
said, are composed, not of one, but of many elements. One
element is the food-producing class, who are called husbandmen; a second, a class of mechanics, who practise the arts 1291 a
without which a city cannot exist;—of these arts some are
absolutely necessary, others contribute to luxury or to the
grace of life. The third class is that of traders, and by traders 10
I mean those who are engaged in buying and selling, whether
in commerce or in retail trade. A fourth class is that of the
serfs or labourers. The warriors make up the fifth class, and
they are as necessary as any of the others, if the country is not
to be the slave of every invader. For how can a state which 11
has any title to the name be of a slavish nature? The state is
independent and self-sufficing, but a slave is the reverse of independent. Hence we see that this subject, though ingeniously,
has not been satisfactorily treated in the Republic [1]. Socrates 12
says that a state is made up of four sorts of people who are
absolutely necessary; these are a weaver, a husbandman,
a shoemaker, and a builder; afterwards, finding that they
are not enough, he adds a smith, and again a herdsman, to
look after the necessary animals; then a merchant, and then
a retail trader. All these together form the complement of the 13
first state, as if a state were established merely to supply the
necessaries of life, rather than for the sake of the good, or
stood equally in need of shoemakers and of husbandmen.
But he does not admit into the state a military class until the

[1] Rep. ii. 369.

iV. 4 country has increased in size, and is beginning to encroach on its neighbour's land, whereupon they go to war. Yet even amongst his four original citizens, or whatever be the number of those whom he associates in the state, there must be some one who will dispense justice and determine what is just.

14 And as the soul may be said to be more truly part of an animal than the body, so the higher parts of states, that is to say, the warrior class, the class engaged in the administration of justice, and in deliberation, which is the special business of political common sense,—these are more essential to the state than the parts which minister to the necessaries of life.

15 Whether their several functions are the functions of different citizens, or of the same—for it may often happen that the same persons are both warriors and husbandmen—is immaterial to the argument. The higher as well as the lower elements are to be equally considered parts of the state, and if so, the military element must be included. There are also the wealthy who minister to the state with their property;

16 these form the seventh class. The eighth class is that of magistrates and of officers; for the state cannot exist without rulers. And therefore some must be able to take office and to

17 serve the state, either always or in turn. There only remains the class of those who deliberate and who judge between disputants; we were just now distinguishing them. If the fair and equitable organization of all these elements is necessary to

1291 b states, then there must also be persons who have the ability of

18 statesmen. [1] Many are of opinion that different functions can be combined in the same individual [1]; for example, the warrior may be a husbandman, or an artisan; or again, the counsellor a judge. And all claim to possess political ability, and

[1] Or, 'Different functions appear to be often combined,' etc.

think that they are quite competent to fill most offices. But **IV. 4**
the same persons cannot be rich and poor at the same time.
For this reason the rich and the poor are regarded in an 19
especial sense as parts of a state. Again, because the rich
are generally few in number, while the poor are many, they
appear to be antagonistic, and as the one or the other prevails
they form the government. Hence arises the common
opinion that there are two kinds of government—democracy
and oligarchy.

I have already explained [1] that there are many differences 20
of constitutions, and to what causes the variety is due. Let
me now show that there are different forms both of democracy
and oligarchy, as will indeed be evident from what has preceded. For both in the common people and in the notables 21
various classes are included; of the common people, one class
are husbandmen, another artisans; another traders, who are
employed in buying and selling; another are the seafaring
class, whether engaged in war or in trade, as ferrymen or as
fishermen. (In many places any one of these classes forms
quite a large population; for example, fishermen at Tarentum
and Byzantium, crews of triremes at Athens, merchant sea-
men at Aegina and Chios, ferrymen at Tenedos.) To the
classes already mentioned may be added day-labourers, and
those who, owing to their needy circumstances, have no
leisure, or those who are not free of birth on both sides; and
there may be other classes as well. The notables again may 22
be divided according to their wealth, birth, virtue, education,
and similar differences.

Of forms of democracy first comes that which is said to
be based strictly on equality. In such a democracy the law

[1] Cp. iii. c. 6.

IV. 4 says that it is just for nobody to be poor, and for nobody to be rich [1]; and that neither should be masters, but both equal.

23 For if liberty and equality, as is thought by some, are chiefly to be found in democracy, they will be best attained when all persons alike share in the government to the utmost. And since the people are the majority, and the opinion of the majority is decisive, such a government must necessarily be

24 a democracy. Here then is one sort of democracy. There is another in which the magistrates are elected according to a certain property qualification, but a low one; he who has the required amount of property has a share in the govern-

1292 a ment, but he who loses his property loses his rights. Another kind is that in which all the citizens who are under no disqualification share in the government, but still the law is

25 supreme. In another, everybody, if he be only a citizen, is admitted to the government, but the law is supreme as before. A fifth form of democracy, in other respects the same, is that in which, not the law, but the multitude, have the supreme

26 power, and supersede the law by their decrees. This is a state of affairs brought about by the demagogues. For in democracies which are subject to the law the best citizens hold the first place, and there are no demagogues; but where the laws are not supreme, there demagogues spring up. For the people becomes a monarch, and is many in one; and the many have the power in their hands, not as individuals, but

27 collectively. Homer says that, 'it is not good to have a rule

---

[1] Or, reading ἄρχειν with Victorius, 'that the poor should no more govern than the rich.' The emendation is not absolutely necessary, though supported by vi. 2. § 9, ἴσον γὰρ τὸ μηθὲν μᾶλλον ἄρχειν τοὺς ἀπόρους ἢ τοὺς εὐπόρους μηδὲ κυρίους εἶναι μόνους ἀλλὰ πάντας ἐξ ἴσου κατ᾽ ἀριθμόν.

of many[1,1], but whether he means this corporate rule, or the **IV. 4**
rule of many individuals, is uncertain. And the people, who
is now a monarch, and no longer under the control of law,
seeks to exercise monarchical sway, and grows into a despot;
the flatterer is held in honour; this sort of democracy being
relatively to other democracies what tyranny is to other forms
of monarchy. The spirit of both is the same, and they alike **28**
exercise a despotic rule over the better citizens. The decrees
of the demos correspond to the edicts of the tyrant; and the
demagogue is to the one what the flatterer is to the other.
Both have great power—the flatterer with the tyrant, the
demagogue with democracies of the kind which we are
describing. The demagogues make the decrees of the people **29**
override the laws, and refer all things to the popular assembly.
And therefore they grow great, because the people have all
things in their hands, and they hold in their hands the votes
of the people, who are too ready to listen to them. Further, **30**
those who have any complaint to bring against the magistrates say, 'let the people be judges'; the people are too
happy to accept the invitation; and so the authority of every
office is undermined. Such a democracy is fairly open to the
objection that it is not a constitution at all; for where the
laws have no authority, there is no constitution. The law **31**
ought to be supreme over all, and the magistracies and the
government should judge only of particulars. So that if
democracy be a real form of government, the sort of constitution in which all things are regulated by decrees is clearly not
a democracy in the true sense of the word, for decrees relate
only to particulars[2].

---

[1] Il. ii. 204.   [2] Cp. N. Eth. v. 10. § 7.

IV. 5   These then are the different kinds of democracies.   Of oligarchies, too, there are different kinds—one where the property qualification for office is so high that the poor, although they form the majority, have no share in the government, yet he who acquires a qualification may obtain a share.

1292 b Another sort is when there is a qualification for office, but a high one, and the vacancies in the governing body are filled by co-optation.   If the election is made out of all the qualified persons, a constitution of this kind inclines to an aristocracy, **2** if out of a privileged class, to an oligarchy.   Another sort of oligarchy is when the son succeeds the father.   There is a fourth form, likewise hereditary, in which the magistrates are supreme and not the law.   Among oligarchies this is what tyranny is among monarchies, and the last-mentioned form of democracy among democracies; and in fact this sort of oligarchy receives the name of a dynasty (or rule of powerful families).

3   These are the different sorts of oligarchies and democracies.   It should however be remembered that in many states [1] the constitution which is established by law, although not democratic, owing to the character and habits of the people, may be administered democratically, and conversely in other states the established constitution may incline to democracy, **4** but may be administered in an oligarchical spirit.   This most often happens after a revolution : for governments do not change at once ; at first the dominant party are content with encroaching a little upon their opponents.   The laws which existed previously continue in force, but the authors of the revolution have the power in their hands.

6   From what has been already said we may safely infer that

[1] Cp. v. i. § 8.

there are so many different kinds of democracies and of **IV. 6**
oligarchies. For it is evident that either all the classes whom
we mentioned must share in the government, or some only and
not others. When the class of husbandmen and of those **2**
who possess moderate fortunes have the supreme power, the
government is administered according to law. For the citizens being compelled to live by their labour have no leisure ;
and so they set up the authority of the law, and attend
assemblies only when necessary. Since they all obtain a **3**
share in the government when they have acquired the qualification which is fixed by the law, nobody is excluded—the
absolute exclusion of any class would be a step towards
oligarchy. But leisure cannot be provided for them unless
there are revenues to support them. This is one sort of
democracy, and these are the causes which give birth to it.
Another kind is based on the mode of election, [1] which
naturally comes next in order [1]; in this, every one to whose
birth there is no objection is eligible, and may share in the
government if he can find leisure. And in such a democracy **4**
the supreme power is vested in the laws, because the state has
no means of paying the citizens. A third kind is when all
freemen have a right to share in the government, but do not
actually share, for the reason which has been already given ;
so that in this form again the law must rule. A fourth kind **5**
of democracy is that which comes latest in the history of **1293 a**
states. In our own day, when cities have far outgrown their
original size, and their revenues have increased, all the citizens
have a place in the government, through the great preponderance of their numbers ; and they all, including the poor
who receive pay, and therefore have leisure to exercise their

[1] Or, ' which is proper to it.'

IV. 6 rights, share in the administration.   Indeed, when they are
6 paid, the common people have the most leisure, for they are.
not hindered by the care of their property, which often fetters
the rich, who are thereby prevented from taking part in the
assembly or in the courts, and so the state is governed by the
7 poor, who are a majority, and not by the laws.   So many
kinds of democracies there are, and they grow out of these
necessary causes.

Of oligarchies, one form is that in which the majority of
the citizens have some property, but not very much ; and this
is the first form, which allows to any one who obtains the
8 required amount the right of sharing in the government.   The
sharers in the government being a numerous body, it follows
that the law must govern, and not individuals.   For in proportion as they are further removed from a monarchical form
of government, and in respect of property have neither so
much as to be able to live without attending to business, nor so
little as to need state support, they must admit the rule of law
9 and not claim to rule themselves.   But if the men of property
in the state are fewer than in the former case, and own more
property, there arises a second form of oligarchy.   For the
stronger they are, the more power they claim, and having this
object in view, they themselves select those of the other
classes who are to be admitted to the government ; but, not
being as yet strong enough to rule without the law, they make
10 the law represent their wishes.   When this power is inten-
sified by a further diminution of their numbers and increase
of their property, there arises a third and further stage of
oligarchy, in which the governing class keep the offices in
their own hands, and the law ordains that the son shall
11 succeed the father.   When, again, the rulers have great

wealth and numerous friends, this sort of dynastia or family **IV. 6**
despotism approaches a monarchy; individuals rule and not
the law.   This is the fourth sort of oligarchy, and is analogous
to the last sort of democracy.

There are still two forms besides democracy and oligarchy; **7**
one of them is universally recognized and included among the
four principal forms of government, which are said to be
(1) monarchy, (2) oligarchy, (3) democracy, and (4) the so-
called aristocracy or government of the best.   But there is also
a fifth, which retains the generic name of polity or constitutional government; this is not common, and therefore has not
been noticed by writers who attempt to enumerate the different kinds of government; like Plato in his books about the **1293 b**
state, they recognize four only.   The term 'aristocracy' **2**
is rightly applied to the form of government which is described in the first part of our treatise: for that only can
be rightly called aristocracy [the government of the best]
which is a government formed of the best men absolutely,
and not merely of men who are good when tried by any given
standard.   In the perfect state the good man is absolutely the
same as the good citizen; whereas in other states the good
citizen is only good relatively to his own form of government.   But there are some states differing from oligarchies **3**
and also differing from the so-called polity or constitutional government; these are termed aristocracies, and in
them magistrates are certainly chosen, both according to their
wealth and according to their merit.   Such a form of government is not the same with the two just now mentioned, and
is termed an aristocracy.   For indeed in states which do not **4**
make virtue the aim of the community, men of merit and
reputation for virtue may be found.   And so where a govern-

IV. 7 ment has regard to wealth, virtue, and numbers, as at Carthage [1], that is aristocracy ; and also where it has regard only to two out of the three, as at Lacedaemon, to virtue and numbers, and the two principles of democracy and virtue
5 temper each other. There are these two forms of aristocracy in addition to the first and perfect state, and there is a third form, viz. the polities which incline towards oligarchy.

8   I have yet to speak of the so-called polity and of tyranny. I put them in this order, not because a polity or constitutional government is to be regarded as a perversion any more than the above-mentioned aristocracies. The truth is, that they all fall short of the most perfect form of government, and so they are reckoned among perversions, and other forms (*sc.* the really perverted forms) are perversions of these, as I
2 said before [2]. Last of all I will speak of tyranny, which I place last in the series because I am enquiring into the constitutions of states, and this is the very reverse of a constitution.

Having explained why I have adopted this order, I will proceed to consider constitutional government ; of which the nature will be clearer now that oligarchy and democracy
3 have been defined. For polity or constitutional government may be described generally as a fusion of oligarchy and democracy ; but the term is usually applied to those forms of government which incline towards democracy, and the term aristocracy to those which incline towards oligarchy, because birth and education are commonly the accompani-
4 ments of wealth. Moreover, the rich already possess the external advantages the want of which is a temptation to crime, and hence they are called noblemen and gentlemen.

[1] Cp. ii. 11. §§ 5–10.   [2] Cp. iii. 7.

And inasmuch as aristocracy seeks to give predominance to **IV. 8**
the best of the citizens, people say also of oligarchies
that they are composed of noblemen and gentlemen. Now 1294 a
it appears to be an impossible thing that the state which 5
is governed by the best citizens should be ill-governed[1], and
equally impossible that the state which is ill-governed should
be governed by the best. But we must remember that good
laws, if they are not obeyed, do not constitute good government. For there are two parts of good government; one 6
is the actual obedience of citizens to the laws, the other
part is the goodness of the laws which they obey; they
may obey bad laws as well as good. And there may be
a further subdivision; they may obey either the best laws
which are attainable to them, or the best absolutely.

The distribution of offices according to merit is a special 7
characteristic of aristocracy, for the principle of an aristocracy
is virtue, as wealth is of an oligarchy, and freedom of a
democracy. In all of them there of course exists the right
of the majority, and whatever seems good to the majority of
those who share in the government has authority. Generally, 8
however, a state of this kind is called a constitutional government [not an aristocracy], for the fusion goes no further
than the attempt to unite the freedom of the poor and the
wealth of the rich, who commonly take the place of the
noble. And as there are three grounds on which men claim 9
an equal share in the government—freedom, wealth, and virtue
(for the fourth or good birth is the result of the two last,
being only ancient wealth and virtue)—it is clear that the
admixture of the two elements, that is to say, of the rich
and poor, is to be called a polity or constitutional government;

---

[1] Omitting ἀλλὰ πονηροκρατουμένην.

IV. 8 and the union of the three is to be called aristocracy or the government of the best, and more than any other form of government, except the true and ideal, has a right to this name.

10 Thus far I have described the different forms of states which exist besides monarchy, democracy, and oligarchy, and what they are, and in what aristocracies differ from one another, and polities from aristocracies—that the two latter are not very unlike is obvious.

9 Next we have to consider how by the side of oligarchy and democracy the so-called polity or constitutional government springs up, and how it should be organized. The nature of it will be at once understood from a comparison of oligarchy and democracy; we must ascertain their different characteristics, and taking a portion from each, put the two 2 together, like the parts of an indenture. Now there are three modes in which fusions of government may be effected. The nature of the fusion will be made intelligible by an example of the manner in which different governments legislate, say concerning the administration of justice. In oligarchies they impose a fine on the rich if they do not serve as judges, and to the poor they give no pay; but in democracies they give 3 pay to the poor and do not fine the rich. Now (1) the union of these two modes[1] is a common or middle term between 1294 b them, and is therefore characteristic of a constitutional government, for it is a combination of both. This is one mode of uniting the two elements. Or (2) a mean may be taken between the enactments of the two: thus democracies require no property qualification, or only a small one, from members of the assembly, oligarchies a high one; here

[1] Cp. c. 13. § 6.

neither of these is the common term, but a mean between them. **IV. 9**
(3) There is a third mode, in which something is borrowed **4**
from the oligarchical and something from the democratical
principle. For example, the appointment of magistrates by
lot is democratical, and the election of them oligarchical;
democratical again when there is no property qualification,
oligarchical when there is. In the aristocratical or constitu- **5**
tional state, one element will be taken from each—from oligarchy the mode of electing to offices, from democracy the
disregard of qualification. Such are the various modes of **6**
combination.

There is a true union of oligarchy and democracy when the
same state may be termed either a democracy or an oligarchy;
those who use both names evidently feel that the fusion
is complete. Such a fusion there is also in the mean; for
both extremes appear in it. The Lacedaemonian constitution, **7**
for example, is often described as a democracy, because it has
many democratical features. In the first place the youth
receive a democratical education. For the sons of the poor
are brought up with the sons of the rich, who are educated
in such a manner as to make it possible for the sons of the
poor to be educated like them. A similar equality prevails **8**
in the following period of life, and when the citizens are
grown up to manhood the same rule is observed; there is
no distinction between the rich and poor. In like manner
they all have the same food at their public tables, and
the rich wear only such clothing as any poor man can
afford. Again, the people elect to one of the two greatest **9**
offices of states, and in the other they share [1]; for they elect
the Senators and share in the Ephoralty. By others the

[1] Cp. ii. 9. § 21.

IV. 9 Spartan constitution is said to be an oligarchy, because it
has many oligarchical elements. That all offices are filled
by election and none by lot, is one of these oligarchical
characteristics; that the power of inflicting death or banish-
ment rests with a few persons is another; and there are
10 others. In a well attempered polity there should appear to
be both elements and yet neither; also the government should
rely on itself, and not on foreign aid, nor on the good will of
a majority of foreign states—they might be equally well-
disposed when there is a vicious form of government—but on
the general willingness of all classes in the state to maintain
the constitution.

Enough of the manner in which a constitutional government,
and in which the so-called aristocracies ought to be framed.

10 Of the nature of tyranny I have still to speak, in order
1295 a that it may have its place in our enquiry, since even tyranny is
reckoned by us to be a form of government, although there is
not much to be said about it. I have already in the former
part of this treatise [1] discussed royalty or kingship according
to the most usual meaning of the term, and considered
whether it is or is not advantageous to states, and what kind
of royalty should be established, and whence, and how it
arises.

2 When speaking of royalty we also spoke of two forms
of tyranny, which are both according to law, and therefore
easily pass into royalty. Among Barbarians there are elected
monarchs who exercise a despotic power; despotic rulers
were also elected in ancient Hellas, called Aesymnetes or
3 dictators. These monarchies, when compared with one
another, exhibit certain differences. And they are, as I

[1] iii. 14-17.

said before, royal, in so far as the monarch rules accord- IV. 10
ing to law and over willing subjects; but they are tyrannical
in so far as he is despotic and rules according to his own
fancy. There is also a third kind of tyranny, which is the
most typical form, and is the counterpart of the perfect
monarchy. This tyranny is just that arbitrary power of an 4
individual which is responsible to no one, and governs all
alike, whether equals or betters, with a view to its own
advantage, not to that of its subjects, and therefore against
their will. No freeman, if he can escape from it, will endure
such a government.

The kinds of tyranny are such and so many, and for the
reasons which I have given.

We have now to enquire what is the best constitution 11
for most states, and the best life for most men, neither
assuming a standard of virtue which is above ordinary persons,
nor an education which is exceptionally favoured by nature
and circumstances, nor yet an ideal state which is an aspiration
only, but having regard to the life in which the majority
are able to share, and to the form of government which states
in general can attain. As to those aristocracies, as they are 2
called, of which we were just now speaking, they either
lie beyond the possibilities of the greater number of states,
or they approximate to the so-called constitutional government, and therefore need no separate discussion. And in
fact the conclusion at which we arrive respecting all these
forms rests upon the same grounds. For if it has been truly 3
said in the Ethics[1] that the happy life is the life according
to unimpeded virtue, and that virtue is a mean, then the
life which is in a mean, and in a mean attainable by every

[1] N. Eth. vii. 13. § 2.

IV. 11 one, must be the best. And the same criteria of virtue
1295 b and vice apply both to cities and to constitutions; for the
constitution is in a figure the life of the city [1].

4   Now in all states there are three elements; one class is
very rich, another very poor, and a third in a mean. It
is admitted that moderation and the mean are best, and therefore it will clearly be best to possess the gifts of fortune
in moderation; for in that condition of life men are most
5 ready to listen to reason. But he who greatly excels in
beauty, strength, birth or wealth, or on the other hand who
is very poor, or very weak, or very much disgraced, finds it
difficult to follow reason [2]. Of these two the one sort grow
into violent and great criminals, the others into rogues and
petty rascals. And two sorts of offences correspond to them [3],
the one committed from violence, the other from roguery.
The petty rogues are disinclined to hold office, whether
military or civil, and their aversion to these two duties is
as great an injury to the state as their tendency to crime.
6 Again, those who have too much of the goods of fortune,
strength, wealth, friends, and the like, are neither willing
nor able to submit to authority. The evil begins at home:
for when they are boys, by reason of the luxury in which
they are brought up [4], they never learn, even at school, the
habit of obedience. On the other hand, the very poor, who
7 are in the opposite extreme, are too degraded. So that the
one class cannot obey, and can only rule despotically; the
other knows not how to command and must be ruled like
slaves. Thus arises a city, not of freemen, but of masters
and slaves, the one despising, the other envying; and nothing

[1] Cp. iii. 3. §§ 7, 8.   [2] Cp. Pl. Rep. iv. 421 c, d ff.
[3] Laws, viii. 831 E.   [4] Cp. v. 9. § 13.

can be more fatal to friendship and good fellowship in states **IV. 11** than this: for good fellowship tends to friendship; when men are at enmity with one another, they would rather not even share the same path. But a city ought to be composed, as far **8** as possible, of equals and similars; and these are generally the middle classes. Wherefore the city which is composed of middle-class citizens is necessarily best governed; they are, as we say, the natural elements of a state. And this is the class of citizens which is most secure in a state, for they do not, like the poor, covet their neighbours' goods; nor do **9** others covet theirs, as the poor covet the goods of the rich; and as they neither plot against others, nor are themselves plotted against, they pass through life safely. Wisely then did Phocylides pray—

'Many things are best in the mean; I desire to be of a middle condition in my city.'

Thus it is manifest that the best political community is **10** formed by citizens of the middle class, and that those states are likely to be well-administered, in which the middle class is large, and larger if possible than both the other classes, or at any rate than either singly; for the addition of the middle class turns the scale, and prevents either of the extremes from being dominant. Great then is the good **11** fortune of a state in which the citizens have a moderate and sufficient property; for where some possess much, and the **1296 a** others nothing, there may arise an extreme democracy, or a pure oligarchy; or a tyranny may grow out of either extreme—either out of the most rampant democracy, or out of an oligarchy; but it is not so likely to arise out of a middle and nearly equal condition. I will explain the reason of this **12**

IV. 11 hereafter, when I speak of the revolutions of states [1]. The mean condition of states is clearly best, for no other is free from faction; and where the middle class is large, there

13 are least likely to be factions and dissensions. For a similar reason large states are less liable to faction than small ones, because in them the middle class is large; whereas in small states it is easy to divide all the citizens into two classes who are either rich or poor, and to leave nothing in the middle.

14 And democracies are safer [2] and more permanent than oligarchies, because they have a middle class which is more numerous and has a greater share in the government; for when there is no middle class, and the poor greatly exceed in number, troubles arise, and the state soon comes to an

15 end. A proof of the superiority of the middle class is that the best legislators have been of a middle condition; for example, Solon, as his own verses testify; and Lycurgus, for he was not a king; and Charondas, and almost all legislators.

16 These considerations will help us to understand why most governments are either democratical or oligarchical. The reason is that the middle class is seldom numerous in them, and whichever party, whether the rich or the common people, transgresses the mean and predominates, draws the government to itself, and thus arises either oligarchy or democracy.

17 There is another reason—the poor and the rich quarrel with one another, and whichever side gets the better, instead of establishing a just or popular government, regards political supremacy as the prize of victory, and the one party sets up

18 a democracy and the other an oligarchy. Both the parties which had the supremacy in Hellas looked only to the

---

[1] Cp. Bk. v.   [2] Cp. v. 1. § 15; 7. § 6.

interest of their own form of government, and established in **IV. 11**
states, the one, democracies, and the other, oligarchies; they
thought of their own advantage, of the public not at all. For 19
these reasons the middle form of government has rarely, if
ever, existed, and among a very few only. One man alone of
all who ever ruled in Hellas was induced to give this middle
constitution to states. But it has now become a habit among 1296 b
the citizens of states, not even to care about equality; all men
are seeking for dominion, or, if conquered, are willing to
submit.

What then is the best form of government, and what makes 20
it the best, is evident; and of other states, since we say that
there are many kinds of democracy and many of oligarchy, it
is not difficult to see which has the first and which the second
or any other place in the order of excellence, now that
we have determined which is the best. For that which 21
is nearest to the best must of necessity be better, and
that which is furthest from it worse, if we are judging
absolutely and not relatively to given conditions : I say
' relatively to given conditions,' since a particular government
may be preferable for some, but another form may be better
for others.

We have now to consider what and what kind of govern- 12
ment is suitable to what and what kind of men. I may begin
by assuming, as a general principle common to all governments, that the portion of the state which desires permanence
ought to be stronger than that which desires the reverse.
Now every city is composed of quality and quantity. By
quality I mean freedom, wealth, education, good birth, and by
quantity, superiority of numbers. Quality may exist in one of 2
the classes which make up the state, and quantity in the

IV. 12 other. For example, the meanly-born may be more in number than the well-born, or the poor than the rich, yet they may not so much exceed in quantity as they fall short in **3** quality; and therefore there must be a comparison of quantity and quality. Where the number of the poor is more than proportioned to the wealth of the rich, there will naturally be a democracy, varying in form with the sort of people who compose it in each case. If, for example, the husbandmen exceed in number, the first form of democracy will then arise; if the artisans and labouring class, the last; and so with the intermediate forms. But where the rich and the notables exceed in quality more than they fall short in quantity, there oligarchy arises, similarly assuming various forms according to the kind of superiority possessed by the oligarchs.

4 The legislator should always include the middle class in his government; if he makes his laws oligarchical, to the middle class let him look; if he makes them democratical, he should equally by his laws try [1] to attach this class to the state [1]. There only can the government ever be stable **1297 a** where the middle class exceeds one or both of the others, and **5** in that case there will be no fear that the rich will unite with the poor against the rulers. For neither of them will ever be willing to serve the other, and if they look for some form of government more suitable to both, they will find none better than this, for the rich and the poor will never consent to rule in turn, because they mistrust one another. The arbiter is always the one trusted, and he who is in the middle is an **6** arbiter. The more perfect the admixture of the political elements, the more lasting will be the state. Many even of

[1] Or, if προσάγεσθαι can govern τοῖς νόμοις, 'to win this class over to his laws.'

those who desire to form aristocratical governments make **IV. 12**
a mistake, not only in giving too much power to the rich, but
in attempting to overreach the people. There comes a time
when out of a false good there arises a true evil, since the
encroachments of the rich are more destructive to the state
than those of the people.

The devices by which oligarchies deceive the people are **13**
five in number; they relate to (1) the assembly; (2) the
magistracies; (3) the courts of law; (4) the use of arms;
(5) gymnastic exercises. (1) The assemblies are thrown
open to all, but either the rich only are fined for non-
attendance, or a much larger fine is inflicted upon them.
(2) As to the magistracies, those who are qualified by **2**
property cannot decline office upon oath, but the poor may.
(3) In the law-courts the rich, and the rich only, are fined
if they do not serve, the poor are let off with impunity, or,
as in the laws of Charondas, a large fine is inflicted on the
rich, and a smaller one on the poor. In some states all **3**
citizens who have registered themselves are allowed to attend
the assembly and to try causes; but if after registration they
do not attend in the assembly or at the courts, heavy fines are
imposed upon them. The intention is that through fear
of the fines they may avoid registering themselves, and then
they cannot sit in the law-courts or in the assembly.
(4) Concerning the possession of arms, and (5) gymnastic **4**
exercises, they legislate in a similar spirit. For the poor are
not obliged to have arms, but the rich are fined for not having
them; and in like manner no penalty is inflicted on the poor
for non-attendance at the gymnasium, and consequently,
having nothing to fear, they do not attend, whereas the rich
are liable to a fine, and therefore they take care to attend.

IV. 13   These are the devices of oligarchical legislators, and
5 in democracies they have counter devices. They pay the poor
for attending the assemblies and the law-courts, and they
6 inflict no penalty on the rich for non-attendance. It is
obvious that he who would duly mix the two principles should
combine the practice of both, and provide that the poor
should be paid to attend, and the rich fined if they do not
attend, for then all will take part; if there is no such combina-
1297 b tion, power will be in the hands of one party only. The
7 government should be confined to those who carry arms. As
to the property qualification, no absolute rule can be laid
down, but we must see what is the highest qualification
sufficiently comprehensive to secure that the number of those
who have the rights of citizens exceeds the number of those
8 excluded. Even if they have no share in office, the poor,
provided only that they are not outraged or deprived of their
property, will be quiet enough.

But to secure gentle treatment for the poor is not an easy
9 thing, since a ruling class is not always humane. And in time
of war the poor are apt to hesitate unless they are fed; when
fed, they are willing enough to fight. In some states the
government is vested, not only in those who are actually
serving, but also in those who have served; among the
Malians, for example, the governing body consisted of the
latter, while the magistrates were chosen from those actually
10 on service. And the earliest government which existed among
the Hellenes, after the overthrow of the kingly power, grew
up out of the warrior class, and was originally taken from the
knights (for strength and superiority in war at that time
depended on cavalry[1]); indeed, without discipline, infantry

[1] Cp. iv. 3. § 3; vi. 7. § 1.

are useless, and in ancient times there was no military know- **IV. 13**
ledge or tactics, and therefore the strength of armies lay
in their cavalry. But when cities increased and the heavy
armed grew in strength, more had a share in the government;
and this is the reason why the states, which we call con- 11
stitutional governments, have been hitherto called democracies.
Ancient constitutions, as might be expected, were oligarchical
and royal; their population being small they had no considerable middle class; the people were weak in numbers and
organization, and were therefore more contented to be
governed.

I have explained why there are various forms of govern- 12
ment, and why there are more than is generally supposed;
for democracy, as well as other constitutions, has more than
one form : also what their differences are, and whence they
arise, and what is the best form of government, speaking
generally, and to whom the various forms of government
are best suited; all this has now been explained.

Having thus gained an appropriate basis of discussion we **14**
will proceed to speak of the points which follow next in
order. We will consider the subject not only in general but
with reference to particular states. All states have three
elements, and the good law-giver has to regard what is
expedient for each state. When they are well-ordered, the
state is well-ordered, and as they differ from one another,
constitutions differ. What is the element first (1) which 2
deliberates about public affairs; secondly (2) which is con- 1298 2
cerned with the magistrates and determines what they should
be, over whom they should exercise authority, and what
should be the mode of electing them; and thirdly (3) which 3
has judicial power?

IV. 14 The deliberative element has authority in matters of war and peace, in making and unmaking alliances; it passes laws, inflicts death, exile, confiscation, audits the accounts of magistrates. All these powers must be assigned either to all the citizens or to some of them, for example, to one or more magistracies; or different causes to different magistracies, or 4 some of them to all, and others of them only to some. That all things should be decided by all is characteristic of democracy; this is the sort of equality which the people desire. But there are various ways in which all may share in the government; they may deliberate, not all in one body, but by turns, as in the constitution of Telecles the Milesian. There are other states in which the boards of magistrates meet and deliberate, but come into office by turns, and are elected out of the tribes and the very smallest divisions of the state, until every one has obtained office in his turn. The citizens, on the other hand, are assembled only for the purposes of legislation, and to consult about the con-5 stitution, and to hear the edicts of the magistrates. In another variety of democracy the citizens form one assembly, but meet only to elect magistrates, to pass laws, to advise about war and peace, and to make scrutinies. Other matters are referred severally to special magistrates, who are elected 6 by vote or by lot out of all the citizens. Or again, the citizens meet about election to offices and about scrutinies, and deliberate concerning war or alliances, while other matters are administered by the magistrates, who, as far as is possible, are elected by vote [1]. I am speaking of those magistracies in 7 which special knowledge is required. A fourth form of democracy is when all the citizens meet to deliberate about

[1] Cp. vi. 2. § 5.

everything, and the magistrates decide nothing, but only make **IV. 14**
the preliminary enquiries; and that is the way in which the
last and worst form of democracy, corresponding, as we
maintain, to the close family oligarchy and to tyranny, is
at present administered. All these modes are democratical.

On the other hand, that some should deliberate about all is
oligarchical. This again is a mode which, like the demo- 8
cratical, has many forms. When the deliberative class, being
elected out of those who have a moderate qualification, are
numerous and they respect and obey the law without alter-
ing it, and any one who has the required qualification shares
in the government, then, just because of this moderation, the
oligarchy inclines towards polity. But when only selected in- 1298 b
dividuals and not the whole people share in the deliberations
of the state, then, although, as in the former case, they observe
the law, the government is a pure oligarchy. Or, again, 9
when those who have the power of deliberation are self-
elected, and son succeeds father, and they and not the laws
are supreme—the government is of necessity oligarchical.
Where, again, particular persons have authority in particular 10
matters—for example, when the whole people decide about
peace and war and hold scrutinies, but the magistrates regulate
everything else, and they are elected either by vote or by lot—
there [1] the form of government is an aristocracy or polity [1].
And if some questions are decided by magistrates elected
by vote, and others by magistrates elected by lot, either
absolutely or out of select candidates, or elected both by
vote and by lot—these practices are partly characteristic of an

---

[1] Reading with several of the MSS. ἀριστοκρατία ἢ πολιτεία, and
omitting μέν. Or, with Bekker's text, ἀριστοκρατία μὲν ἢ πολιτεία,
'the government is an aristocracy.'

IV. 14 aristocratical government, and partly of a pure constitutional government.

11   These are the various forms of the deliberative body ; they correspond to the various forms of government.   And the government of each state is administered according to one or 12 other of the principles which have been laid down.   Now it is for the interest of democracy, according to the most prevalent notion of it (I am speaking of that extreme form of democracy, in which the people are supreme even over the laws), with a view to better deliberation to adopt the custom of oligarchies respecting courts of law.   For in oligarchies the rich who are wanted to be judges are compelled to attend under pain of a fine, whereas in democracies the poor are paid to attend.   And this practice of oligarchies should be adopted by democracies in their public assemblies, for they will advise better if they all deliberate together—the people 13 with the notables and the notables with the people.   It is also a good plan that those who deliberate should be elected by vote or by lot in equal numbers out of the different classes ; and that if the people greatly exceed in number those who have political training, pay should not be given to all, but only to as many as would balance the number of the notables, or that the number in excess should be eliminated 14 by lot.   But in oligarchies either certain persons should be chosen out of the mass, or a class of officers should be appointed such as exist in some states, who are termed *probuli* and guardians of the law ; and the citizens should occupy themselves exclusively with matters on which these have previously deliberated ; for so the people will have a share in the deliberations of the state, but will not be able 15 to disturb the principles of the constitution.   Again, in

oligarchies either the people ought to accept the measures **IV. 14** of the government, or not to pass anything contrary to them; or, if all are allowed to share in counsel, the decision should rest with the magistrates. The opposite of what is done in constitutional governments should be the rule in oligarchies; the veto of the majority should be final, their assent not final, but the proposal should be referred back to the magistrates. Whereas in constitutional governments they take the contrary **16** course; the few have the negative not the affirmative power; the affirmation of everything rests with the multitude. **1299 a**

These, then, are our conclusions respecting the deliberative, that is, the supreme element in states.

Next we will proceed to consider the distribution of **15** offices; this, too, being a part of politics concerning which many questions arise:—What shall their number be? Over what shall they preside, and what shall be their duration? Sometimes they last for six months, sometimes for less; sometimes they are annual, whilst in other cases offices are held for still longer periods. Shall they be for life or for a long term of years; or, if for a short term only, shall the same persons hold them over and over again, or once only? Also about the appointment to them—from whom are they to be chosen, by whom, and how? We should **2** first be in a position to say what are the possible varieties of them, and then we may proceed to determine which are suited to different forms of government. But what are to be included under the term 'offices'? That is a question not quite so easily answered. For a political community requires many officers; and not every one who is chosen by vote or by lot is to be regarded as a ruler. In the first place there are the priests, who must be distinguished from political

IV. 15 officers; masters of choruses and heralds, even ambassadors,
3 are elected by vote [but still they are not political officers].
Some duties of superintendence again are political, extending
either to all the citizens in a single sphere of action, like
the office of the general who superintends them when they
are in the field, or to a section of them only, like the
inspectorships of women or of youth. Other offices are
concerned with household management, like that of the corn
measurers who exist in many states and are elected officers.
There are also menial offices which the rich have executed by
4 their slaves.   Speaking generally, they are to be called offices
to which the duties are assigned of deliberating about certain
measures and of judging and commanding, especially the last;
for to command is the especial duty of a magistrate. But the
question is not of any importance in practice; no one has ever
brought into court the meaning of the word, although such
problems have a speculative interest.

5   What kinds of offices, and how many, are necessary to the
existence of a state, and which, if not necessary, yet conduce
to its well-being, are much more important considerations,
6 affecting all states, but more especially small ones.   For in
great states it is possible, and indeed necessary, that every
office should have a special function; where the citizens are
numerous, many may hold office.   And so it happens that
vacancies occur in some offices only after long intervals, or
the office is held once only; and certainly every work is
1299 b better done which receives of the sole [1], and not the divided,
7 attention of the worker.   But in small states it is necessary
to combine many offices in a few hands [2], since the small
number of citizens does not admit of many holding office:—

[1] Cp. ii. 2. § 6.   [2] Cp. vi. 8.

for who will there be to succeed them? And yet small **IV. 15**
states at times require the same offices and laws as large ones;
the difference is that the one want them often, the others only
after long intervals. Hence there is no reason why the care 8
of many offices should not be imposed on the same person,
for they will not interfere with each other. When the
population is small, offices should be like the spits which also
serve to hold a lamp[1]. We must first ascertain how many
magistrates are necessary in every state, and also how many
are not exactly necessary, but are nevertheless useful, and
then there will be no difficulty in judging what offices can be
combined in one. We should also know when local tribunals 9
are to have jurisdiction over many different matters, and when
authority should be centralized: for example, should one
person keep order in the market and another in some other
place, or should the same person be responsible everywhere?
Again, should offices be divided according to the subjects
with which they deal, or according to the persons with whom
they deal: I mean to say, should one person see to good
order in general, or one look after the boys, another after the
women, and so on? Further, under different constitutions, 10
should the magistrates be the same or different? For
example, in democracy, oligarchy, aristocracy, monarchy,
should there be the same magistrates, although they are
elected, not out of equal or similar classes of citizens, but
differently under different constitutions—in aristocracies, for
example, they are chosen from the educated, in oligarchies
from the wealthy, and in democracies from the free—or are
there different offices proper to different constitutions[2], and

---

[1] Cp. Note on i. 2. § 3. [2] See note.

IV 15 may the same be suitable to some, but unsuitable to others? For in some states it may be convenient that the same office should have a more extensive, in other states a narrower 11 sphere. Special offices are peculiar to certain forms of government:—for example, [to oligarchies] that of probuli, which is not a democratic office, although a bule or council is. There must be some body of men whose duty is to prepare measures for the people in order that they may not be diverted from their business; when these are few in number, the state inclines to an oligarchy: or rather the probuli must always be 12 few, and are therefore an oligarchical element. But when both institutions exist in a state, the probuli are a check on the council; for the counsellor is a democratic element, but the probuli are oligarchical. Even the power of the council disappears when democracy has taken that extreme 1300 a form, in which the people themselves are always meeting and 13 deliberating about everything. This is the case when the members of the assembly are wealthy or receive pay; for they have nothing to do and are always holding assemblies and deciding everything for themselves. A magistracy which controls the boys or the women, or any similar office, is suited to an aristocracy rather than to a democracy; for how can the magistrates prevent the wives of the poor from going out of doors? Neither is it an oligarchical office; for the wives of the oligarchs are too fine to be controlled.

14 Enough of these matters. I will now enquire into the appointment of offices. There are three questions to be answered, and the combinations of answers give all possible differences: first, who appoints? secondly, from whom? and 15 thirdly, how? Each of these three may further differ in three ways: (1) All the citizens, or only some, appoint;

(2) Either the magistrates are chosen out of all or out of **IV. 15** some who are distinguished either by a property qualification, or by birth, or merit, or for some special reason, as at Megara only those were eligible who had returned from exile and fought together against the democracy; (3) They may be appointed either by vote or by lot.   Again, these several 16 modes may be combined; I mean that some officers may be elected by some, others by all, and some again out of some, and others out of all, and some by vote and others by lot.   Each of these differences admits of four variations. 17 (1) Either all may elect out of all by vote, or all out of all by lot; and either out of all collectively or by sections, as, for example, by tribes, and wards, and phratries, until all the citizens have been gone through; or the citizens may be in all cases eligible indiscriminately, and in some cases they may be elected by vote, and in some by lot.   Again, (2) if only 18 some appoint, they may appoint out of all by vote, or out of all by lot; or out of some by vote, out of some by lot, and some offices may be appointed in one way and some in another; I mean if they are appointed by all they may be appointed partly by vote and partly by lot[1].   Thus there will be twelve forms of appointment without including the two combinations in the mode of election.   Of these varieties two 19 are democratic forms, namely, when the choice is made by all the people out of all by vote or by lot, or by both, that is to say, some by lot and some by vote.   The cases in which they do not all appoint at one time, but some appoint out of all or out of some by vote or by lot or by both (I mean some by lot and some by vote), or some out of all and others out

---

[1] i. e. partly out of all and partly out of some, and partly by vote and partly by lot (see infra c. 16. § 6).

IV. 15 of some both by lot and vote, are characteristic of a polity or
20 constitutional government. That some should be appointed
out of all by vote or by lot or by both, is oligarchical, and still
more·oligarchical when some are elected from all and some
from some. That some should be elected out of all and
some out of some, or again some by vote and others by
1300 b lot, is characteristic of a constitutional government, which
21 inclines to an aristocracy. That some should be chosen out
of some, and some taken by lot out of some, is oligarchical
[1] though not equally oligarchical [1]; oligarchical, too, is the
appointment of some out of some in both ways, and of some
out of all. But that all should elect by vote out of some is
aristocratical.

22   These are the different ways of constituting magistrates,
and in this manner officers correspond to different forms
of government:—which are proper to which, or how they
ought to be established, will be evident when we determine
the nature of their powers [2]. By powers I mean such power
as a magistrate exercises over the revenue or in defence of
the country; for there are various kinds of power : the power
of the general, for example, is not the same with that which
regulates contracts in the market.

16   Of the three parts of government, the judicial remains
to be considered, and this we shall divide on the same
principle. There are three points on which the varieties
of law-courts depend—the persons from whom they are
appointed, the matters with which they are concerned, and the
manner of their appointment. I mean, (1) are the judges
taken from all, or from some only ? (2) how many kinds of

---

[1] These words are bracketed by Bekker in both editions.
[2] Omitting καί with some MSS. and the old translator.

law-courts are there? (3) are the judges chosen by vote or IV. 16
by lot?

First, let me determine how many kinds of law-courts 2
there are. They are eight in number: One is the court of
audits or scrutinies; a second takes cognizance of [ordinary]
offences against the state; a third is concerned with treason
against the government; the fourth determines disputes respecting penalties, whether raised by magistrates or by private
persons; the fifth decides the more important civil cases;
the sixth tries cases of homicide, which are of various kinds, 3
(*a*) premeditated, (*b*) unpremeditated, (*c*) cases in which the
guilt is confessed but the justice is disputed; and there may
be a fourth court (*d*) in which murderers who have fled from
justice are tried after their return; such as the Court of
Phreatto is said to be at Athens. But cases of this sort
rarely happen at all even in large cities. The different kinds
of homicide may be tried either by the same or by different
courts. (7) There are courts for strangers:—of these there 4
are two subdivisions, (*a*) for the settlement of their disputes
with one another, (*b*) for the settlement of disputes between
them and the citizens. And besides all these there must be
(8) courts for small suits about sums of a drachma up to five
drachmas, or a little more, which have to be determined, but
they do not require many judges.

Nothing more need be said of these small suits, nor of the 5
courts for homicide and for strangers:—I would rather speak
of political cases, which, when mismanaged, create division and
disturbances in states.

Now if all the citizens judge, in all the different cases
which I have distinguished, they may be appointed by vote
or by lot, or sometimes by lot and sometimes by vote. Or

IV. 16 when a certain class of causes are tried, the judges who decide them may be appointed, some by vote, and some by lot.

1301 a These then are the four modes of appointing judges from the
6 whole people, and there will be likewise four modes, if they are elected from a part only; for they may be appointed from some by vote and judge in all causes; or they may be appointed from some by lot and judge in all causes; or they may be elected in some cases by vote, and in some cases taken by lot, or some courts, even when judging the same causes, may be composed of members some appointed by vote and some by lot. These then are the ways in which the aforesaid judges may be appointed.

7 Once more, the modes of appointment may be combined, I mean, that some may be chosen out of the whole people, others out of some, some out of both; for example, the same tribunal may be composed of some who were elected out of all, and of others who were elected out of some, either by vote or by lot or by both.

8 In how many forms law-courts can be established has now been considered. The first form, viz. that in which the judges are taken from all the citizens, and in which all causes are tried, is democratical; the second, which is composed of a few only who try all causes, oligarchical; the third, in which some courts are taken from all classes, and some from certain classes only, aristocratical and constitutional.

BOOK V

THE design which we proposed to ourselves is now nearly **V. 1**
completed[1].   Next in order follow the causes of revolution
in states, how many, and of what nature they are ; what
elements work ruin in particular states, and out of what, and
into what they mostly change ; also what are the elements of
preservation in states generally, or in a particular state, and
by what means each state may be best preserved : these
questions remain to be considered.

In the first place we must assume as our starting-point **2**
that in the many forms of government which have sprung up
there has always been an acknowledgement of justice and[2]
proportionate equality, although mankind fail in attaining
them, as indeed I have already explained[3].   Democracy, **3**
for example, arises out of the notion that those who are
equal in any respect are equal in all respects; because men
are equally free, they claim to be absolutely equal.   Oligarchy
is based on the notion that those who are unequal in one
respect are in all respects unequal ; being unequal, that is, in
property, they suppose themselves to be unequal absolutely.
The democrats think that as they are equal they ought to be **4**

---

[1] Cp. iv. c. 2.
[2] Reading καί with the MSS. and Bekker's 1st ed.
[3] Cp. iii. 9. §§ 1–4.

V. 1 equal in all things; while the oligarchs, under the idea that
they are unequal, claim too much, which is one form of
5 inequality. All these forms of government have a kind of
justice, but, tried by an absolute standard, they are faulty;
and, therefore, both parties, whenever their share in the
government does not accord with their preconceived ideas,
6 stir up revolution.   Those who excel in virtue have the best
1301 b right of all to rebel (for they alone can with reason be deemed
absolutely unequal)[1], but then they are of all men the least
7 inclined to do so[2]. There is also a superiority which is
claimed by men of rank; for they are thought noble because
they spring from wealthy and virtuous ancestors[3].   Here
8 then, so to speak, are opened the very springs and fountains
of revolution; and hence arise two sorts of changes in governments; the one affecting the constitution, when men seek to
change from an existing form into some other, for example,
from democracy into oligarchy, and from oligarchy into democracy, or from either of them into constitutional government or
aristocracy, and conversely; the other not affecting the constitution, when, without disturbing the form of government,
whether oligarchy, or monarchy, or any other, they try to get
9 the administration into their own hands[4].   Further, there is
a question of degree; an oligarchy, for example, may become
more or less oligarchical, and a democracy more or less democratical; and in like manner the characteristics of the other
forms of government may be more or less strictly maintained.
10 Or, the revolution may be directed against a portion of the
constitution only, e. g. the establishment or overthrow of
a particular office : as at Sparta it is said that Lysander

[1] Cp. iii. 13. § 25.   [2] Cp. c. 4. § 12.
[3] Cp. iv. 8. § 9.   [4] Cp. iv. 5. § 3.

attempted to overthrow the monarchy, and king Pausanias [1] **V. 1**
the ephoralty. At Epidamnus, too, the change was partial.
For instead of phylarchs or heads of tribes, a council was
appointed; but to this day the magistrates are the only **11**
members of the ruling class who are compelled to go to the
Heliaea when an election takes place, and the office of the
single archon [2] [survives, which] is another oligarchical feature.
Everywhere inequality is a cause of revolution, but an inequality in which there is no proportion, for instance, a perpetual monarchy among equals; and always it is the desire of
equality which rises in rebellion.

Now equality is of two kinds, numerical and proportional; **12**
by the first I mean sameness or equality in number or size;
by the second, equality of ratios. For example, the excess of
three over two is equal to the excess of two over one;
whereas four exceeds two in the same ratio in which two
exceeds one, for two is the same part of four that one is of
two, namely, the half. As I was saying before [3], men agree **13**
about justice in the abstract, that it is treating others according
to their deserts, but there is a difference of opinion about the
application of the principle; some think that if they are equal
in any respect they are equal absolutely, others that if they are
unequal in any respect they are unequal in all. Hence there **14**
are two principal forms of government, democracy and oligarchy; for good birth and virtue are rare, but wealth and **1302 a**
numbers are more common. In what city shall we find
a hundred persons of good birth and of virtue? whereas the
poor everywhere abound. That a state should be ordered,
simply and wholly, according to either kind of equality, is not

---

[1] Cp. vii. 14. § 20.   [2] Cp. iii. 16. § 1.
[3] Cp. § 2; iii. 9. §§ 1–4.

V. 1 a good thing; the proof is the fact that such forms of govern-
15 ment never last. They are originally based on a mistake, and,
as they begin badly, cannot fail to end badly. The inference
is that both kinds of equality should be employed; numerical
in some cases, and proportionate in others.

Still democracy appears to be safer and less liable to revo-
16 lution than oligarchy [1]. For in oligarchies [2] there is the double
danger of the oligarchs falling out among themselves and also
with the people; but in democracies [3] there is only the danger
of a quarrel with the oligarchs. No dissension worth mentioning arises among the people themselves. And we may
further remark that a government which is composed of the
middle class more nearly approximates to democracy than to
oligarchy [4], and is the safest of the imperfect forms of
government.

2 In considering how dissensions and political revolutions
arise, we must first of all ascertain the beginnings and causes
of them which affect constitutions generally. They may be
said to be three in number; and we have now to give an out-
line of each. We want to know (1) what is the feeling?
and (2) what are the motives of those who make them?
2 (3) whence arise political disturbances and quarrels? The
universal and chief cause of this revolutionary feeling has been
already mentioned; viz. the desire of equality, when men think
that they are equal to others who have more than themselves;
or, again, the desire of inequality and superiority, when con-
ceiving themselves to be superior they think that they have
3 not more but the same or less than their inferiors; pretensions
which may and may not be just. Inferiors revolt in order

---

[1] Cp. iv. 11. § 14.   [2] Cp. c. 6.
[3] Cp. c. 5.   [4] Omitting ἡ before τῶν ὀλίγων.

that they may be equal, and equals that they may be superior. **V. 2**
Such is the state of mind which creates revolutions. The
motives for making them are the desire of gain and honour,
or the fear of dishonour and loss ; the authors of them want
to divert punishment or dishonour from themselves or their
friends. The causes and reasons of these motives and dis- 4
positions which are excited in men, about the things which
I have mentioned, viewed in one way, may be regarded as
seven, and in another as more than seven. Two of them 5
have been already noticed [1] ; but they act in a different
manner, for men are excited against one another by the love
of gain and honour—not, as in the case which I have just
supposed, in order to obtain them for themselves, but at seeing 1302 b
others, justly or unjustly, engrossing them. Other causes are 6
insolence, fear, love of superiority, contempt, disproportionate
increase in some part of the state ; causes of another sort are
election intrigues, carelessness, neglect about trifles, dissimi-
larity of elements.

What share insolence and avarice have in creating revolu- 3
tions, and how they work, is plain enough. When the
magistrates are insolent and grasping they conspire against
one another and also against the constitution from which they
derive their power, making their gains either at the expense of
individuals or of the public. It is evident, again, what an 2
influence honour exerts and how it is a cause of revolution. Men
who are themselves dishonoured and who see others obtaining
honours rise in rebellion ; the honour or dishonour when un-
deserved is unjust, and just when awarded according to
merit. Again, superiority is a cause of revolution when one 3
or more persons have a power which is too much for the

[1] Supra §§ 2, 3.

V. 3 state and the power of the government; this is a condition of affairs out of which there arises a monarchy, or a family oligarchy. And, therefore, in some places, as at Athens and Argos, they have recourse to ostracism[1]. But how much better to provide from the first that there should be no such pre-eminent individuals instead of letting them come into existence and then finding a remedy.

4   Another cause of revolution is fear. Either men have committed wrong, and are afraid of punishment, or they are expecting to suffer wrong and are desirous of anticipating their enemy[2]. Thus at Rhodes the notables conspired against the people through fear of the suits that were brought 5 against them. Contempt is also a cause of insurrection and revolution; for example, in oligarchies—when those who have no share in the state are the majority, they revolt, because they think that they are the stronger. Or, again, in democracies, the rich despise the disorder and anarchy of the state; at Thebes, for example, where, after the battle of Oenophyta, the bad administration of the democracy led to its ruin. At Megara the fall of the democracy was due to a defeat occasioned by disorder and anarchy. And at Syracuse the democracy was overthrown before the tyranny of Gelo arose; at Rhodes before the insurrection.

6   Political revolutions also spring from a disproportionate increase in any part of the state. For as a body is made up of many members, and every member ought to grow in proportion[3], that symmetry may be preserved, but loses its nature if the foot be four cubits long and the rest of the 1303 a body two spans; and, should the abnormal increase be one of

---

[1] Cp. iii. 13. § 15.   [2] Cp. c. 5. § 2.
[3] Cp. iii. 13. § 21.

quality as well as of quantity, may even take the form of **V. 3**
another animal : even so a state has many parts, of which
some one may often grow imperceptibly ; for example, the
number of poor in democracies and in constitutional states.
And this disproportion may sometimes happen by an accident, **7**
as at Tarentum, from a defeat in which many of the notables
were slain in a battle with the Iapygians just after the
Persian War, the constitutional government in consequence
becoming a democracy ; or, as was the case at Argos, where
after the losses inflicted in 'the Battle of the Seventh Day'
by Cleomenes the Lacedaemonian, the Argives were compelled to admit to citizenship some of their perioeci : and at
Athens, when, after frequent defeats of their infantry in the
times of the Peloponnesian War, the notables were reduced
in number, because the soldiers had to be taken from the
roll of citizens.   Revolutions arise from this cause in **8**
democracies as well as in other forms of government, but not
to so great an extent.   When the rich [1] grow numerous or
properties increase, the form of government changes into an
oligarchy or a government of families.   Forms of government **9**
also change—sometimes even without revolution, owing to
election contests, as at Heraea (where, instead of electing
their magistrates, they took them by lot, because the electors
were in the habit of choosing their own partisans) ; or owing
to carelessness, when disloyal persons are allowed to find
their way into the highest offices, as at Oreum, where, upon
the accession of Heracleodorus to office, the oligarchy was
overthrown, and changed by him into a constitutional and
democratical government.

---

[1] Reading εὐπόρων.

V. 3   Again, the revolution may be accomplished by small
10 degrees; I mean that a great change may sometimes slip
into the constitution through neglect of a small matter; at
Ambracia, for instance, the qualification for office, small
at first, was eventually reduced to nothing. For the
Ambraciots thought that a small qualification was much the
same as none at all.

11   Another cause of revolution is difference of races which do
not at once acquire a common spirit; for a state is not the
growth of a day, neither is it a multitude brought together
by accident. Hence the reception of strangers in colonies,
either at the time of their foundation or afterwards, has
generally produced revolution; for example, the Achaeans
who joined the Troezenians in the foundation of Sybaris,
being the more numerous, afterwards expelled them; hence
12 the curse fell upon Sybaris. At Thurii the Sybarites
quarrelled with their fellow-colonists; thinking that the land
belonged to them, they wanted too much of it and were
driven out. At Byzantium the new colonists were detected
in a conspiracy, and were expelled by force of arms; the
people of Antissa, who had received the Chian exiles, fought
with them, and drove them out; and the Zancleans, after
having received the Samians, were driven by them out of
13 their own city. The citizens of Apollonia on the Euxine,
after the introduction of a fresh body of colonists, had a
revolution; the Syracusans, after the expulsion of their
1303 b tyrants, having admitted strangers and mercenaries to the
rights of citizenship, quarrelled and came to blows; the
people of Amphipolis, having received Chalcidian colonists,
were nearly all expelled by them.

14   Now, in oligarchies the masses make revolution under the

idea that they are unjustly treated, because, as I said before, **V**. 3 they are equals, and have not an equal share, and in democracies the notables revolt, because they are not equals, and yet have only an equal share.

Again, the situation of cities is a cause of revolution when 15 the country is not naturally adapted to preserve the unity of the state. For example, the Chytrians at Clazomenae did not agree with the people of the island; and the people of Colophon quarrelled with the Notians; at Athens, too, the inhabitants of the Piraeus are more democratic than those who live in the city. For just as in war, the impediment of 16 a ditch, though ever so small, may break a regiment, so every cause of difference, however slight, makes a breach in a city. The greatest opposition is confessedly that of virtue and vice; next comes that of wealth and poverty; and there are other antagonistic elements, greater or less, of which one is this difference of place.

In revolutions the occasions may be trifling, but great 4 interests are at stake. Trifles are most important when they concern the rulers, as was the case of old at Syracuse; for the Syracusan constitution was once changed by a love-quarrel of two young men, who were in the government. The story is that while one of them was away from home 2 his beloved was gained over by his companion, and he to revenge himself seduced the other's wife. They then drew all the members of the ruling class into their quarrel and made a revolution. We learn from this story that we should 3 be on our guard against the beginnings of such evils, and should put an end to the quarrels of chiefs and mighty men. The mistake lies in the beginning—as the proverb says, 'Well begun is half done'—so an error at the beginning,

V. 4 though quite small, has the proportion of a half to the whole
4 matter. In general, when the notables quarrel, the whole city
is involved, as happened in Hestiaea after the Persian War.
The occasion was the division of an inheritance; one of
two brothers refused to give an account of their father's
property and the treasure which he had found : so the poorer
of the two quarrelled with him and enlisted in his cause
the popular party, the other, who was very rich, the wealthy
classes.

5   At Delphi, again, a quarrel about a marriage was the
1304 a beginning of all the troubles which followed. In this case the
bridegroom, fancying some occurrence to be of evil omen,
came to the bride, and went away without taking her.
Whereupon her relations, thinking that they were insulted
by him, put some of the sacred treasure [among his offerings]
while he was sacrificing, and then slew him, pretending that
6 he had been robbing the temple. At Mitylene, too, a dispute about heiresses was the beginning of many misfortunes,
and led to the war with the Athenians in which Paches took
their city. A wealthy citizen, named Timophanes, left two
daughters; Doxander, another citizen, wanted to obtain them
for his sons, but he was rejected in his suit, whereupon
he stirred up a revolution, and instigated the Athenians (of
7 whom he was proxenus) to interfere. A similar quarrel about
an heiress arose at Phocis between Mnaseas the father of
Mnason, and Euthycrates the father of Onomarchus ; this
was the beginning of the Sacred War. A marriage-quarrel
was also the cause of a change in the government of
Epidamnus. A certain man bethrothed his daughter secretly
to a person whose father, having been made a magistrate,
fined the father of the girl, and the latter, stung by the insult,

conspired with the unenfranchised classes to overthrow the **V. 4** state.

Governments also change into oligarchy or into democracy 8 or into a constitutional government because the magistrates, or some other section of the state, increase in power or renown. Thus at Athens the reputation gained by the court of the Areopagus, in the Persian War, seemed to tighten the reins of government. On the other hand, the victory of Salamis [1], which was gained by the common people who served in the fleet, and won for the Athenians the empire of the sea, strengthened the democracy. At Argos, the notables, 9 having distinguished themselves against the Lacedaemonians in the battle of Mantinea, attempted to put down the democracy. At Syracuse, the people having been the chief authors of the victory in the war with the Athenians, changed the constitutional government into democracy. At Chalcis, the people, uniting with the notables, killed Phoxus the tyrant, and then seized the government. At Ambracia [2], the people, in like manner, having joined with the conspirators in expelling the tyrant Periander, transferred the government to themselves. And generally, it should be remembered that 10 those who have secured power to the state, whether private citizens, or magistrates, or tribes, or any other part or section of the state, are apt to cause revolutions. For either envy of their greatness draws others into rebellion, or they themselves, in their pride of superiority, are unwilling to remain on a level with others.

Revolutions break out when opposite parties, e.g. the rich 11 and the poor, are equally balanced, and there is little or 1304 b

[1] Cp. ii. 12. § 5; viii. 6. § 11.
[2] Cp. supra c. 3. § 10, and infra c. 10. § 16.

V. 4 nothing between them; for, if either party were manifestly
12 superior, the other would not risk an attack upon them. And,
for this reason, those who are eminent in virtue do not stir up
insurrections, being always a minority. Such are the beginnings
and causes of the disturbances and revolutions to which every
form of government is liable.

Revolutions are effected in two ways, by force and by
fraud. Force may be applied either at the time of making the
13 revolution or afterwards. Fraud, again, is of two kinds; for
(1) sometimes the citizens are deceived into a change of
government, and afterwards they are held in subjection against
their will. This was what happened in the case of the Four
Hundred, who deceived the people by telling them that the
king would provide money for the war against the Lacedaemonians, and when the deception was over, still endeavoured
to retain the government. (2) In other cases the people are
persuaded at first, and afterwards, by a repetition of the
persuasion, their goodwill and allegiance are retained. The
revolutions which affect constitutions generally spring from
the above-mentioned causes [1].

5   And now, taking each constitution separately, we must see
what follows from the principles already laid down.

Revolutions in democracies are generally caused by the intemperance of demagogues, who either in their private capacity
lay information against rich men until they compel them
to combine (for a common danger unites even the bitterest
enemies), or coming forward in public they stir up the people
against them. The truth of this remark is proved by a
2 variety of examples. At Cos the democracy was overthrown
because wicked demagogues arose, and the notables combined.

[1] Cp. supra c. 2. § 1.

At Rhodes the demagogues not only provided pay for the V. 5 multitude, but prevented them from making good to the trierarchs the sums which had been expended by them; and they, in consequence of the suits which were brought against them, were compelled to combine and put down the democracy [1]. The democracy at Heraclea was overthrown 3 shortly after the foundation of the colony by the injustice of the demagogues, which drove out the notables, who came back in a body and put an end to the democracy. Much in 4 the same manner the democracy at Megara [2] was overturned; there the demagogues drove out many of the notables in order that they might be able to confiscate their property. At length the exiles, becoming numerous, returned, and engaging and defeating the people, established an oligarchy. The same 1305 a thing happened with the democracy of Cyme which was overthrown by Thrasymachus. And we may observe that in most 5 states the changes have been of this character. For sometimes the demagogues, in order to curry favour with the people, wrong the notables and so force them to combine;—either they make a division of their property, or diminish their incomes by the imposition of public services, and sometimes they bring accusations against the rich that they may have their wealth to confiscate [3].

Of old, the demagogue was also a general, and then demo- 6 cracies changed into tyrannies. Most of the ancient tyrants were originally demagogues [4]. They are not so now, but 7 they were then; and the reason is that they were generals and not orators, for oratory had not yet come into fashion. Whereas in our day, when the art of rhetoric has made such

[1] Cp. supra c. 3. § 4.   [2] Cp. c. 3. § 5, and iv. 15. § 15.
[3] Cp. infra c. 8. § 20.   [4] Cp. c. 10. § 4; Plato, Rep. viii. 565 D.

V. 5 progress, the orators lead the people, but their ignorance of
military matters prevents them from usurping power; at any
8 rate instances to the contrary are few and slight.   Formerly
tyrannies were more common than they are now, because
great power was often placed in the hands of individuals;
thus a tyranny arose at Miletus out of the office of the Pry-
tanis, who had supreme authority in many important matters [1].
Moreover, in those days, when cities were not large, the
people dwelt in the fields, busy at their work; and their chiefs,
9 if they possessed any military talent, seized the opportunity,
and winning the confidence of the masses by professing their
hatred of the wealthy, they succeeded in obtaining the tyranny.
Thus at Athens Peisistratus led a faction against the men of
the plain [2], and Theagenes at Megara slaughtered the cattle
of the wealthy, which he found by the river side where they
10 had put them to graze.   Dionysius, again, was thought worthy
of the tyranny because he denounced Daphnaeus and the rich;
his enmity to the notables won for him the confidence of the
people.   Changes also take place from the ancient to the
latest form of democracy; for where there is a popular election of the magistrates and no property qualification, the
aspirants for office get hold of the people, and contrive at
11 last even to set them above the laws.   A more or less complete cure for this state of things is for the separate tribes,
and not the whole people, to elect the magistrates.

These are the principal causes of revolutions in democracies.

6   There are two patent causes of revolutions in oligarchies
[one coming from without, the other from within the govern-
ment]: (1) First, when the oligarchs oppress the people,

---

[1] Cp. infra c. 10. § 5.   [2] See Herod. i. 59.

for then anybody is good enough to be their champion, **V. 6**
especially if he be himself a member of the oligarchy, as 1305 b
Lygdamis at Naxos, who afterwards came to be tyrant. But 2
revolutions which commence outside the governing class may
be further subdivided. Sometimes, when the government is
very exclusive, the revolution is brought about by persons of
the wealthy class who are excluded, as happened at Massalia
and Istros and Heraclea, and other cities. Those who had 3
no share in the government created a disturbance, until first
the elder brothers, and then the younger, were admitted; for
in some places father and son, in others elder and younger
brothers, do not hold office together. At Massalia the oligarchy became more like a constitutional government, but at
Istros ended in a democracy, and at Heraclea was enlarged
to 600. At Cnidos, again, the oligarchy underwent a con- 4
siderable change. For the notables fell out among themselves,
because only a few shared in the government; there existed
among them the rule already mentioned, that father and son
could not hold office together, and, if there were several
brothers, only the eldest was admitted. The people took
advantage of the quarrel, and choosing one of the notables to
be their leader, attacked and conquered the oligarchs, who
were divided, and division is always a source of weakness.
The city of Erythrae, too, in old times was ruled, and ruled 5
well, by the Basilidae, but the people took offence at the
narrowness of the oligarchy and changed the government.

(2) Of internal causes of revolutions in oligarchies one is
the personal rivalry of the oligarchs, which leads them to
play the demagogue. Now, the oligarchical demagogue is of 6
two sorts: either (1) he practises upon the oligarchs themselves (for, although the oligarchy are quite a small number,

V. 6 there may be a demagogue among them, as at Athens the party of Charicles predominated among the Thirty, that of Phrynichus in the Four Hundred); or (2) the oligarchs may play the demagogue with the people. This was the case at Larissa, where the guardians of the citizens endeavoured to gain over the people because they were elected by them; and such is the fate of all oligarchies in which the magistrates are elected, as at Abydos, not by the class to which they belong, but by the heavy-armed or by the people, although they may be required to have a high qualification, or to be members of **7** a political club; or, again, where the law-courts are independent of the government, the oligarchs flatter the people in order to obtain a decision in their own favour, and so they change the constitution; this happened at Heraclea in Pontus. Again, oligarchies change whenever any attempt is made to narrow them; for then those who desire equal rights are compelled **8** to call in the people. Changes in the oligarchy also occur when the oligarchs waste their private property by extravagant living; for then they want to innovate, and **1306 a** either try to make themselves tyrants, or install some one else in the tyranny, as Hipparinus did Dionysius at Syracuse, and as at Amphipolis [1] a man named Cleotimus introduced Chalcidian colonists, and when they arrived, stirred them up **9** against the rich. For a like reason in Aegina the person who carried on the negotiation with Chares endeavoured to revolutionize the state. Sometimes a party among the oligarchs try to create a political change; sometimes they rob the treasury, and then, either the other oligarchs quarrel with the thieves, as happened at Apollonia in Pontus, or they with the other oligarchs. But an oligarchy which is at unity

---

[1] Cp. c. 3. § 13.

with itself is not easily destroyed from within; of this we **V. 6**
may see an example at Pharsalus, for there, although the 10
rulers are few in number, they govern a large city, because
they have a good understanding among themselves.

Oligarchies, again, are overthrown when another oligarchy
is created within the original one, that is to say, when the 11
whole governing body is small and yet they do not all share
in the highest offices. Thus at Elis the governing body was
a small senate; and very few ever found their way into it,
because, although in number ninety, the senators were elected
for life and out of certain families in a manner similar to the
Lacedaemonian elders. Oligarchy is liable to revolutions 12
alike in war and in peace; in war because, not being able to
trust the people, the oligarchs are compelled to hire mercenaries, and the general who is in command of them often
ends in becoming a tyrant, as Timophanes did at Corinth; or
if there are more generals than one they make themselves into
a company of tyrants[1]. Sometimes the oligarchs, fearing
this danger, give the people a share in the government because
their services are necessary to them. And in time of peace, 13
from mutual distrust, the two parties hand over the defence
of the state to the army and to an arbiter between the two
factions who often ends the master of both. This happened
at Larissa when Simos and the Aleuadae had the government,
and at Abydos in the days of Iphiades and the political clubs.
Revolutions also arise out of marriages or lawsuits which lead 14
to the overthrow of one party among the oligarchs by another.
Of quarrels about marriages I have already mentioned[2] some
instances; another occurred at Eretria, where Diagoras overturned the oligarchy of the knights because he had been

---

[1] δυναστεία.   [2] Cp. c. 4. §§ 5–7.

V. 6 wronged about a marriage. A revolution at Heraclea, and
15 another at Thebes, both arose out of decisions of law-courts
upon a charge of adultery; in both cases the punishment was
just, but executed in the spirit of party, at Heraclea upon
1306 b Eurytion, and at Thebes upon Archias; for their enemies
were jealous of them and so had them pilloried in the
16 agora. Many oligarchies have been destroyed by some
members of the ruling class taking offence at their excessive
despotism; for example, the oligarchy at Cnidus and at
Chios.

Changes of constitutional governments, and also of oligarchies which limit the office of counsellor, judge, or other
magistrate to persons having a certain money qualification,
17 often occur by accident. The qualification may have been
originally fixed according to the circumstances of the time, in
such a manner as to include in an oligarchy a few only, or
in a constitutional government the middle class. But after
a time of prosperity, whether arising from peace or some
other good fortune, the same property becomes many times
as large, and then everybody participates in every office; this
happens sometimes gradually and insensibly, and sometimes
18 quickly. These are the causes of changes and revolutions in
oligarchies.

We must remark generally, both of democracies and oligarchies, that they sometimes change, not into the opposite
forms of government, but only into another variety of the
same class; I mean to say, from those forms of democracy
and oligarchy which are regulated by law into those which are
arbitrary, and conversely.

7 In aristocracies revolutions are stirred up when a few only
share in the honours of the state; a cause which has been

already shown to affect oligarchies; for an aristocracy is **V. 7**
a sort of oligarchy, and, like an oligarchy, is the government
of a few, although the few are the virtuous and not the
wealthy; hence the two are often confounded. And revo- 2
lutions will be most likely to happen, and must happen, when
the majority of the people are high-spirited, and have a notion
that they are as good as their rulers. Thus at Lacedaemon
the so-called Partheniae, who were the [illegitimate] sons of
the Spartan peers, attempted a revolution, and, being detected,
were sent away to colonize Tarentum. Again, revolutions
occur when great men who are at least of equal merit are
dishonoured by those higher in office, as Lysander was by 3
the kings of Sparta : or, when a brave man is excluded from
the honours of the state, like Cinadon, who conspired against
the Spartans under Agesilaus; or, again, when some are very
poor and others very rich, a state of society which is most
often the result of war, as at Lacedaemon in the days of the
Messenian War; this is proved from the poem of Tyrtaeus, 4
entitled ' Good Order'; for he speaks of certain citizens who 1307 a
were ruined by the war and wanted to have a redistribution of
the land. Again, revolutions arise when an individual who
is great, and might be greater, wants to rule alone, as at Lacedaemon, Pausanias, who was general in the Persian War, or
like Hanno at Carthage.

Constitutional governments and aristocracies are commonly 5
overthrown owing to some deviation from justice in the constitution itself; the cause of the downfall is, in the former,
the ill-mingling of the two elements democracy and oligarchy;
in the latter, of the three elements, democracy, oligarchy, and
virtue, but especially democracy and oligarchy. For to combine these is the endeavour of constitutional governments;

V. 7 and most of the so-called aristocracies have a like aim[1], but
6 differ from polities by the addition of virtue; hence some of
them are more and some less permanent. Those which
incline more to oligarchy are called aristocracies, and those
which incline to democracy constitutional governments. And
therefore the latter are the safer of the two; for the greater
the number, the greater the strength, and when men are equal
7 they are contented. But the rich, if the government gives
them power, are apt to be insolent and avaricious; and, in
general, whichever way the constitution inclines, in that direction it changes as either party gains strength, a constitutional
government becoming a democracy, an aristocracy, an oli-
8 garchy. But the process may be reversed, and aristocracy
may change into democracy. This happens when the poor,
under the idea that they are being wronged, force the constitution to take an opposite form. In like manner constitutional
governments change into oligarchies. The only stable principle of government is equality according to proportion, and
for every man to enjoy his own.

9 What I have just mentioned actually happened at Thurii[2],
where the qualification for office, though at first high, was
reduced, and the magistrates increased in number. The
notables had previously acquired the whole of the land
contrary to law; for the government tended to oligarchy, and
they were able to encroach. But the people, who had been
trained by war, soon got the better of the guards kept by the
oligarchs, until those who had too much gave up their land.

10 Again, since all aristocratical governments incline to oligarchy, the notables are apt to be grasping; thus at Lacedaemon, where property has passed into few hands[3], the notables

[1] Cp. iv. c. 7.   [2] Cp. c. 3. § 12.   [3] Cp. ii. 9. § 14.

can do too much as they like, and are allowed to marry whom **V. 7** they please. The city of Locri was ruined by a marriage connexion with Dionysius, but such a thing could never have happened in a democracy, or in a well-balanced aristocracy.

I have already remarked that in all states revolutions are 11 occasioned by trifles [1]. In aristocracies, above all, they are of 1307 ʙ a gradual and imperceptible nature. The citizens begin by giving up some part of the constitution, and so with greater ease the government change something else which is a little more important, until they have undermined the whole fabric of the state. At Thurii there was a law that generals should 12 only be re-elected after an interval of five years, and some high-spirited young men who were popular with the soldiers of the guard, despising the magistrates and thinking that they would easily gain their purpose, wanted to abolish this law and allow their generals to hold perpetual commands; for they well knew that the people would be glad enough to elect them. Whereupon the magistrates who had charge of these matters, 13 and who are called councillors, at first determined to resist, but they afterwards consented, thinking that, if only this one law was changed, no further inroad would be made on the constitution. But other changes soon followed which they in vain attempted to oppose; and the state passed into the hands of the revolutionists who established a dynastic oligarchy.

All constitutions are overthrown either from within or from 14 without; the latter, when there is some government close at hand having an opposite interest, or at a distance, but powerful. This was exemplified in the old times of the Athenian and the Lacedaemonian supremacies; the Athenians everywhere

[1] c. 4. § 1.

V. 7 put down the oligarchies, and the Lacedaemonians the democracies[1].

I have now explained what are the chief causes of revolutions and dissensions in states.

8   We have next to consider what means there are of preserving states in general, and also in particular cases. In the first place it is evident that if we know the causes which destroy states, we shall also know the causes which preserve them; for opposites produce opposites, and destruction is the opposite of preservation[2].

2   In all well-attempered governments there is nothing which should be more jealously maintained than the spirit of obedience to law, more especially in small matters; for transgression creeps in unperceived and at last ruins the state, just as the constant recurrence of small expenses in time eats

3 up a fortune. The change does not take place all at once, and therefore is not observed; the mind is deceived, as in the fallacy which says that 'if each part is little, then the whole is little.' And this is true in one way, but not in another, for the whole and the all are not little, although they are made up of littles.

4   In the first place, then, men should guard against the beginning of change, and in the second place they should not

1808 a rely upon the political devices of which I have already spoken[3], invented only to deceive the people, for they are

5 proved by experience to be useless. Further we note that oligarchies as well as aristocracies may last, not from any inherent stability in such forms of government, but because the rulers are on good terms both with the unenfranchised and

---

[1] Cp. iv. 11. § 18.   [2] Cp. Nic. Eth. v. 1. § 4.
[3] Cp. iv. 13. § 1.

with the governing classes, not maltreating any who are **V.8**
excluded from the government, but introducing into it the
leading spirits among them[1]. They should never wrong the
ambitious in a matter of honour, or the common people in
a matter of money; and they should treat one another and
their fellow-citizens in a spirit of equality. The equality **6**
which the friends of democracy seek to establish for the
multitude is not only just but likewise expedient among equals.
Hence, if the governing class are numerous, many democratic
institutions are useful; for example, the restriction of the
tenure of offices to six months, that all those who are of
equal rank may share in them. Indeed, equals or peers when
they are numerous become a kind of democracy, and therefore
demagogues are very likely to arise among them, as I have
already remarked[2]. The short tenure of office prevents oli- **7**
garchies and aristocracies from falling into the hands of
families; it is not easy for a person to do any great harm
when his tenure of office is short, whereas long possession
begets tyranny in oligarchies and democracies. For the
aspirants to tyranny are either the principal men of the state,
who in democracies are demagogues and in oligarchies
members of ruling houses, or those who hold great offices,
and have a long tenure of them[3].

States are preserved when their destroyers are at a distance, **8**
and sometimes also because they are near, for the fear of them
makes the government keep in hand the state. Wherefore the
ruler who has a care of the state should invent terrors, and
bring distant dangers near, in order that the citizens may be on
their guard, and, like sentinels in a night-watch, never relax
their attention. He should endeavour too by help of the laws **9**

[1] vi. 7. § 4.   [2] Supra c. 6. § 6.   [3] Cp. c. 5. § 6.

V. 8 to control the contentions and quarrels of the notables, and to prevent those who have not hitherto taken part in them from being drawn in. No ordinary man can discern the beginning of evil[1], but only the true statesman.

10 As to the change produced in oligarchies and constitutional governments[2] by the alteration of the qualification, when this arises, not out of any variation in the census but only out of the increase of money, it is well to compare the general valuation of property with that of past years, annually in those cities in which the census is taken annually, and in larger 1308 b cities every third or fifth year. If the whole is many times greater or many times less than when the rates were fixed at the previous census, there should be power given by law to raise or lower the qualification as the amount is greater or less.

11 Where in the absence of any such provision the standard is raised, a constitutional government passes into an oligarchy, and an oligarchy is narrowed to a rule of families; where the standard is lowered, constitutional government becomes democracy, and oligarchy either constitutional government or democracy.

12 It is a principle common to democracy, oligarchy[3], and every other form of government not to allow the disproportionate increase of any citizen, but to give moderate honour for a long time rather than great honour for a short time. For men are easily spoilt; not every one can bear prosperity. But if this rule is not observed, at any rate the honours which are given all at once should be taken away by degrees and not all at once. Especially should the laws provide against any one

[1] Cp. c. 4. §§ 1–3.   [2] Cp. c. 3. § 8; c. 6. §§ 16–18.

[3] Or, adding καὶ μοναρχίᾳ, 'monarchy,' with many MSS. and Bekker's first edition.

having too much power, whether derived from friends or **V. 8**
money; if he has, he and his followers should be sent out of
the country[1]. And since innovations creep in through the 13
private life of individuals, there ought to be a magistracy which
will have an eye to those whose life is not in harmony with
the government, whether oligarchy or democracy or any other.
And for a like reason an increase of prosperity in any part of
the state should be carefully watched. The proper remedy 14
for this evil is always to give the management of affairs and
offices of state to opposite elements; such opposites are the
virtuous and the many, or the rich and the poor. Another
way is to combine the poor and the rich in one body, or to
increase the middle class: thus an end will be put to the
revolutions which arise from inequality.

But above all every state should be so administered and so 15
regulated by law that its magistrates cannot possibly make
money[2]. In oligarchies special precautions should be used
against this evil. For the people do not take any great 16
offence at being kept out of the government—indeed they are
rather pleased than otherwise at having leisure for their private
business—but what irritates them is to think that their rulers
are stealing the public money; then they are doubly annoyed;
for they lose both honour and profit. If office brought no 17
profit, then and then only could democracy and aristocracy be
combined; for both notables and people might have their 1309 a
wishes gratified. All would be able to hold office, which is
the aim of democracy, and the notables would be magistrates,
which is the aim of aristocracy. And this result may be 18
accomplished when there is no possibility of making money

---

[1] Cp. c. 3. § 3; iii. 13. § 15.　　　[2] Cp. c. 12. § 14.

V. 8 out of the offices; for the poor will not want to have them
when there is nothing to be gained from them—they would
rather be attending to their own concerns; and the rich, who
do not want money from the public treasury, will be able to
take them; and so the poor will keep to their work and grow
rich, and the notables will not be governed by the lower class.

19 In order to avoid peculation of the public money, the transfer
of the revenue should be made at a general assembly of the
citizens, and duplicates of the accounts deposited with the
different brotherhoods, companies, and tribes. And honours
should be given by law to magistrates who have the reputation

20 of being incorruptible. In democracies the rich should be
spared; not only should their property not be divided, but
their incomes also, which in some states are taken from them
imperceptibly, should be protected. It is a good thing to
prevent the wealthy citizens, even if they are willing, from
undertaking expensive and useless public services, such as the
giving of choruses, torch-races, and the like. In an oligarchy,
on the other hand, great care should be taken of the poor, and
lucrative offices should go to them; if any of the wealthy
classes insult them, the offender should be punished more
severely [1] than one of their own class for a like offence [1].
Provision should be made that estates pass by inheritance and
not by gift, and no person should have more than one inheritance; for in this way properties will be equalized, and more

21 of the poor rise to competency. It is also expedient both in
a democracy and in an oligarchy to assign to those who have
less share in the government (for example, to the rich in
a democracy and to the poor in an oligarchy) an equality or
preference in all but the principal offices of state. The latter

[1] Or, 'tnan if he had wronged one of his own class.'

should be entrusted chiefly or only to members of the govern- **V. 8** ing class.

There are three qualifications required in those who have to fill the highest offices—(1) first of all, loyalty to the **9** established constitution; (2) the greatest administrative capacity; (3) virtue and justice of the kind proper to each form of government; for, if what is just is not the same in all governments, the quality of justice must also differ. There may be a doubt however, when all these qualities do not meet **2** in the same person, how the selection is to be made; suppose, for example, a good general is a bad man and not a friend to **1309 b** the constitution, and another man is loyal and just, which should we choose? In making the election ought we not to consider two points? what qualities are common, and what are rare. Thus in the choice of a general, we should regard his skill rather than his virtue; for few have military skill, **3** but many have virtue. In keeping watch or in any office of stewardship, on the other hand, the opposite rule should be observed; for more virtue than ordinary is required in the holder of such an office, but the necessary knowledge is of a sort which all men possess.

It may, however, be asked what a man wants with virtue if **4** he have political ability and is loyal, since these two qualities alone will make him do what is for the public interest. But may not men have both of them and yet be deficient in self-control? If, knowing and loving their own interests, they do not always attend to them, may they not be equally negligent of the interests of the public?

Speaking generally, we may say that whatever legal enact- **5** ments are held to be for the interest of states, all these preserve states. And the great preserving principle is the one which

V. 9 has been repeatedly mentioned [1]—to have a care that the loyal
6 citizens should outnumber the disloyal.   Neither should we
forget the mean, which at the present day is lost sight of in
perverted forms of government: for many practices which
appear to be democratical are the ruin of democracies, and
many which appear to be oligarchical are the ruin of oligarchies.
7 Those who think that all virtue is to be found in their own
party principles push matters to extremes; they do not consider that disproportion destroys a state.   A nose which varies
from the ideal of straightness to a hook or snub may still be
of good shape and agreeable to the eye; but if the excess be
very great, all symmetry is lost, and the nose at last ceases to
be a nose at all on account of some excess in one direction or
defect in the other; and this is true of every other part of the
8 human body.   The same law of proportion equally holds in
states.   Oligarchy or democracy, although a departure from
the most perfect form, may yet be a good enough government,
but if any one attempts to push the principles of either to an
extreme, he will begin by spoiling the government and end by
9 having none at all.   Wherefore the legislator and the statesman ought to know what democratical measures save and
what destroy a democracy, and what oligarchical measures save
or destroy an oligarchy.   For neither the one nor the other
can exist or continue to exist unless both rich and poor are
included in it.   If equality of property is introduced, the state
1310 a must of necessity take another form; for when by laws carried
to excess one or other element in the state is ruined, the constitution is ruined.
10   There is an error common both to oligarchies and to
democracies:—in the latter the demagogues, when the multi-

[1] Cp. iv. 12. § 1; vi. 6. § 2.

tude are above the law, are always cutting the city in two by **V. 9** quarrels with the rich, whereas they should always profess to be maintaining their cause; just as in oligarchies, the oligarchs should profess to maintain the cause of the people, and should take oaths the opposite of those which they now take. For **11** there are cities in which they swear—'I will be an enemy to the people, and will devise all the harm against them which I can;' but they ought to exhibit and to entertain the very opposite feeling; in the form of their oath there should be an express declaration—'I will do no wrong to the people.'

But of all the things which I have mentioned, that which most contributes to the permanence of constitutions is the adaptation of education to the form of government[1], and yet in our own day this principle is universally neglected. The **12** best laws, though sanctioned by every citizen of the state, will be of no avail unless the young are trained by habit and education in the spirit of the constitution, if the laws are democratical, democratically, or oligarchically if the laws are oligarchical. For there may be a want of self-discipline in states as well as in individuals. Now, to have been educated **13** in the spirit of the constitution is not to perform the actions in which oligarchs or democrats delight, but those by which the existence of an oligarchy or of a democracy is made possible. Whereas among ourselves the sons of the ruling class in an oligarchy live in luxury[2], but the sons of the poor are hardened by exercise and toil, and hence they are both more inclined and better able to make a revolution[3]. And in democracies **14** of the more extreme type there has arisen a false idea of freedom which is contradictory to the true interests of the

---

[1] Cp. i. 13 § 15.   [2] Cp. iv. 11. § 6.

[3] Cp. Pl. Rep. viii. 556 D.

V. 9 state. For two principles are characteristic of democracy, the
15 government of the majority and freedom. Men think that
what is just is equal; and that equality is the supremacy of
the popular will; and that freedom and equality mean the
doing what a man likes. In such democracies every one lives
as he pleases, or in the words of Euripides, 'according to his
fancy.' But this is all wrong; men should not think it
slavery to live according to the rule of the constitution; for it
is their salvation.

I have now discussed generally the causes of the revolution
and destruction of states, and the means of their preservation
and continuance.

10 I have still to speak of monarchy, and the causes of its
destruction and preservation. What I have said already
1310 b respecting other forms of government applies almost equally
2 to royal and to tyrannical rule. For royal rule is of the
nature of an aristocracy, and a tyranny is a compound of
oligarchy and democracy in their most extreme forms; it is
therefore most injurious to its subjects, being made up of two
evil forms of government, and having the perversions and
3 errors of both. These two forms of monarchy differ in their
very origin. The appointment of a king is the resource of
the better classes against the people, and he is elected by
them out of their own number, because either he himself or
his family excel in virtue and virtuous actions; whereas a
tyrant is chosen from the people to be their protector against
the notables, and in order to prevent them from being injured.
4 History shows that almost all tyrants have been demagogues
who gained the favour of the people by their accusation of the
5 notables[1]. At any rate this was the manner in which the

[1] Cp. c. 5. § 6; Plato, Rep. 565 D.

tyrannies arose in the days when cities had increased in power. **V. 10**
Others which were older originated in the ambition of kings
wanting to overstep the limits of their hereditary power and
become despots. Others again grew out of the class which
were chosen to be chief magistrates; for in ancient times the
people who elected them gave the magistrates, whether civil or
religious, a long tenure. Others arose out of the custom
which oligarchies had of making some individual supreme over
the highest offices. In any of these [1] ways an ambitious man **6**
had no difficulty, if he desired, in creating a tyranny, since he
had the power in his hands already, either as king or as one of
the officers of state [2]. Thus Pheidon at Argos and several
others were originally kings, and ended by becoming tyrants;
Phalaris, on the other hand, and the Ionian tyrants, acquired
the tyranny by holding great offices. Whereas Panaetius at
Leontini, Cypselus at Corinth, Peisistratus at Athens, Dionysius at Syracuse, and several others who afterwards became
tyrants, were at first demagogues.

And so, as I was saying, royalty ranks with aristocracy, for **7**
it is based upon merit, whether of the individual or of his
family, or on benefits conferred [3], or on these claims with
power added to them. For all who have obtained this honour **8**
have benefited, or had in their power to benefit, states and
nations; some, like Codrus, have prevented the state from
being enslaved in war; others, like Cyrus, have given their
country freedom, or have settled or gained a territory, like the
Lacedaemonian, Macedonian, and Molossian kings [4]. The **9**
idea of a king is to be a protector of the rich against unjust **1311 a**

[1] Retaining τούτοις, which is omitted in Bekker's second edition,
apparently by mistake.
[2] Cp. c. 5. § 8. [3] Cp. iii. 14. § 12. [4] Cp. c. 11. § 2.

V. 10 treatment, of the people against insult and oppression. Whereas a tyrant, as has often been repeated, has no regard to any public interest, but only to his private ends; his aim is plea-
10 sure, the aim of a king, honour. Wherefore also in their desires they differ; the tyrant is desirous of riches, the king, of what brings honour. And the guards of a king are citizens, but of a tyrant mercenaries[1].

11   That tyranny has all the vices both of democracy and oligarchy is evident. As of oligarchy so of tyranny, the end is wealth; (for by wealth only can the tyrant maintain either his guard or his luxury). Both mistrust the people, and therefore deprive them of their arms. Both agree too in injuring the people and driving them out of the city and
12 dispersing them. From democracy tyrants have borrowed the art of making war upon the notables and destroying them secretly or openly, or of exiling them because they are rivals and stand in the way of their power; and also because plots against them are contrived by men of this class, who either
13 want to rule or escape subjection. Hence Periander advised Thrasybulus[2] to cut off the tops of the tallest ears of corn, meaning that he must always put out of the way the citizens who overtop the rest. And so, as I have already intimated, the beginnings of change are the same in monarchies as in other forms of government; subjects attack their sovereigns out of fear or contempt, or because they have been unjustly treated by them. And of injustice, the most common form is insult, another is confiscation of property.

14   The ends sought by conspiracies against monarchies, whether tyrannies or royalties, are the same as the ends sought by conspiracies against other forms of government.

[1] Cp. iii. 14. § 7.   [2] Cp. iii. 13. § 16.

Monarchs have great wealth and honour which are objects of **V. 10** desire to all mankind. The attacks are made sometimes against their lives, sometimes against the office; where the sense of insult is the motive, against their lives. Any sort of 15 insult (and there are many) may stir up anger, and when men are angry, they commonly act out of revenge, and not from ambition. For example, the attempt made upon the Peisistratidae arose out of the public dishonour offered to the sister of Harmodius and the insult to himself. He attacked the tyrant for his sister's sake, and Aristogeiton joined in the attack for the sake of Harmodius. A conspiracy was also 16 formed against Periander, the tyrant of Ambracia, because, when drinking with a favourite youth, he asked him whether 1311 b by this time he was not with child by him. Philip, too, was attacked by Pausanias because he permitted him to be insulted by Attalus and his friends, and Amyntas the little, by Derdas, because he boasted of having enjoyed his youth. Evagoras of Cyprus, again, was slain by the eunuch to revenge an insult; for his wife had been carried off by Evagoras' son. Many 17 conspiracies have originated in shameful attempts made by sovereigns on the persons of their subjects. Such was the attack of Crataeus upon Archelaus; he had always hated the connexion with him, and so, when Archelaus, having promised him one of his two daughters in marriage, did not give him either of them, but broke his word and married the elder to the king of Elymaea, when he was hard pressed in a war against Sirrhas and Arrhibaeus, and the younger to his own son Amyntas, under the idea that he would then be less likely to quarrel with the son of Cleopatra—Crataeus made this slight a pretext for attacking Archelaus, though even a less reason would have sufficed, for the real cause of the estrange-

V. 10 ment was the disgust which he felt at his connexion with the
18 king.   And from a like motive Hellanocrates of Larissa conspired with him; for when Archelaus, who was his lover, did
not fulfil his promise of restoring him to his country, he
thought that the connexion between them had originated, not
in affection, but in the wantonness of power.   Parrhon, too,
and Heracleides of Aenos, slew Cotys in order to avenge
their father, and Adamas revolted from Cotys in revenge for
the wanton outrage which he had committed in mutilating him
when a child.

19   [1] Many, too, irritated at blows inflicted on the person which
they deemed an insult, have either killed or attempted to kill
officers of state and royal princes by whom they have been
injured [1].   Thus, at Mitylene, Megacles and his friends
attacked and slew the Penthalidae, as they were going about
and striking people with clubs.   At a later date Smerdis, who
had been beaten and torn away from his wife by Penthilus,
20 slew him.   In the conspiracy against Archelaus, Decamnichus
stimulated the fury of the assassins and led the attack; he was
enraged because Archelaus had delivered him to Euripides to
be scourged; for the poet had been irritated at some remark
made by Decamnichus on the foulness of his breath.   Many
other examples might be cited of murders and conspiracies
which have arisen from similar causes.

21   Fear is another motive which has caused conspiracies as
well in monarchies as in more popular forms of government.
Thus Artapanes conspired against Xerxes and slew him,
fearing that he would be accused of hanging Darius against
his orders—he being under the impression that Xerxes would

---

[1] Or: ' Many persons too, even of those connected with the government or the royal family,' taking τῶν περί, etc. with the subject.

forget what he had said in the middle of a meal, and that the **V. 10** offence would be forgiven.

Another motive is contempt, as in the case of Sardanapulus, 1312 a whom some one saw carding wool with his women, if the 22 story-tellers say truly; and the tale may be true, if not of him, of some one else[1]. Dion attacked the younger Dionysius 23 because he despised him, and saw that he was equally despised by his own subjects, and that he was always drunk. Even the friends of a tyrant will sometimes attack him out of contempt; for the confidence which he reposes in them breeds contempt, and they think that they will not be found out. The expectation of success is likewise a sort of contempt; 24 the assailants are ready to strike, and think nothing of the danger, because they seem to have the power in their hands. Thus generals of armies attack monarchs; as, for example, Cyrus attacked Astyages, despising the effeminacy of his life, and believing that his power was worn out. Thus, again, Seuthes the Thracian conspired against Amadocus, whose general he was.

And sometimes men are actuated by more than one motive, 25 like Mithridates, who conspired against Ariobarzanes, partly out of contempt and partly from the love of gain.

Bold natures, placed by their sovereigns in a high military position, are most likely to make the attempt in the expectation of success; for courage is emboldened by power, and the union of the two inspires them with the hope of an easy victory.

Attempts of which the motive is ambition arise from other causes. There are men who will not risk their lives in the 26 hope of gains and rewards however great, but who nevertheless

[1] Cp. i. 11. § 8.

V. 10 regard the killing of a tyrant simply as an extraordinary action
which will make them famous and honourable in the world;
27 they wish to acquire, not a kingdom, but a name.   It is rare,
however, to find such men; he who would kill a tyrant must
28 be prepared to lose his life if he fail.   He must have the
resolution of Dion, who, when he made war upon Dionysius,
took with him very few troops, saying, 'that whatever measure
of success he might attain would be enough for him, even if
he were to die the moment he landed; such a death would be
welcome to him.'   But this is a temper to which few can
attain.

29   Once more, tyrannies, like all other governments, are
1312 b destroyed from without by some opposite and more powerful
form of government.   That such a government will have the
will to attack them is clear; for the two are opposed in
30 principle; and all men, if they can, do what they will.
Democracy is also antagonistic to tyranny, on the principle of
Hesiod, 'Potter hates Potter,' because they are nearly akin,
for the extreme form of democracy is tyranny, and royalty
and aristocracy are both alike opposed to tyranny, because
they are constitutions of a different type.   And therefore the
Lacedaemonians put down most of the tyrannies, and so
did the Syracusans during the time when they were well
governed.

31   Again, tyrannies are destroyed from within, when the
reigning family are divided among themselves, as that of
Gelo was, and more recently that of Dionysius; in the case of
Gelo because Thrasybulus, the brother of Hiero, flattered the
son of Gelo and led him into excesses in order that he might
rule in his name.   Whereupon the family conspired to get rid
of Thrasybulus and save the tyranny; but the party who con-

spired [1] with them seized the opportunity and drove them all **V. 10**
out. In the case of Dionysius, Dion, his own relative, **32**
attacked and expelled him with the assistance of the people;
he afterwards perished himself.

There are two chief motives which induce men to attack
tyrannies—hatred and contempt. Hatred of tyrants is
inevitable, and contempt is also a frequent cause of their
destruction. Thus we see that most of those who have **33**
acquired, have retained their power, but those who have
inherited [2], have lost it, almost at once; for living in luxurious
ease, they have become contemptible, and offer many oppor-
tunities to their assailants. Anger, too, must be included
under hatred, and produces the same effects. It is oftentimes **34**
even more ready to strike—the angry are more impetuous in
making an attack, for they do not listen to reason. And men
are very apt to give way to their passions when they are
insulted. To this cause is to be attributed the fall of the
Peisistratidae and of many others. Hatred is more reasonable, **35**
but anger is accompanied by pain, which is an impediment to
reason, whereas hatred is painless [3].

In a word, all the causes which I have mentioned as
destroying the last and most unmixed form of oligarchy, and
the extreme form of democracy, may be assumed to affect
tyranny; indeed the extreme forms of both are only tyrannies
distributed among several persons. Kingly rule is little **36**
affected by external causes, and is, therefore, lasting; it is
generally destroyed from within. And there are two ways
in which the destruction may come about; (1) when the **1313 a**

---

[1] Omitting κατ' inserted by Bekker in 2nd ed.
[2] Cp. Plato, Laws, iii. 695.
[3] Cp. Rhetoric, ii. 4. § 31.

V. 10 members of the royal family quarrel among themselves, and
(2) when the kings attempt to administer the state too much
37 after the fashion of a tyranny, and to extend their authority
contrary to the law. There are now no royalties; monarchies,
where they exist, are [1] tyrannies. For the rule of a king is
over voluntary subjects, and he is supreme in all important
matters; but in our own day men are more upon an equality,
and no one is so immeasurably superior to others as to represent adequately the greatness and dignity of the office. Hence
mankind will not, if they can help, endure it, and any one who
obtains power by force or fraud is at once thought to be
38 a tyrant. In hereditary monarchies a further cause of destruction is the fact that kings often fall into contempt, and,
although possessing not tyrannical but only royal power, are
apt to outrage others. Their overthrow is then readily
effected; for there is an end to the king when his subjects
do not want to have him, but the tyrant lasts, whether they
like him or not.

The destruction of monarchies is to be attributed to these
and the like causes.

11   And they are preserved, to speak generally, by the opposite
causes; or, if we consider them separately, (1) royalty is
preserved by the limitation of its powers. The more restricted the functions of kings, the longer their power will last
unimpaired; for then they are more moderate and not so
despotic in their ways; and they are less envied by their
2 subjects. This is the reason why the kingly office has lasted
so long among the Molossians. And for a similar reason it
has continued among the Lacedaemonians, because there it
was always divided between two, and afterwards further

---

[1] Omitting καί with Bekker's 2nd ed.

limited by Theopompus in various respects, more particularly **V. 11**
by the establishment of the Ephoralty. He diminished the
power of the kings, but established on a more lasting basis
the kingly office, which was thus made in a certain sense not
less, but greater. There is a story that when his wife once **3**
asked him whether he was not ashamed to leave to his sons
a royal power which was less than he had inherited from his
father, he replied, 'No indeed, for the power which I leave
to them will be more lasting.'

As to (2) tyrannies, they are preserved in two most **4**
opposite ways. One of them is the old traditional method in
which most tyrants administer their government. Of such
arts Periander of Corinth is said to have been the great
master, and many similar devices may be gathered from the
Persians in the administration of their government. There **5**
are also the ancient prescriptions for the preservation of
a tyranny, in so far as this is possible; viz. that the tyrant
should lop off those who are too high; he must put to death
men of spirit: he must not allow common meals, clubs,
education, and the like; he must be upon his guard against **1313 b**
anything which is likely to inspire either courage or confidence
among his subjects; he must prohibit literary assemblies or
other meetings for discussion, and he must take every means
to prevent people from knowing one another (for acquaintance
begets mutual confidence). Further, he must compel the **6**
inhabitants to appear in public and live [1] at his gates [1]; then
he will know what they are doing; if they are always kept
under, they will learn to be humble. In short, he should
practise these and the like Persian and barbaric arts which all
have the same object. A tyrant should also endeavour to **7**

[1] Or, 'at their doors.'

V. 11 know what each of his subjects says or does, and should
employ spies, like the 'female detectives' at Syracuse, and
the eavesdroppers whom Hiero was in the habit of sending to
any place of resort or meeting; for the fear of informers
prevents people from speaking their minds, and if they do,
8 they are more easily found out.   Another art of the tyrant is
to sow quarrels among the citizens; friends should be
embroiled with friends, the people with the notables, and the
rich with one another.   Also he should impoverish his
subjects; he thus provides money for the support of his
guards [1], and the people, having to keep hard at work, are
9 prevented from conspiring.   The Pyramids of Egypt afford
an example of this policy; also the offerings of the family of
Cypselus, and the building of the temple of Olympian Zeus
by the Peisistratidae, and the great Polycratean monuments at
Samos; all these works were alike intended to occupy the
10 people and keep them poor.   Another practice of tyrants is
to multiply taxes, after the manner of Dionysius at Syracuse,
who contrived that within five years his subjects should bring
into the treasury their whole property.   The tyrant is also
fond of making war in order that his subjects may have something to do and be always in want of a leader.   And whereas
the power of a king is preserved by his friends, the characteristic of a tyrant is to distrust his friends, because he knows
that all men want to overthrow him, and they above all have
the power [2].

[1] Reading ἤ τε with Bekker's 2nd ed.

[2] This, which is probably the meaning of the passage, cannot be
elicited from the text as it stands.   The addition is required of some
such phrase as αὐτὸν καθελεῖν, which is not wholly without manuscript
authority.

Again, the evil practices of the last and worst forms of **V. 11**
democracy are all found in tyrannies. Such are the power **11**
given to women in their families in the hope that they will
inform against their husbands, and the licence which is allowed
to slaves in order that they may betray their masters; for
slaves and women do not conspire against tyrants; and they
are of course friendly to tyrannies and also to democracies,
since under them they have a good time. For the people too
would fain be a monarch, and therefore by them, as well as by **12**
the tyrant, the flatterer is held in honour; in democracies he
is the demagogue; and the tyrant also has his humble companions who flatter him. 1314 a

Hence tyrants are always fond of bad men, because they
love to be flattered, but no man who has the spirit of a freeman in him will demean himself by flattery; good men love
others, but they do not flatter anybody. Moreover the bad **13**
are useful for bad purposes; 'nail knocks out nail,' as the
proverb says. It is characteristic of a tyrant to dislike every
one who has dignity or independence; he wants to be alone in
his glory, but any one who claims a like dignity or asserts his
independence encroaches upon his prerogative, and is hated by
him as an enemy to his power. Another mark of a tyrant is **14**
that he likes foreigners better than citizens, and lives with
them and invites them to his table; for the one are enemies,
but the others enter into no rivalry with him.

Such are the notes of the tyrant and the arts by which he
preserves his power; there is no wickedness too great for him.
All that we have said may be summed up under three heads,
which answer to the three aims of the tyrant. These are, **15**
(1) the humiliation of his subjects; he knows that a mean-
spirited man will not conspire against anybody: (2) the crea-

V. 11 tion of mistrust among them; for a tyrant is not overthrown
until men begin to have confidence in one another; and this
is the reason why tyrants are at war with the good; they are
under the idea that their power is endangered by them, not
only because they will not be ruled despotically, but also
because they are loyal to one another, and to other men, and
do not inform against one another or against other men:
16 (3) the tyrant desires that his subjects shall be incapable of
action, for no one attempts what is impossible, and they will
not attempt to overthrow a tyranny, if they are powerless.
Under these three heads the whole policy of a tyrant may be
summed up, and to one or other of them all his ideas may be
referred: (1) he sows distrust among his subjects; (2) he
takes away their power; (3) he humbles them.

17   This then is one of the two methods by which tyrannies
are preserved; and there is another which proceeds upon
18 a different principle of action. The nature of this latter
method may be gathered from a comparison of the causes
which destroy kingdoms, for as one mode of destroying
kingly power is to make the office of king more tyrannical, so
the salvation of a tyranny is to make it more like the rule of
a king. But of one thing the tyrant must be careful; he
must keep power enough to rule over his subjects, whether
they like him or not, for if he once gives this up he gives up
19 his tyranny. But though power must be retained as the
foundation, in all else the tyrant should act or appear to act in
1314 b the character of a king. In the first place he should pretend
a care of the public revenues, and not waste money in making
presents of a sort at which the common people get excited
when they see their miserable earnings taken from them and
lavished on courtesans and strangers and artists. He should

give an account of what he receives and of what he spends **V. 11**
(a practice which has been adopted by some tyrants); for
then he will seem to be the manager of a household rather
than a tyrant; nor need he fear that, while he is the lord of **20**
the city, he will ever be in want of money.   Such a policy is
much more advantageous for the tyrant when he goes from
home, than to leave behind him a hoard, for then the garrison
who remain in the city will be less likely to attack his power;
and a tyrant, when he is absent from home, has more reason
to fear the guardians of his treasure than the citizens, for the
one accompany him, but the others remain behind.   In the **21**
second place, he should appear to collect taxes and to require
public services only for state purposes; and that he may form
a fund in case of war, he ought to make himself the guardian
and treasurer of them, as if they belonged, not to him, but to
the public.   He should appear, not harsh, but dignified, and
when men meet him they should look upon him with reverence,
and not with fear.   Yet it is hard for him to be respected if **22**
he inspires no respect, and therefore whatever virtues he may
neglect, at least he should maintain the character of a statesman, and produce the impression that he is one.   Neither he
nor any of his associates should ever be guilty of the least
offence against modesty towards the young of either sex who
are his subjects, and the women of his family should observe **23**
a like self-control towards other women; the insolence of
women has ruined many tyrannies.   In the indulgence of
pleasures he should be the opposite of our modern tyrants,
who not only begin at dawn and pass whole days in sensuality,
but want other men to see them, that they may admire their
happy and blessed lot.   In these things a tyrant should be **24**
especially moderate, or at any rate should not parade his vices

V. 11 to the world; for a drunken and drowsy tyrant is soon despised and attacked; not so he who is temperate and wide awake. His conduct should be the very reverse of nearly everything which has been said before about tyrants. He ought to adorn and improve his city, as though he were not **25** a tyrant, but the guardian of the state. Also he should **1315 a** appear to be particularly earnest in the service of the Gods; for if men think that a ruler is religious and has a reverence for the Gods, they are less afraid of suffering injustice at his hands, and they are less disposed to conspire against him, because they believe him to have the very Gods fighting on **26** his side. At the same time his religion must not be thought foolish. And he should honour men of merit, and make them think that they would not be held in more honour by the citizens if they had a free government. The honour he should distribute himself, but the punishment should be in- **27** flicted by officers and courts of law. It is a precaution which is taken by all monarchs not to make one person great; but if one, then two or more should be raised, that they may look sharply after one another. If after all some one has to be made great, he should not be a man of bold spirit; for such dispositions are ever most inclined to strike. And if any one is to be deprived of his power, let it be diminished gradually, **28** not taken from him all at once[1]. The tyrant should abstain from all outrage; in particular from personal violence and from wanton conduct towards the young. He should be especially careful of his behaviour to men who are lovers of honour; for as the lovers of money are offended when their property is touched, so are the lovers of honour and the **29** virtuous when their honour is affected. Therefore a tyrant

[1] Cᴅ c. 8. § 12.

ought either not to use force at all, or he should be thought **V. 11**
only to employ fatherly correction, and not to trample upon
others; and his acquaintance with youth should be supposed
to arise from affection, and not from the insolence of power,
and in general he should compensate the appearance of dishonour by the increase of honour.

Of those who attempt assassination they are the most 30
dangerous, and require to be most carefully watched who do
not care to survive, if they effect their purpose. Therefore 31
special precaution should be taken about any who think that
either they or their relatives have been insulted; for when
men are led away by passion to assault others they are regard-
less of themselves. As Heracleitus says, 'It is difficult to
fight against anger; for a man will buy revenge with life[1].'

And whereas states consist of two classes, of poor men 32
and of rich, the tyrant should lead both to imagine that they
are preserved and prevented from harming one another by his
rule, and whichever of the two is stronger he should attach
to his government; for, having this advantage, he has no
need either to emancipate slaves or to disarm the citizens;
either party added to the force which he already has, will
make him stronger than his assailants.

But enough of these details;—what should be the general 33
policy of the tyrant is obvious. He ought to show himself to
his subjects in the light, not of a tyrant, but of the master of
a household and of a king. He should not appropriate what 1315 b
is theirs, but should be their guardian; he should be moderate,
not extravagant in his way of life; he should be the companion of the notables, and the hero of the multitude. For 34
then his rule will of necessity be nobler and happier, because

[1] Fragm. 69 (ed. Mullach).

V. 11 he will rule over better men [1] whose spirits are not crushed, over men to whom he himself is not an object of hatred, and of whom he is not afraid. His power too will be more lasting   Let his disposition be virtuous, or at least half virtuous; and if he must be wicked, let him be half wicked only.

12   Yet no forms of government are so short-lived as oligarchy and tyranny.   The tyranny which lasted longest was that of Orthagoras and his sons at Sicyon; this continued for a hundred years.   The reason was that they treated their subjects with moderation, and to a great extent observed the laws; and in various ways gained the favour of the people by the care which they took of them.   Cleisthenes, in particular, **2** was respected for his military ability.   If report may be believed, he crowned the judge who decided against him in the games; and, as some say, the sitting statue in the Agora of Sicyon is the likeness of this person.   A similar story is told of Peisistratus, who is said on one occasion to have allowed himself to be summoned and tried before the Areopagus.

3   Next in duration to the tyranny of Orthagoras was that of the Cypselidae at Corinth, which lasted seventy-three years and six months: Cypselus reigned thirty years, Periander forty-four, and Psammetichus the son of Gordius three. **4** Their continuance was due to similar causes: Cypselus was a popular man, who during the whole time of his rule never had a body-guard; and Periander, although he was a tyrant, **5** was a great soldier.   Third in duration was the rule of the Peisistratidae at Athens, but it was interrupted; for Peisistratus was twice driven out, so that during three-and-thirty

[1] Cp. i. 5. § 2.

years he reigned only seventeen; and his sons reigned **V. 12**
eighteen—altogether thirty-five years. Of other tyrannies,
that of Hiero and Gelo at Syracuse was the most lasting.
Even this, however, was short, not more than eighteen years **6**
in all; for Gelo continued tyrant for seven years, and died in
the eighth; Hiero reigned for ten years, and Thrasybulus
was driven out in the eleventh month. In fact, tyrannies
generally have been of quite short duration.

I have now gone through all the causes by which consti- **7**
tutional governments and monarchies are either destroyed or **1316 a**
preserved.

In the Republic of Plato[1], Socrates treats of revolutions,
but not well, for he mentions no cause of change which
peculiarly affects the first or perfect state. He only says **8**
that nothing is abiding, but that all things change in a certain
cycle; and that the origin of the change is a base of numbers
which are in the ratio of four to three, and this when combined with a figure of five gives two harmonies—(he means
when the number of this figure becomes solid); he conceives
that nature will then produce bad men who will not submit
to education; in which latter particular he may very likely
be not far wrong, for there may well be some men who
cannot be educated and made virtuous. But why is such **9**
a cause of change peculiar to his ideal state, and not rather
common to all states, nay to everything which comes into
being at all? [2] Or how is the state specially changed by
the agency of time, which, as he declares, makes all things
change? And things which did not begin together, change
together[2], for example, if something has come into being the

[1] Rep. viii. 546.
[2] Placing a note of interrogation after μεταβάλλειν. Or: 'And

V. 12 day before the completion of the cycle, it will change with it. Further, why should the perfect state change into the Spartan?
10 for governments more often take an opposite form than one akin to them. The same remark is applicable to the other changes; he says that the Spartan constitution changes into an oligarchy, and this into a democracy, and this again
11 into a tyranny. And yet the contrary happens quite as often; for a democracy is even more likely to change into an oligarchy than into a monarchy. Further, he never says whether tyranny is, or is not, liable to revolutions, and if it is, what is the cause of them, or into what form it changes. And the reason is, that he could not very well have told: for there is no rule; according to him it should revert to the first and
12 best, and then there would be a complete cycle. But in point of fact a tyranny often changes into a tyranny, as that at Sicyon changed from the tyranny of Myron into that of Cleisthenes; into oligarchy, as the tyranny of Antileon did at Chalcis; into democracy, as that of Gelo did at Syracuse; into aristocracy, as at Carthage, and the tyranny of Charilaus
13 at Lacedaemon. Often an oligarchy changes into a tyranny, like most of the ancient oligarchies in Sicily; for example, the oligarchy at Leontini changed into the tyranny of Panaetius; that at Gela into the tyranny of Cleander; that at Rhegium into the tyranny of Anaxilaus; the same thing has
14 happened in many other states. And it is absurd to suppose that the state changes into oligarchy merely because [as Plato

in the period of time which, as he says, makes all things change, things which did not begin together change together.'

Bekker in his 2nd edition has altered the reading of the MSS. διά τε τοῦ χρόνου to διά γε τὸν χρόνον. The rendering of the text agrees with either reading; that of the note with the reading of the MSS. only.

says[1]] the ruling class are lovers and makers of money, **V. 12** and not because the very rich think it unfair that the very poor 1316 b should have an equal share in the government with themselves. Moreover, in many oligarchies there are laws against making money in trade. But at Carthage, which is a democracy, there is no such prohibition; and yet to this day the Carthaginians have never had a revolution. It is absurd too for him 15 to say that an oligarchy is two cities, one of the rich, and the other of the poor[2]. Is not this just as much the case in the Spartan constitution, or in any other in which either all do not possess equal property, or in which all are not equally good men? Nobody need be any poorer than he was before, 16 and yet the oligarchy may change all the same into a democracy, if the poor form the majority; and a democracy may change into an oligarchy, if the wealthy class are stronger than the people, and the one are energetic, the other indifferent. Once more, although the causes of revolutions are 17 very numerous, he mentions only one[3], which is, that the citizens become poor through dissipation and debt, as though he thought that all, or the majority of them, were originally rich. This is not true: though it is true that when any of the leaders lose their property they are ripe for revolution; but, when anybody else, it is no great matter. And an 18 oligarchy does not more often pass into a democracy than into any other form of government. Again, if men are deprived of the honours of state, and are wronged, and insulted, they make revolutions, and change forms of government, even although they have not wasted their substance because they

---

[1] Rep. viii. 550 E.   [2] Rep. viii. 551 D.
[3] Rep. viii. 555 D.

V. 12 might do what they liked—of which extravagance he declares excessive freedom to be the cause [1].

Finally, although there are many forms of oligarchies and democracies, Socrates speaks of their revolutions as though there were only one form of either of them.

[1] Rep. viii. 564.

BOOK VI

W<small>E</small> have now considered the varieties of the deliberative **VI. 1**
or supreme power in states, and the various arrangements of
law-courts and state offices, and which of them are adapted
to different forms of government[1]. We have also spoken of
the destruction and preservation of states, how and from what
causes they arise[2].

Of democracy and all other forms of government there are **2**
many kinds; and it will be well to assign to them severally
the modes of organization which are proper and advantageous
to each, adding what remains to be said about them. More- **3**
over, we ought to consider the various combinations of these
modes themselves[3]; for such combinations make constitutions
overlap one another, so that aristocracies have an oligarchical
character, and constitutional governments incline to democracies[4].

When I speak of the combinations which remain to be **4**
considered, and thus far have not been considered by us,
I mean such as these:—when the deliberative part of the
government and the election of officers is constituted oligarchically, and the law-courts aristocratically, or when the
courts and the deliberative part of the state are oligarchical,
and the election to offices aristocratical, or when in any other
way there is a want of harmony in the composition of a state.

I have shown already what forms of democracy are suited **5**

---

[1] Bk. iv. 14–16.   [2] Bk. v.
[3] Cp. Bk. iv. 7–9.   [4] Cp. iv. 8. § 3.

VI. 1 to particular cities, and what of oligarchy to particular peoples, and to whom each of the other forms of government is suited. **6** Further, we must not only show which of these governments is the best for each state, but also briefly proceed to consider [1] how these and other forms of government are to be established.

First of all let us speak of democracy, which will also bring to light the opposite form of government commonly **7** called oligarchy. For the purposes of this enquiry we need to ascertain all the elements and characteristics of democracy, since from the combinations of these the varieties of demo- **8** cratic government arise. There are several of these differing from each other, and the difference is due to two causes. One (1) has been already mentioned [2]—differences of population; for the popular element may consist of husbandmen, or of mechanics, or of labourers, and if the first of these be added to the second, or the third to the two others, not only does the democracy become better or worse, but its **9** very nature is changed. A second cause (2) remains to be mentioned: the various properties and characteristics of democracy, when variously combined, make a difference. For one democracy will have less and another will have more, and another will have all of these characteristics. There is an advantage in knowing them all, whether a man wishes to establish some new form of democracy, or only to remodel **10** an existing one [3]. Founders of states try to bring together all the elements which accord with the ideas of the several constitutions; but this is a mistake of theirs, as I have already remarked [4] when speaking of the destruction and preservation

---

[1] Cp. iv. 2. § 5.   [2] Cp. iv. 4. § 21.
[3] Cp. iv. 1. § 7.   [4] v. 9. § 7.

of states.   We will now set forth the requirements, ethical **VI. 1**
character, and aims of such states.

The basis of a democratic state is liberty; which, according **2**
to the common opinion of men, can only be enjoyed in such **1317 b**
a state—this they affirm to be the great end of every democracy[1].   One principle of liberty is for all to rule and be **2**
ruled in turn, and indeed democratic justice is the application
of numerical not proportionate equality; whence it follows
that the majority must be supreme, and that whatever the
majority approve must be the end and the just.   Every citizen,
it is said, must have equality, and therefore in a democracy
the poor have more power than the rich, because there are
more of them, and the will of the majority is supreme.   This, **3**
then, is one note of liberty which all democrats affirm to
be the principle of their state.   Another is that a man should
live as he likes[2].   This, they say, is the privilege of a freeman;
and, on the other hand, not to live as a man likes is the mark
of a slave.   This is the second characteristic of democracy, **4**
whence has arisen the claim of men to be ruled by none,
if possible, or, if this is impossible, to rule and be ruled
in turns; and so it coincides with the freedom based upon
equality [which was the first characteristic].

[3] Such being our foundation and such the nature of de- **5**
mocracy, its characteristics are as follows[3]:—the election
of officers by all out of all; and that all should rule over
each, and each in his turn over all; that the appointment
to all offices, or to all but those which require experience and

---

[1] Cp. Plato Rep. viii. 557 foll.   [2] Cp. v. 9. § 15.
[3] Or (taking ἀρχή in the sense of 'beginning'), 'Such being our
foundation, and such being the principle from which we start, the
characteristics of democracy are as follows.'

VI. 2 skill[1], should be made by lot; that no property qualification should be required for offices, or only a very low one; that no one should hold the same office twice, or not often, except in the case of military offices; that the tenure of all offices, or of as many as possible, should be brief; that all men should sit in judgment, or that judges selected out of all should judge in all matters, or in most, or in the greatest and most important—such as the scrutiny of accounts, the constitution, and private contracts; that the assembly should be supreme over all causes, or at any rate over the most important, and

6 the magistrates over none or only over a very few[2]. Of all institutions, a council is the most democratic[3] when there is not the means of paying all the citizens, but when they are paid even this is robbed of its power; for the people then draw all cases to themselves, as I said in the previous dis-

7 cussion[4]. The next characteristic of democracy is payment for services; assembly, law-courts, magistrates, everybody receives pay, when it is to be had; or when it is not to be had for all, then it is given to the law-courts and to the stated assemblies, to the council and to the magistrates, or at least to any of them who are compelled to have their meals together. And whereas oligarchy is characterized by birth, wealth, and education, the notes of democracy appear to be

8 the opposite of these—low birth, poverty, mean employment. Another note is that no magistracy is perpetual, but if any

1318 a such have survived some ancient change in the constitution it should be stripped of its power, and the holders should be elected by lot and no longer by vote. These are points common to all democracies; but democracy and demos in

---

[1] Cp. iv. 14. § 6.   [2] See note.

[3] Cp. iv. 15. § 11.   [4] Cp. iv. 6. § 5.

their truest form are based upon the recognized principle of **VI. 2**
democratic justice, that all should count equally; for equality
implies that the rich should have no more share in the government than the poor [1], and should not be the only rulers, but
that all should rule equally according to their numbers [2]. And
in this way men think that they will secure equality and
freedom in their state.

Next comes the question, How is this equality to be ob- **3**
tained? Is the qualification to be so distributed that five
hundred rich shall be equal to a thousand poor? and shall we
give the thousand a power equal to that of the five hundred?
or, if this is not to be the mode, ought we, still retaining the
same ratio, to take equal numbers from each and give them
the control of the elections [3] and of the courts?—Which, **2**
according to the democratical notion, is the juster form of the
constitution—this or one based on numbers only? Democrats say that justice is that to which the majority agree,
oligarchs that to which the wealthier class; in their opinion
the decision should be given according to the amount of
property. In both principles there is some inequality and **3**
injustice. For if justice is the will of the few, any one
person who has more wealth than all the rest of his class put
together, ought, upon the oligarchical principle, to have the
sole power—but this would be tyranny; or if justice is the
will of the majority, as I was before saying [4], they will
unjustly confiscate the property of the wealthy minority. To **4**

[1] Transposing ἀπόρους and εὐπόρους, with Bekker's 2nd ed.
[2] Cp. iv. 4. § 22.
[3] Reading with Bekker's 2nd ed. αἱρέσεων from conjecture for
διαιρέσεων, which is the reading of the MSS. See note.
[4] Cp. iii. 10. § 1.

VI. 3 find a principle of equality in which they both agree we must
enquire into their respective ideas of justice.

Now they agree in saying that whatever is decided by the
majority of the citizens is to be deemed law. Granted :—but
not without some reserve ; since there are two classes out of
which a state is composed,—the poor and the rich,—that
is to be deemed law on which both or the greater part
of both agree ; and if they disagree, that which is approved
by the majority, that is by those who have the higher qualifi-
5 cation. For example, suppose that there are ten rich and
twenty poor, and some measure is approved by six of the rich
and is disapproved by fifteen of the poor, and the remaining
four of the rich join with the party of the poor, and the
remaining five of the poor with that of the rich ; in such
a case the will of those whose qualifications, when both sides
6 are added up, are the greatest, should prevail. If they turn
out to be equal, there is no greater difficulty than at present,
when, if the assembly or the courts are divided, recourse
1318 b is had to the lot, or to some similar expedient. But, although
it may be difficult in theory to know what is just and equal,
the practical difficulty of inducing those to forbear who can,
if they like, encroach, is far greater, for the weaker are
always asking for equality and justice, but the stronger [1] care
for none of these things [1].

4   Of the four kinds of democracy, as was said in the previous
discussion [2], the best is that which comes first in order ; it is
also the oldest of them all. I am speaking of them according
to the natural classification of their inhabitants. For the best
material of democracy is an agricultural population [3] ; there is

---

[1] Or, 'care nothing for the weaker.'   [2] Cp. iv. 4. § 22.
[3] Cp. iv. 6. § 2.

no difficulty in forming a democracy where the mass of the **VI. 4**
people live by agriculture or tending of cattle. Being poor, **2**
they have no leisure, and therefore do not often attend the
assembly, and not having the necessaries of life they are always
at work, and do not covet the property of others. Indeed,
they find their employment pleasanter than the cares of government or office where no great gains can be made out of them,
for the many are more desirous of gain than of honour[1].
A proof is that even the ancient tyrannies were patiently endured **3**
by them, as they still endure oligarchies, if they are allowed
to work and are not deprived of their property; for some of
them grow quickly rich and the others are well enough off.
Moreover they have the power of electing the magistrates **4**
and calling them to account[2]; their ambition, if they have
any, is thus satisfied; and in some democracies, although they
do not all share in the appointment of offices, except through
representatives elected in turn out of the whole people, as at
Mantinea, yet, if they have the power of deliberating, the
many are contented. Even this form of government may be **5**
regarded as a democracy, and was such at Mantinea. Hence
it is both expedient and customary in such a democracy that
all should elect to offices, and conduct scrutinies, and sit in
the law-courts, but that the great offices should be filled up by
election and from persons having a qualification; the greater
requiring a greater qualification, or, if there be no offices for
which a qualification is required, then those who are marked
out by special ability should be appointed. Under such a **6**
form of government the citizens are sure to be governed well
(for the offices will always be held by the best persons; the
people are willing enough to elect them and are not jealous of

---

[1] iv. 13. § 8.   [2] Cp. ii. 12. § 5.

VI. 4 the good).   The good and the notables will then be satisfied, for they will not be governed by men who are their inferiors, and the persons elected will rule justly, because others will call

7 them to account.   Every man should be responsible to others, nor should any one be allowed to do just as he pleases; for where absolute freedom is allowed there is nothing to restrain

1319 a the evil which is inherent in every man.   But the principle of responsibility secures that which is the greatest good in states; the right persons rule and are prevented from doing wrong,

8 and the people have their due.   It is evident that this is the best kind of democracy, and why? because the people are drawn from a certain class.   The ancient laws of many states which aimed at making the people husbandmen were excellent.   They provided either that no one should possess more than a certain quantity of land, or that, if he did, the land should not be within a certain distance from the town or the acropolis.

9 Formerly in many states there was a law forbidding any one to sell his original allotment of land[1].   There is a similar law attributed to Oxylus, which is to the effect that there should be a certain portion of every man's property on which he could

10 not borrow money.   A useful corrective to the evil of which I am speaking would be the law of the Aphytaeans, who, although they are numerous, and do not possess much land, are all of them husbandmen.   For their properties are reckoned in the census, not entire, but only in such small portions [2] that even the poor may have more than the amount required[2].

11   Next best to an agricultural, and in many respects similar, are a pastoral people, who live by their flocks; they are the

[1] Cp. ii. 7. § 7.

[2] Or, ' that the qualification of the poor may exceed that of the rich.'

best trained of any for war, robust in body and able to camp VI. 4
out. The people of whom other democracies consist are far 12
inferior to them, for their life is inferior; there is no room for
moral excellence in any of their employments, whether they
be mechanics or traders or labourers. Besides, people of this 13
class can readily come to the assembly, because they are con-
tinually moving about in the city and in the agora; whereas
husbandmen are scattered over the country and do not meet,
or equally feel the want of assembling together. Where the 14
territory extends to a distance from the city, there is no
difficulty in making an excellent democracy or constitutional
government, for the people are compelled to settle in the
country; and even if there is a town population the assembly
ought not to meet when the country people cannot come. We 15
have thus explained how the first and best form of democracy
should be constituted; it is clear that the other or inferior
sorts will deviate in a regular order, and the population which 1319 b
is excluded will at each stage be of a lower kind.

The last form of democracy, that in which all share alike, is
one which cannot be borne by all states, and will not last long
unless well regulated by laws and customs. The more general
causes which tend to destroy this or other kinds of government
have now been pretty fully considered[1]. In order to constitute 16
such a democracy and strengthen the people, the leaders have
been in the habit of including as many as they can, and making
citizens not only of those who are legitimate, but even of the
illegitimate, and of those who have only one parent a citizen,
whether father or mother[2]; for nothing of this sort comes
amiss to such a democracy. This is the way in which dema- 17
gogues proceed; whereas the right thing would be to make

[1] Cp. v. 5.   [2] Cp. iii. 5. § 7.

VI. 4 no more additions when the number of the commonalty exceeds that of the notables or of the middle class,—beyond this not to go.   When in excess of this point the state becomes disorderly, and the notables grow excited and impatient of the democracy, as in the insurrection at Cyrene; for no notice is taken of a little evil, but when it increases it strikes the eye.

18 Measures like those which Cleisthenes[1] passed when he wanted to increase the power of the democracy at Athens, or such as were taken by the founders of popular government at Cyrene,

19 are useful in the extreme form of democracy.   Fresh tribes and brotherhoods should be established; the private rites of families should be restricted and converted into public ones; in short, every contrivance should be adopted which will mingle the citizens with one another and get rid of old connexions.

20 Again, the measures which are taken by tyrants appear all of them to be democratic; such, for instance, as the licence permitted to slaves (which may be to a certain extent advantageous) and also that of women and children, and the allowing everybody to live as he likes[2].   Such a government will have many supporters, for most persons would rather live in a disorderly than in a sober manner.

5   The mere establishment of a democracy is not the only or principal business of the legislator, or of those who wish to create such a state, for any state, however badly constituted, may last one, two, or three days; a far greater difficulty is the

2 preservation of it.   The legislator should therefore endeavour to have a firm foundation according to the principles already laid down concerning the preservation and destruction of states[3]; he should guard against the destructive elements, and should

---

[1] Cp. iii. 2. § 3; v. 3. § 5.   [2] Cp. v. 11. § 11.
[3] Cp. Bk. v.

make laws, whether written or unwritten, which will contain VI. 5
all the preservatives of states.   He must not think the truly 1320 a
democratical or oligarchical measure to be that which will give
the greatest amount of democracy or oligarchy, but that which
will make them last longest [1].   The demagogues of our own 3
day often get property confiscated [2] in the law-courts in order
to please the people.   But those who have the welfare of the
state at heart should counteract them, and make a law that the
property of the condemned which goes into the treasury should
not be public but sacred.   Thus offenders will be as much
afraid, for they will be punished all the same, and the people,
having nothing to gain, will not be so ready to condemn the
accused.   Care should also be taken that state trials are as 4
few as possible, and heavy penalties should be inflicted on
those who bring groundless accusations ; for it is the practice
to indict, not members of the popular party, but the notables,
although the citizens ought to be all equally attached to the
state, or at any rate should not regard their rulers as enemies.

Now, since in the last and worst form of democracy the 5
citizens are very numerous, and can hardly be made to assemble
unless they are paid, and to pay them when there are no
revenues presses hardly upon the notables (for the money
must be obtained by a property-tax and confiscations and corrupt practices of the courts, things which have before now
overthrown many democracies) ; where, I say, there are no
revenues, the government should hold few assemblies, and the
law-courts should consist of many persons, but sit for a few
days only.   This system has two advantages : first, the rich 6
do not fear the expense, even although they are unpaid themselves when the poor are paid ; and secondly, causes are better

[1] Cp. v. 11. §§ 2, 3.   [2] Cp. v. 5. § 5.

VI. 5 tried, for wealthy persons, although they do not like to be long absent from their own affairs, do not mind going for a few
7 days to the law-courts.   Where there are revenues the demagogues should not be allowed after their manner to distribute the surplus; the poor are always receiving and always wanting more and more, for such help is like water poured into a leaky cask.   Yet the true friend of the people should see that they be not too poor, for extreme poverty lowers the character of
8 the democracy; measures also should be taken which will give them lasting prosperity; and as this is equally the interest of all classes, the proceeds of the public revenues should be accumulated and distributed among them, if possible, in such quantities as may enable them to purchase a little farm, or, at any
1320 b rate, make a beginning in trade and husbandry.   And if this
9 benevolence cannot be extended to all, money should be distributed in turn according to tribes or other divisions, and in the meantime the rich should pay the fee for the attendance of the poor at the necessary assemblies; and should in return be excused from useless public services.   By administering the state in this spirit the Carthaginians retain the affections of the people; their policy is from time to time to send some of
10 them into their dependent towns, where they grow rich [1].   It is also worthy of a generous and sensible nobility to divide the poor amongst them, and give them the means of going to work. The example of the people of Tarentum is also well deserving of imitation, for, by sharing the use of their own property with
11 the poor, they gain their good will [2].   Moreover, they divide all their offices into two classes, one-half of them being elected by vote, the other by lot; the latter, that the people may participate in them, and the former, that the state may be better

---

[1] Cp. ii. 11. § 15.   [2] Cp. ii. 5. § 8.

administered. A like result may be gained by dividing the **VI. 5**
same offices [1], so as to have two classes of magistrates, one
chosen by vote, the other by lot.

Enough has been said of the manner in which democracies **6**
ought to be constituted.

From these considerations there will be no difficulty in seeing what should be the constitution of oligarchies. We must
put together in our minds each form of oligarchy by reasoning
from its opposite, calculating the structure of each in relation
to that of the opposite democracy.

The first and best attempered of oligarchies is akin to a con- **2**
stitutional government. In this there ought to be two standards
of qualification; the one high, the other low—the lower
qualifying for the humbler yet indispensable offices and the
higher for the superior ones. He who acquires the prescribed
qualification should have the rights of citizenship. The nature
of those admitted should be such as will make the entire **3**
governing body stronger than those who are excluded, and the
new citizen should be always taken out of the better class of the
people. The principle, narrowed a little, gives another form
of oligarchy; until at length we reach the most cliquish and
tyrannical of them all, answering to the extreme democracy,
which, being the worst, requires vigilance in proportion to its **4**
badness. For as healthy bodies and ships well provided with
sailors may undergo many mishaps and survive them, whereas
sickly constitutions and rotten ill-manned ships are ruined by
the very least mistake, so do the worst forms of government **1321 a**
require the greatest care. The populousness of democracies **5**
generally preserves them (for number is to democracy in the
place of justice based on proportion); whereas the preservation

[1] Reading τῆς αὐτῆς ἀρχῆς with Bekker's 2nd ed.

VI. 6 of an oligarchy clearly depends on an opposite principle, viz. good order.

7   As there are four chief divisions of the common people—husbandmen, mechanics, retail traders, labourers; so also there are four kinds of military forces—the cavalry, the heavy infantry, the light-armed troops, the navy [1]. When the country is adapted for cavalry, then a strong oligarchy is likely to be established.   For the security of the inhabitants depends upon a force of this sort, and only rich men can afford to keep horses.   The second form of oligarchy prevails when there are heavy infantry [2]; for this service is better suited to the rich

2 than to the poor.   But the light-armed and the naval element are wholly democratic; and nowadays, when they are so numerous, if the two parties quarrel, the oligarchy are often worsted by them in the struggle.   A remedy for this state of things may be found in the practice of generals who combine a proper contingent of light-armed troops with cavalry and

3 heavy-armed.   And this is the way in which the poor get the better of the rich in civil contests; being lightly armed, they fight with advantage against cavalry and heavy infantry.   An oligarchy which raises such a force out of the lower classes raises a power against itself.   And therefore, since the ages of the citizens vary and some are older and some younger, the fathers should have their own sons, while they are still young, taught the agile movements of light-armed troops; and some, when they grow up, should be selected out of the youth, and

4 become light-armed warriors in reality.   The oligarchy should also yield a share in the government to the people, either, as I said before, to those who have a property qualification [3], or, as

---

[1] Cp. iv. 3. §§ 2, 3.   [2] Reading ὁπλίτην with Bekker's 1st ed.
[3] Cp. c. 6. § 2.

in the case of Thebes [1], to those who have abstained for a **VI. 7**
certain number of years from mean employments, or, as at
Massalia, to men of merit who are selected for their worthi-
ness, whether [previously] citizens or not.   The magistracies **5**
of the highest rank, which ought to be in the hands of the
governing body, should have expensive duties attached to them,
and then the people will not desire them and will take no
offence at the privileges of their rulers when they see that
they pay a heavy fine for their dignity.   It is fitting also that **6**
the magistrates on entering office should offer magnificent
sacrifices or erect some public edifice, and then the people who
participate in the entertainments, and like to see the city
decorated with votive offerings and buildings, will not desire
an alteration in the government, and the notables will have
memorials of their munificence.   This, however, is anything **7**
but the fashion of our modern oligarchs, who are as covetous
of gain as they are of honour; oligarchies like theirs may be
well described as petty democracies.   Enough of the manner 1321 b
in which democracies and oligarchies should be organized.

Next in order follows the right distribution of offices, their **8**
number, their nature, their duties, of which indeed we have
already spoken [2]. No state can exist not having the necessary
offices, and no state can be well administered not having the
offices which tend to preserve harmony and good order.   In **2**
small states, as we have already remarked [3], there need not be
many of them, but in larger there must be a larger number,
and we should carefully consider which offices may properly
be united and which separated.

First among necessary offices is that which has the care of **3**

[1] Cp. iii. 5. § 7.   [2] Cp. iv. 15.
[3] Cp. iv. 15. §§ 5–7.

VI. 8 the market; a magistrate should be appointed to inspect contracts and to maintain order. For in every state there must inevitably be buyers and sellers who will supply one another's wants; this is the readiest way to make a state self-sufficing and so fulfil the purpose for which men come together into one

4 state[1]. A second office of a similar kind undertakes the supervision and embellishment of public and private buildings, the maintaining and repairing of houses and roads, the prevention of disputes about boundaries and other concerns of a like nature.

5 This is commonly called the office of City-warden, and has various departments, which, in more populous towns, are shared among different persons, one, for example, taking charge of the

6 walls, another of the fountains, a third of harbours. There is another equally necessary office, and of a similar kind, having to do with the same matters without the walls and in the country :—the magistrates who hold this office are called Wardens of the country, or Inspectors of the woods. Besides these three there is a fourth office of receivers of taxes, who have under their charge the revenue which they distribute among the various departments; these are called Receivers or

7 Treasurers. Another officer registers all private contracts, and decisions of the courts, all public indictments, and also all preliminary proceedings. This office again is sometimes subdivided, in which case one officer is appointed over all the rest. These officers are called Recorders or Sacred Recorders, Presidents, and the like.

8 Next to these comes an office of which the duties are the most necessary and also the most difficult, viz. that to which is committed the execution of punishments, or the exaction of

---

[1] Cp. i. 2. § 8; Nic. Eth. v. 6. § 4; Pl. Rep. ii. 369.

fines from those who are posted up according to the registers; **VI. 8**
and also the custody of prisoners.   The difficulty of this office 1322 a
arises out of the odium which is attached to it; no one will 9
undertake it unless great profits are to be made, and any one who
does is loth to execute the law.   Still the office is necessary;
for judicial decisions are useless if they take no effect; and if
society cannot exist without them, neither can it exist without the execution of them.   It is an office which, being so 10
unpopular, should not be entrusted to one person, but divided
among several taken from different courts.   In like manner
an effort should be made to distribute among different persons
the writing up of those who are registered as public debtors.
Some sentences should be executed by officers who have other
functions; penalties for new offences should be exacted by new
offices; and as regards those which are not new, when one
court has given judgment, another should exact the penalty; for
example, the wardens of the city should exact the fines imposed
by the wardens of the agora, and others again should exact the
fines imposed by them.   For penalties are more likely to be 11
exacted when less odium attaches to the exaction of them;
but a double odium is incurred when the judges who have
passed also execute the sentence, and if they are always the
executioners, they will be the enemies of all.

In many places one magistracy has the custody of the
prisoners, while another executes the sentence, as, for example,
'the Eleven' at Athens.   It is well to separate off the jailor- 12
ship, and try by some device to render the office less unpopular.
For it is quite as necessary as that of the executioner; but
good men do all they can to avoid it, and worthless persons
cannot safely be trusted with it; for they themselves require a
guard, and are not fit to guard others.   There ought not there- 13

VI. 8 fore to be a single or permanent officer set apart for this duty ;
but it should be entrusted to the young, wherever they are
organized into a band or guard, and different magistrates acting
in turn should take charge of it.

These are the indispensable officers, and should be ranked
first :—next in order follow others, equally necessary, but of
14 higher rank, and requiring great experience and fidelity.   Such
are the offices to which are committed the guard of the city,
and other military functions.   Not only in time of war but of
peace their duty will be to defend the walls and gates, and to
muster and marshal the citizens.   In some states there are
many such offices ; in others there are a few only, while small
15 states are content with one ; these officers are called generals
1322 b or commanders.   Again, if a state has cavalry or light-armed
troops or archers or a naval force, it will sometimes happen
that each of these departments has separate officers, who are
called admirals, or generals of cavalry or of infantry.   And
there are subordinate officers called naval and military captains,
and captains of horse ; having others under them :—all these
16 are included in the department of war.   Thus much of military
command.

But since many, not to say all, of these offices handle the
public money, there must of necessity be another office which
examines and audits them, and has no other functions.   Such
officers are called by various names—Scrutineers, Auditors,
17 Accountants, Controllers.   Besides all these offices there is
another which is supreme over them, and to this, which in a
democracy presides over the assembly, is often entrusted both
the introduction and the ratification of measures.   For that
power which convenes the people must of necessity be the
head of the state.   In some places they are called 'probuli,'

because they hold previous deliberations, but in a democracy **VI.** 8
more commonly 'councillors[1].' These are the chief political 18
offices.

Another set of officers is concerned with the maintenance
of religion ; priests and guardians see to the preservation and
repair of the temples of the gods and to other matters of religion.
One office of this sort may be enough in small places, but in 19
larger ones there are a great many besides the priesthood ; for
example, superintendents of sacrifices, guardians of shrines,
treasurers of the sacred revenues.   Nearly connected with these 20
there are also the officers appointed for the performance of the
public sacrifices, except any which the law assigns to the
priests ; such officers derive their dignity from the public hearth
of the city.   They are sometimes called archons, sometimes
kings[2], and sometimes prytanes.

These, then, are the necessary offices, which may be summed 21
up as follows : offices concerned with matters of religion, with
war, with the revenue and expenditure, with the market, with
the city, with the harbours, with the country ; also with the
courts of law, with the records of contracts, with execution of
sentences, with custody of prisoners, with audits and scrutinies
and accounts of magistrates ; lastly, there are those which preside over the public deliberations of the state.   There are like- 22
wise magistracies characteristic of states which are peaceful
and prosperous, and at the same time have a regard to good
order : such as the offices of guardians of women, guardians of
the laws, guardians of children, and directors of gymnastics ;
also superintendents of gymnastic and Dionysiac contests, and 1323 :
of other similar spectacles.   Some of these are clearly not 23
democratic offices ; for example, the guardianships of women

[1] Cp. iv. 15. § 11.   [2] Cp. iii. 14. § 14.

VI. 8 and children [1]—the poor, not having any slaves, must employ both their women and children as servants.

24　　Once more: there are three forms of the highest elective offices in states—guardians of the law, probuli, councillors,—of these, the guardians of the law are an aristocratical, the probuli an oligarchical, the council a democratical institution. Enough of the different kinds of offices.

[1] Cp. iv. 15. § 13.

BOOK VII

He who would duly enquire about the best form of a state
ought first to determine which is the most eligible life; while
this remains uncertain the best form of the state must also be
uncertain; for, in the natural order of things, those may be
expected to lead the best life who are governed in the best
manner of which their circumstances admit. We ought there- **2**
fore to ascertain, first of all, which is the most generally eligible
life, and then whether the same life is or is not best for the state
and for individuals.

Assuming that enough has been already said in exoteric
discourses concerning the best life, we will now only repeat
the statements contained in them. Certainly no one will dispute **3**
the propriety of that partition of goods which separates them
into three classes[1], viz. external goods, goods of the body,
and goods of the soul, or deny that the happy man must have
all three. For no one would maintain that he is happy who **4**
has not in him a particle of courage or temperance or justice
or prudence, who is afraid of every insect which flutters past
him, and will commit any crime, however great, in order to
gratify his lust of meat or drink, who will sacrifice his dearest
friend for the sake of half a farthing, and is as feeble and false
in mind as a child or a madman. These propositions are **5**
universally acknowledged as soon as they are uttered[2], but men

---

[1] Cp. N. Eth. i. 8. § 2.

[2] Omitting ὥσπερ, which is bracketed by Bekker in his second
edition.

VII. 1 differ about the quantity which is desirable or the relative superiority of this or that good. Some think that a very moderate amount of virtue is enough, but set no limit to their desires of wealth, property, power, reputation, and the like.

6 To whom we reply by an appeal to facts, which easily prove that mankind do not acquire or preserve virtue by the help of **1323 b** external goods, but external goods by the help of virtue, and that happiness, whether consisting in pleasure or virtue, or both, is more often found with those who are most highly cultivated in their mind and in their character, and have only a moderate share of external goods, than among those who possess external goods to a useless extent but are deficient in higher qualities; and this is not only matter of experience, but, if reflected upon, will easily appear to be in accordance with **7** reason. For, whereas external goods have a limit, like any other instrument [1], and all things useful are of such a nature that where there is too much of them they must either do harm, or at any rate be of no use, to their possessors, every good of the soul, the greater it is, is also of greater use, if the epithet **8** 'useful' as well as 'noble' is appropriate to such subjects. No proof is required to show that the best state of one thing in relation to another is proportioned to the degree of excellence by which the natures corresponding to those states are separated from each other: so that, if the soul is more noble than our possessions or our bodies, both absolutely and in relation to us, it must be admitted that the best state of either **9** has a similar ratio to the other. Again, it is for the sake of the soul that goods external and goods of the body are eligible at all, and all wise men ought to choose them for the sake of the soul, and not the soul for the sake of them.

[1] Cp. i. 8. § 15.

Let us acknowledge then that each one has just so much of **VII. 1** happiness as he has of virtue and wisdom, and of virtuous and [10] wise action.   God is a witness to us of this truth [1]; for he is happy and blessed, not by reason of any external good, but in himself and by reason of his own nature.   And herein of necessity lies the difference between good fortune and happiness; for external goods come of themselves, and chance is the author of them, but no one is just or temperate by or through chance [2]. In like manner, and by a similar train of argument, the happy [11] state may be shown to be that which is [morally] best and which acts rightly; and rightly it cannot act without doing right actions, and neither individual nor state can do right actions without virtue and wisdom.   Thus the courage, justice, and [12] wisdom of a state have the same form and nature as the qualities which give the individual who possesses them the name of just, wise, or temperate.

Thus much may suffice by way of preface: for I could not [13] avoid touching upon these questions, neither could I go through all the arguments affecting them; these must be reserved for another discussion.

Let us assume then that the best life, both for individuals and states, is the life of virtue, having external goods enough for the performance of good actions.   If there are any who con-   1324 a trovert our assertion, we will in this treatise pass them over, [14] and consider their objections hereafter.

There remains to be discussed the question, Whether the **2** happiness of the individual is the same as that of the state, or different?   Here again there can be no doubt—no one denies that they are the same.   For those who hold that the well-being [2]

---

[1] Cp. c. 3. § 10; N. Eth. x. 8. § 7; Met. xii. 7.
[2] Ethics i. 9. § 6.

VII. 2 of the individual consists in his wealth, also think that riches make the happiness of the whole state, and those who value most highly the life of a tyrant deem that city the happiest which rules over the greatest number; while they who approve an individual for his virtue say that the more virtuous a city **3** is, the happier it is. Two points here present themselves for consideration: first (1), which is the more eligible life, that of a citizen who is a member of a state, or that of an alien who has no political ties; and again (2), which is the best form of constitution or the best condition of a state, either on the supposition that political privileges are given to all, or **4** that they are given to a majority only? Since the good of the state and not of the individual is the proper subject of political thought and speculation, and we are engaged in a political discussion, while the first of these two points has a secondary interest for us, the latter will be the main subject of our enquiry.

5 Now it is evident that the form of government is best in which every man, whoever he is, can act for the best and live happily. But even those who agree in thinking that the life of virtue is the most eligible raise a question, whether the life of business and politics is or is not more eligible than one which is wholly independent of external goods, I mean than a contemplative life, which by some is maintained to be the **6** only one worthy of a philosopher. For these two lives—the life of the philosopher and the life of the statesman—appear to have been preferred by those who have been most keen in the pursuit of virtue, both in our own and in other ages. Which is the better is a question of no small moment; for the wise man, like the wise state, will necessarily regulate his **7** life according to the best end. There are some who think that while a despotic rule over others is the greatest injustice, **VII. 2** to exercise a constitutional rule over them, even though not unjust, is a great impediment to a man's individual well-being. Others take an opposite view; they maintain that the true life of man is the practical and political, and that every virtue admits of being practised, quite as much by statesmen and rulers as by private individuals. Others, again, are of opinion that **1324 b 8** arbitrary and tyrannical rule alone consists with happiness; indeed, [1] in some states the entire aim of the laws[1] is to give men despotic power over their neighbours. And, therefore, **9** although in most cities the laws may be said generally to be in a chaotic state, still, if they aim at anything, they aim at the maintenance of power: thus in Lacedaemon and Crete the system of education and the greater part of the laws are framed with a view to war[2]. And in all nations which are able to **10** gratify their ambition military power is held in esteem, for example among the Scythians and Persians and Thracians and Celts. In some nations there are even laws tending to stimulate the warlike virtues, as at Carthage, where we are told that men obtain the honour of wearing as many armlets as they have served campaigns. There was once a law in Macedonia that he who **11** had not killed an enemy should wear a halter, and among the Scythians no one who had not slain his man was allowed to drink out of the cup which was handed round at a certain feast. Among the Iberians, a warlike nation, the number of enemies whom a man has slain is indicated by the number of spits which are fixed in the earth round his tomb; and there are numerous **12**

[1] Or, inserting καί before νόμων (apparently the reading of the old translator), 'in some cases the entire aim both of the constitution and the laws.'

[2] Cp. Plato, Laws, i. 633 ff

VII. 2 practices among other nations of a like kind, some of them established by law and others by custom.   Yet to a reflecting mind it must appear very strange that the statesman should be always considering how he can dominate and tyrannize over **13** others, whether they will or not.   How can that which is not even lawful be the business of the statesman or the legislator?   Unlawful it certainly is to rule without regard to justice, for there may be might where there is no right. The other arts and sciences offer no parallel; a physician is not expected to persuade or coerce his patients, nor a pilot **14** the passengers in his ship.   Yet many appear to think that a despotic government is a true political form, and what men affirm to be unjust and inexpedient in their own case they are not ashamed of practising towards others; they demand justice for themselves, but where other men are concerned **15** they care nothing about it.   Such behaviour is irrational; unless the one party is born to command, and the other born to serve, in which case men have a right to command, not indeed all their fellows, but only those who are intended to be subjects; just as we ought not to hunt mankind, whether for food or sacrifice, but only the animals which are intended for food or sacrifice, that is to say, such wild **16** animals as are eatable.   And surely there may be a city **1325 a** happy in isolation, which we will assume to be well-governed (for it is quite possible that a city thus isolated might be well-administered and have good laws); but such a city would not be constituted with any view to war or the conquest of **17** enemies—all that sort of thing must be excluded.   Hence we see very plainly that warlike pursuits, although generally to be deemed honourable, are not the supreme end of all things, but only means.   And the good lawgiver should

enquire how states and races of men and communities **VII. 2**
may participate in a good life, and in the happiness which is
attainable by them.   His enactments will not be always the **18**
same ;   and where there are neighbours [1] he will have to deal
with them according to their characters, and to see what
duties are to be performed towards each.   The end at which
the best form of government should aim may be properly
made a matter of future consideration [2].

Let us now address those who, while they agree that the **3**
life of virtue is the most eligible, differ about the manner
of practising it.   For some renounce political power, and
think that the life of the freeman is different from the life of
the statesman and the best of all ; but others think the life
of the statesman best.   The argument of the latter is that
he who does nothing cannot do well, and that virtuous
activity is identical with happiness.   To both we say : ' you
are partly right and partly wrong.'   The first class are right
in affirming that the life of the freeman is better than the
life of the despot ; for there is nothing grand or noble **2**
in having the use of a slave, in so far as he is a slave ;
or in issuing commands about necessary things.   But it is
an error to suppose that every sort of rule is despotic like
that of a master over slaves, for there is as great a difference
between the rule over freemen and the rule over slaves as
there is between slavery by nature and freedom by nature,
about which I have said enough at the commencement of
this treatise [3].   And it is equally a mistake to place inac- **3**
tivity above action, for happiness is activity, and the actions of
the just and wise are the realization of much that is noble.

---

[1] Cp. ii. 6. § 7 ; 7. § 14.   [2] Cp. c. 14.
[3] Cp. i. c. 5, 6, 7.

VII. 3   But perhaps some one, accepting these premises, may still maintain that supreme power is the best of all things, because the possessors of it are able to perform the greatest number **4** of noble actions.   If so, the man who is able to rule, instead of giving up anything to his neighbour, ought rather to take away his power ; and the father should make no account of his son, nor the son of his father, nor friend of friend ; they should not bestow a thought on one another in comparison with this higher object, for the best is the most eligible and 'doing well' is the best.   There might be some **1325 b** truth in such a view if we assume that robbers and plunderers **5** attain the chief good.   But this can never be ; and hence we infer the view to be false.   For the actions of a ruler cannot really be honourable, unless he is as much superior to other men as a husband is to a wife, or a father to his children, or a master to his slaves.   And therefore he who violates the law can never recover by any success, however great, what he has already lost in departing from virtue.   For equals share alike in the honourable and the just, as is just **6** and equal.   But that the unequal should be given to equals, and the unlike to those who are like, is contrary to nature, and nothing which is contrary to nature is good.   If, therefore, there is any one [1] superior in virtue and in the power of performing the best actions, him we ought to follow and **7** obey, but he must have the capacity for action as well as virtue.

If we are right in our view, and happiness is assumed to be virtuous activity, the active life will be the best, both for **8** the city collectively, and for individuals.   Not that a life of action must necessarily have relations to others, as some

[1] Cp. iii, 13. § 25, and 17. § 7.

persons think, nor are those ideas only to be regarded **VII. 3**
as practical which are pursued for the sake of practical results,
but much more the thoughts and contemplations which are
independent and complete in themselves; since virtuous
activity, and therefore action, is an end, and even in the case
of external actions the directing mind is most truly said
to act.   Neither, again, is it necessary that states which are **9**
cut off from others and choose to live alone should be inactive;
for there may be activity also in the parts; there are many
ways in which the members of a state act upon one another.
The same thing is equally true of every individual.   If this **10**
were otherwise, God and the universe, who have no external
actions over and above their own energies[1], would be far enough
from perfection.   Hence it is evident that the same life is
best for each individual, and for states, and for mankind
collectively.

   Thus far by way of introduction.   In what has preceded **4**
I have discussed other forms of government; in what
remains, the first point to be considered is what should be the
conditions of the ideal or perfect state; for the perfect state **2**
cannot exist without a due supply of the means of life.   And
therefore we must presuppose many purely imaginary conditions[2], but nothing impossible.   There will be a certain
number of citizens, a country in which to place them, and the
like.   As the weaver or shipbuilder or any other artisan **3**
must have the material proper for his work (and in proportion **1326 a**
as this is better prepared, so will the result of his art be
nobler), so the statesman or legislator must also have the
materials suited to him.

   First among the materials required by the statesman is **4**

[1] Cp. c. I. § 10.   [2] Cp. ii. 6. § 7.

VII. 4 population : he will consider what should be the number and character of the citizens, and then what should be the size and character of the country.   Most persons think that a state in order to be happy ought to be large; but even if they are right, they have no idea what is a large and what a small

5 state.   For they judge of the size of the city by the number of the inhabitants; whereas they ought to regard, not their number, but their power.   A city too, like an individual, has a work to do; and that city which is best adapted to the fulfilment of its work is to be deemed greatest, in the same sense of the word great in which Hippocrates might be called greater, not as a man, but as a physician, than some one

6 else who was taller.   And even if we reckon greatness by numbers, we ought not to include everybody, for there must always be in cities a multitude of slaves and sojourners and foreigners; but we should include those only who are members of the state, and who form an essential part of it.   The number of the latter is a proof of the greatness of a city; but a city which produces numerous artisans and comparatively few soldiers cannot be great, for a great city is not to be confounded

7 with a populous one.   Moreover, experience shows that a very populous city can rarely, if ever, be well governed ; since all cities which have a reputation for good government have a limit of population.   We may argue on grounds of reason, and

8 the same result will follow.   For law is order, and good law is good order; but a very great multitude cannot be orderly : to introduce order into the unlimited is the work of a divine power—of such a power as holds together the universe.   Beauty

9 is realized in number and magnitude[1], and the state which combines magnitude with good order must necessarily be the most

[1] Cp. Poet. 7. § 4.

beautiful.   To the size of states there is a limit, as there is to **VII. 4**
other things, plants, animals, implements; for none of these **10**
retain their natural power when they are too large or too small,
but they either wholly lose their nature, or are spoiled.   For
example[1], a ship which is only a span long will not be a ship
at all, nor a ship a quarter of a mile long ; yet there may be
a ship of a certain size, either too large or too small, which
will still be a ship, but bad for sailing.   In like manner a state **1326 b**
when composed of too few is not as a state ought to be, self-   **11**
sufficing ; when of too many, though self-sufficing in all mere
necessaries, it is a nation and not a state, being almost incapable of constitutional government.   For who can be the general
of such a vast multitude, or who the herald, unless he have the
voice of a Stentor ?

   A state then only begins to exist when it has attained
a population sufficient for a good life in the political community : it may indeed somewhat exceed this number.   But, **12**
as I was saying, there must be a limit.   What should be
the limit will be easily ascertained by experience.   For both
governors and governed have duties to perform ; the special
functions of a governor are to command and to judge.   But **13**
if the citizens of a state are to judge and to distribute offices
according to merit, then they must know each other's
characters ; where they do not possess this knowledge,
both the election to offices and the decision of lawsuits
will go wrong.   When the population is very large they
are manifestly settled at haphazard, which clearly ought
not to be.   Besides, in an overpopulous state foreigners and **14**
metics will readily acquire the rights of citizens, for who will
find them out ?   Clearly, then, the best limit of the population

[1] Cp. v. 9. § 7.

VII. **4** of a state is the largest number which suffices for the purposes of life, and can be taken in at a single view. Enough concerning the size of a city.

5   Much the same principle will apply to the territory of the state: every one would agree in praising the state which is most entirely self-sufficing; and that must be the state which is all-producing, for to have all things and to want nothing is sufficiency. In size and extent it should be such as may enable the inhabitants to live temperately and liberally

2 in the enjoyment of leisure[1]. Whether we are right or wrong in laying down this limit we will enquire more precisely hereafter[2], when we have occasion to consider what is the right use of property and wealth: a matter which is much disputed, because men are inclined to rush into one of two extremes, some into meanness, others into luxury.

3   It is not difficult to determine the general character of the territory which is required; there are, however, some points on which military authorities should be heard; they tell us that it should be difficult of access to the enemy, and

1327 a easy of egress to the inhabitants. Further, we require that the land as well as the inhabitants of whom we were just now speaking should be taken in at a single view, for a country which is easily seen can be easily protected. As to the position of the city, if we could have what we wish, it should

4 be well situated in regard both to sea or land. This then is one principle, that it should be a convenient centre for the protection of the whole country: the other is, that it should be suitable for receiving the fruits of the soil, and also for the bringing in of timber and any other products.

6   Whether a communication with the sea is beneficial to

---

[1] Cp. ii. 6. § 9.   [2] Cp. c. 8–10 infra (?).

a well-ordered state or not is a question which has often been **VII. 6**
asked.   It is argued that the introduction of strangers brought
up under other laws, and the increase of population, will be
adverse to good order (for a maritime people will always have
a crowd of merchants coming and going), and that intercourse
by sea is inimical to good government[1].   Apart from these **2**
considerations, it would be undoubtedly better, both with
a view to safety and to the provision of necessaries, that the
city and territory should be connected with the sea; the **3**
defenders of a country, if they are to maintain themselves
against an enemy, should be easily relieved both by land and
by sea; and even if they are not able to attack by sea and
land at once, they will have less difficulty in doing mischief
to their assailants on one element, if they themselves can use
both.   Moreover, it is necessary that they should import from **4**
abroad what is not found in their own country, and that they
should export what they have in excess; for a city ought to
be a market, not indeed for others, but for herself.

Those who make themselves a market for the world only
do so for the sake of revenue, and if a state ought not to
desire profit of this kind it ought not to have such an
emporium.   Nowadays we often see in countries and cities **5**
dockyards and harbours very conveniently placed outside the
city, but not too far off; and they are kept in dependence by
walls and similar fortifications.   Cities thus situated manifestly reap the benefit of intercourse with their ports; and
any harm which is likely to accrue may be easily guarded
against by the laws, which will pronounce and determine who
may hold communication with one another, and who may not.

There can be no doubt that the possession of a moderate **6**

[1] Cp. Plato, Laws, iv. 704 ff.

VII. 6 naval force is advantageous to a city; the citizens require
1327 b such a force for their own needs, and they should also
be formidable to their neighbours in certain cases[1], or,
if necessary, able to assist them by sea as well as by land.
7 The proper number or magnitude of this naval force is
relative to the character of the state; for if her function
is to take a leading part in politics[2], her naval power should
be commensurate with the scale of her enterprises. The
population of the state need not be much increased, since
8 there is no necessity that the sailors should be citizens: the
marines who have the control and command will be freemen,
and belong also to the infantry; and wherever there is
a dense population of Perioeci and husbandmen, there will
always be sailors more than enough. Of this we see
instances at the present day. The city of Heraclea, for
example, although small in comparison with many others, can
9 man a considerable fleet. Such are our conclusions respecting the territory of the state, its harbour, its towns, its
relations to the sea, and its maritime power.

7   Having spoken of the number of the citizens, we will
proceed to speak of what should be their character. This is
a subject which can be easily understood by any one who
casts his eye on the more celebrated states of Hellas,
and generally on the distribution of races in the habitable
2 world.   Those who live in a cold climate and in [northern]
Europe are full of spirit, but wanting in intelligence and
skill; and therefore they keep their freedom, but have
no political organization, and are incapable of ruling over
others. Whereas the natives of Asia are intelligent and

---

[1] Cp. ii. 6. § 7.

[2] Reading πολιτικόν with the MSS. and Bekker's first edition.

inventive, but they are wanting in spirit, and therefore they are **VII. 7**
always in a state of subjection and slavery.   But the Hellenic **3**
race, which is situated between them, is likewise intermediate
in character, being high-spirited and also intelligent [1].   Hence
it continues free, and is the best governed of any nation, and,
if it could be formed into one state, would be able to rule the
world.   There are also similar differences in the different tribes **4**
of Hellas ; for some of them are of a one-sided nature, and
are intelligent or courageous only, while in others there is a
happy combination of both qualities.   And clearly those whom
the legislator will most easily lead to virtue may be expected
to be both intelligent and courageous.   Some [like Plato [2]] **5**
say that the guardians should be friendly towards those
whom they know, fierce towards those whom they do not
know.   Now, passion is the quality of the soul which begets **1328 a**
friendship and inspires affection ; notably the spirit within us
is more stirred against our friends and acquaintances than
against those who are unknown to us, when we think that we
are despised by them ; for which reason Archilochus, com- **6**
plaining of his friends, very naturally addresses his soul in these
words,

   ' For wert thou not plagued on account of friends [3] ? '

The power of command and the love of freedom are in all
men based upon this quality, for passion is commanding and
invincible.   Nor is it right to say that the guardians should be **7**
fierce towards those whom they do not know, for we ought
not to be out of temper with any one ; and a lofty spirit is not

---

[1] Cp. Plato, Rep. iv. 435 E, 436 A.   [2] Rep. ii. 375.
[3] Or : ' For surely thou art not plagued on account of thy friends ? '
The line is probably corrupt.   Better to read with Bergk, σὺ γὰρ δὴ παρὰ
φίλων ἀπάγχεο, ' for thou indeed wert plagued by friends.'

VII. 7 fierce by nature, but only when excited against evil-doers. And this, as I was saying before, is a feeling which men show most strongly towards their friends if they think they **8** have received a wrong at their hands: as indeed is reasonable; for, besides the actual injury, they seem to be deprived of a benefit by those who owe them one. Hence the saying,

> 'Cruel is the strife of brethren[1];'

and again,

> 'They who love in excess also hate in excess[1].'

9 Thus we have nearly determined the number and character of the citizens of our state, and also the size and nature of their territory. I say 'nearly,' for we ought not to require the same minuteness in theory as in fact[2].

8 As in other natural compounds the conditions of a composite whole are not necessarily organic parts of it, so in a state or in any other combination forming a unity not everything **2** is a part, which is a necessary condition[3]. The members of an association have necessarily some one thing the same and common to all, in which they share equally or unequally; **3** for example, food or land or any other thing. But where there are two things of which one is a means and the other an end, they have nothing in common except that the one receives what the other produces. Such, for example, is the relation in which workmen and tools stand to their work; the house and the builder have nothing in common, but **4** the art of the builder is for the sake of the house. And so states require property, but property, even though living beings are included in it[4], is no part of a state; for a state is

---

[1] Eurip. Frag. 51 Dindorf.   [2] Cp. 12. § 9, infra.
[3] Cp. iii. 5. § 2.   [4] Cp. i. 4. § 2.

not a community of living beings only, but a community **VII. 8**
of equals, aiming at the best life possible. Now, whereas **5**
happiness is the highest good, being a realization and perfect
practice of virtue, which some attain, while others have little
or none of it, the various qualities of men are clearly the
reason why there are various kinds of states and many forms
of government ; for different men seek after happiness in
different ways and by different means, and so make for **1328 b**
themselves different modes of life and forms of government.
We must see also how many things are indispensable to **6**
the existence of a state, for what we call the parts of a state
will be found among them. Let us then enumerate the
functions of a state, and we shall easily elicit what we want :

First, there must be food ; secondly, arts, for life requires **7**
many instruments ; thirdly, there must be arms, for the
members of a community have need of them in order to
maintain authority both against disobedient subjects and
against external assailants ; fourthly, there must be a certain
amount of revenue, both for internal needs and for the
purposes of war ; fifthly, or rather first, there must be a care
of religion, which is commonly called worship ; sixthly, and
most necessary of all, there must be a power of deciding what
is for the public interest, and what is just in men's dealings
with one another.

These are the things which every state may be said to **8**
need. For a state is not a mere aggregate of persons, but
a union of them sufficing for the purposes of life [1] ; and
if any of these things be wanting, it is simply impossible
that the community can be self-sufficing. A state then **9**

---

[1] Cp. supra, c. 5. § 1.

VII. 8 should be framed with a view to the fulfilment of these functions. There must be husbandmen to procure food, and artisans, and a warlike and a wealthy class, and priests, and judges to decide what is just [1] and expedient.

9   Having determined these points, we have in the next place to consider whether all ought to share in every sort of occupation. Shall every man be at once husbandman, artisan, councillor, judge, or shall we suppose the several occupations just mentioned assigned to different persons? or, thirdly, shall some employments be assigned to individuals and others common to all? The question, however, does not occur in every state;

2 as we were saying, all may be shared by all, or not all by all, but only some by some [2]; and hence arise the differences of states, for in democracies all share in all, in oligarchies the

3 opposite practice prevails. Now, since we are here speaking of the best form of government, and that under which the state will be most happy (and happiness, as has been already said, cannot exist without virtue [3]), it clearly follows that in the state which is best governed the citizens who are absolutely and not merely relatively just men must not lead the life of mechanics or tradesmen, for such a life is ignoble and inimical

4 to virtue [4]. Neither must they be husbandmen, since leisure is

1329 a necessary both for the development of virtue and the performance of political duties.

    Again, there is in a state a class of warriors, and another of councillors, who advise about the expedient and determine matters of law, and these seem in an especial manner parts of a state. Now, should these two classes be distinguished, or

5 are both functions to be assigned to the same persons? Here

---

[1] Reading δικαίων with Bekker in his second edition.

[2] Cp. iv. 4 and 14.   [3] Cp. c. 8. § 5.   [4] Cp. Plato, Laws, xi. 919.

again there is no difficulty in seeing that both functions will in **VII. 9**
one way belong to the same, in another, to different persons.
To different persons in so far as their employments are suited
to different ages of life, for the one requires wisdom, and the
other strength. But on the other hand, since it is an impossible thing that those who are able to use or to resist force
should be willing to remain always in subjection, from this
point of view the persons are the same ; for those who carry
arms can always determine the fate of the constitution. It **6**
remains therefore that both functions of government should be
entrusted to the same persons, not, however, at the same time,
but in the order prescribed by nature, who has given to young
men strength and to older men wisdom. Such a distribution
of duties will be expedient and also just, for it is in accordance
with desert. Besides, the ruling class should be the owners of **7**
property, for they are citizens, and the citizens of a state should
be in good circumstances ; whereas mechanics or any other
class whose art excludes the art of virtue have no share in the
state. This follows from our first principle, for happiness cannot exist without virtue, and a city is not to be termed happy
in regard to a portion of the citizens, but in regard to them all [1].
And clearly property should be in their hands, since the hus- **8**
bandmen will of necessity be slaves or barbarians or Perioeci [2].

Of the classes enumerated there remain only the priests, and
the manner in which their office is to be regulated is obvious.
No husbandman or mechanic should be appointed to it ; for **9**
the Gods should receive honour from the citizens only. Now
since the body of the citizens is divided into two classes, the
warriors and the councillors ; and it is beseeming that the
worship of the Gods should be duly performed, and also a

---

[1] Cp. ii. 5. §§ 27, 28.　　　[2] Cp. infra, c. 10. §§ 13, 14.

VII. 9 rest provided in their service for those who from age have given up active life—to the old men of these two classes should be assigned the duties of the priesthood.

10 We have shown what are the necessary conditions, and what the parts of a state: husbandmen, craftsmen, and labourers of all kinds are necessary to the existence of states, but the parts of the state are the warriors and councillors. And these are distinguished severally from one another, the distinction being in some cases permanent, in others not.

10 It is no new or recent discovery of political philosophers
1329 b that the state ought to be divided into classes, and that the warriors should be separated from the husbandmen. The system has continued in Egypt and in Crete to this day, and was established, as tradition says, by a law of Sesostris in
2 Egypt and of Minos in Crete. The institution of common tables also appears to be of ancient date, being in Crete as
3 old as the reign of Minos, and in Italy far older. The Italian historians say that there was a certain Italus king of Oenotria, from whom the Oenotrians were called Italians, and who gave the name of Italy to the promontory of Europe lying between the Scylletic and Lametic Gulfs, which are distant from one
4 another only half a day's journey. They say that this Italus converted the Oenotrians from shepherds into husbandmen, and besides other laws which he gave them, was the founder of their common meals; even in our day some who are derived from him retain this institution and certain other laws of his.
5 On the side of Italy towards Tyrrhenia dwelt the Opici, who are now, as of old, called Ausones; and on the side towards Iapygia and the Ionian Gulf, in the district called Syrtis [1], the

---

[1] Retaining the reading of the MSS., which Bekker in his second edition has altered into Σιρῖτις, a conjecture of Goettling's.

Chones, who are likewise of Oenotrian race.   From this part VII. 10
of the world originally came the institution of common tables; [6]
the separation into castes [which was much older] from Egypt,
for the reign of Sesostris is of far greater antiquity than that
of Minos.   It is true indeed that these and many other things 7
have been invented several times over [1] in the course of ages,
or rather times without number; for necessity may be supposed
to have taught men the inventions which were absolutely required, and when these were provided, it was natural that other
things which would adorn and enrich life should grow up by
degrees.   And we may infer that in political institutions the
same rule holds.   Egypt [2] witnesses to the antiquity of all 8
things, for the Egyptians appear to be of all people the most
ancient; and they have laws and a regular constitution [existing
from time immemorial].   We should therefore make the best
use of what has been already discovered [3], and try to supply
defects.

I have already remarked that the land ought to belong to 9
those who possess arms and have a share in the government [4],
and that the husbandmen ought to be a class distinct from them;
and I have determined what should be the extent and nature
of the territory.   Let me proceed to discuss the distribution
of the land, and the character of the agricultural class; for
I do not think that property ought to be common, as some

---

[1] Cp. Plato, Laws, iii. 676; Aristotle, Metaph. xi. 8. 1074 b. 10; and
Pol. ii. 5. § 16 (note).

[2] Cp. Metaph. i. 1. § 16; Meteor. i. 14. 352 b. 19; Plato, Timaeus,
22 B; Laws, ii. 656, 657.

[3] Reading, with Bekker in his second edition, εὐρημένοις: which may
have been altered into εἰρημένοις from a confusion of εἴρηται πρότερον
in § 9 infra.

[4] Cp. supra, c. 9. §§ 5-7.

VII. 10 maintain[1], but only that by friendly consent there should be
1330 a a common use of it; and that no citizen should be in want of
subsistence.

As to common meals, there is a general agreement that a well-
10 ordered city should have them; and we will hereafter explain
what are our own reasons for taking this view. They ought,
however, to be open to all the citizens[2]. And yet it is not
easy for the poor to contribute the requisite sum out of their
private means, and to provide also for their household. The
expense of religious worship should likewise be a public charge.

11 The land must therefore be divided into two parts, one public
and the other private, and each part should be subdivided,
half of the public land being appropriated to the service of
the Gods, and the other half used to defray the cost of the
common meals; while of the private land, half should be
near the border, and the other near the city, so that each
citizen having two lots they may all of them have land in both
places; there is justice and fairness in such a division[3], and it
tends to inspire unanimity among the people in their border
12 wars. Where there is not this arrangement, some of them are
too ready to come to blows with their neighbours, while others
are so cautious that they quite lose the sense of honour.
Wherefore there is a law in some places which forbids those
who dwell near the border to take part in public deliberations
about wars with neighbours, on the ground that their interests
13 will pervert their judgment. For the reasons already mentioned,
then, the land should be divided in the manner described.

---

[1] Cp. ii. 5.   [2] Cp. ii. 9. § 31.

[3] Cp. Plato, Laws, v. 745, where the same proposal is found. Aristotle,
in Book ii. 6. § 15, condemns the division of lots which he here
adopts.

The very best thing of all would be that the husbandmen should **VII. 10**
be slaves, not all of the same race[1] and not spirited, for if
they have no spirit they will be better suited for their work,
and there will be no danger of their making a revolution. The
next best thing would be that they should be Perioeci of foreign
race[2], and of a like inferior nature; some of them should be 14
the slaves of individuals, and employed on the private estates
of men of property, the remainder should be the property of
the state and employed on the common land[3]. I will hereafter
explain what is the proper treatment of slaves, and why it is
expedient that liberty should be always held out to them as
the reward of their services.

We have already said that the city should be open to the **11**
land and to the sea[4], and to the whole country as far
as possible. In respect of the place itself our wish would
be to find a situation for it, fortunate in four things. The
first, health—this is a necessity: cities which lie towards the 2
east, and are blown upon by winds coming from the east,
are the healthiest; next in healthfulness are those which are
sheltered from the north wind, for they have a milder winter.
The site of the city should likewise be convenient both 1330 b
for political administration and for war. With a view to the 3
latter it should afford easy egress to the citizens, and
at the same time be inaccessible and difficult of capture to
enemies[5]. There should be a natural abundance of springs
and fountains in the town or, if there is a deficiency of them,
great reservoirs may be established for the collection of
rain-water, such as will not fail when the inhabitants are cut

---

[1] Cp. Plato, Laws, vi. 777. [2] Cp. c. 9. § 8.
[3] Cp. ii. 7. § 23. [4] Cp. c. 5. § 3.
[5] Repetition of c. 5. § 3.

VII. 11 off from the country by war.   Special care should be taken
4 of the health of the inhabitants, which will depend chiefly on
the healthiness of the locality and of the quarter to which they
are exposed, and secondly, on the use of pure water; this
latter point is by no means a secondary consideration.   For
the elements which we use most and oftenest for the support
of the body contribute most to health, and among these
5 are water and air.   Wherefore, in all wise states, if there is
a want of pure water, and the supply is not all equally good,
the drinking water ought to be separated from that which is
used for other purposes.

As to strongholds, what is suitable to different forms of
government varies: thus an acropolis is suited to an oligarchy
or a monarchy, but a plain to a democracy; neither to an
6 aristocracy, but rather a number of strong places.   The
arrangement of private houses is considered to be more
agreeable and generally more convenient if the streets are
regularly laid out after the modern fashion which Hippodamus [1] introduced; but for security in war the antiquated
mode of building, which made it difficult for strangers to get
out of a town and for assailants to find their way in, is
7 preferable.   A city should therefore adopt both plans of
building: it is possible to arrange the houses irregularly,
as husbandmen plant their vines in what are called ' clumps.'
The whole town should not be laid out in straight lines, but
only certain quarters and regions; thus security and beauty
will be combined.

8   As to walls, those who say [2] that cities making any
pretension to military virtue should not have them, are quite
out of date in their notions;   and they may see the cities

---

[1] Cp. ii. 8. § 1.   [2] Cp. Plato, Laws, vi. 778, 779.

which prided themselves on this fancy confuted by facts. **VII. 11**
True, there is little courage shown in seeking for safety 9
behind a rampart when an enemy is similar in character
and not much superior in number; but the superiority of the
besiegers may be and often is beyond the power of men to
resist, and too much for the valour of a few; and if they
are to be saved and to escape defeat and outrage, the strongest 1331 a
wall will be the best defence of the warrior, more especially
now that catapults and siege engines have been brought
to such perfection. To have no walls would be as foolish 10
as to choose a site for a town in an exposed country, and to
level the heights; or as if an individual were to leave his
house unwalled, lest the inmates should become cowards.
Nor must we forget that those who have their cities surrounded 11
by walls may either take advantage of them or not, but cities
which are unwalled have no choice.

If our conclusions are just, not only should cities have
walls, but care should be taken to make them ornamental,
as well as useful for warlike purposes, and adapted to resist
modern inventions. For as the assailants of a city do 12
all they can to gain an advantage, so the defenders should
make use of any means of defence which have been already
discovered, and should devise and invent others, for when
men are well prepared no enemy even thinks of attacking
them.

As the walls are to be divided by guardhouses and towers 13
built at suitable intervals, and the body of citizens must
be distributed at common tables, the idea will naturally
occur that we should establish some of the common tables
in the guardhouses. The arrangement might be as follows: 2
the principal common tables of the magistrates will occupy

VII. 12 a suitable place, and there also will be the buildings appropriated to religious worship except in the case of those rites which the law or the Pythian oracle has restricted to a 3 special locality[1]. The site should be a spot seen far and wide, which gives due elevation to virtue and towers over the neighbourhood. Near this spot should be established an agora, such as that which the Thessalians call the 'freemen's 4 agora'; from this all trade should be excluded, and no mechanic, husbandman, or any such person allowed to enter, unless he be summoned by the magistrates. It would be a charming use of the place, if the gymnastic exercises of 5 the elder men were performed there. For [2] in this noble practice different ages should be separated[2], and some of the magistrates should stay with the boys, while the grown-up men remain with the magistrates [i. e. in the freeman's agora]; for the presence of the magistrates is the best mode 1331 b of inspiring true modesty and ingenuous fear. There should 6 also be a traders' agora, distinct and apart from the other, in a situation which is convenient for the reception of goods both by sea and land.

But in speaking of the magistrates we must not forget another section of the citizens, viz. the priests, for whom public tables should likewise be provided in their proper 7 place near the temples. The magistrates who deal with contracts, indictments, summonses, and the like, and those who have the care of the agora and of the city respectively, ought to be established near the agora and in some public place of meeting; the neighbourhood of the traders' agora will be a suitable spot; the upper agora we devote to

---

[1] Cp. Plato, Laws, v. 738; vi. 759, 778; viii. 848.

[2] Or 'this institution should be divided according to ages.'

the life of leisure, the other is intended for the necessities of VII. 12
trade.

The same order should prevail[1] in the country, for there 8
too the magistrates, called by some 'Inspectors of Forests,'
and by others 'Wardens of the Country,' must have guardhouses and common tables while they are on duty ; temples
should also be scattered throughout the country, dedicated,
some to Gods, and some to heroes.

But it would be a waste of time for us to linger over 9
details like these. The difficulty is not in imagining but in
carrying them out. We may talk about them as much as we
like, but the execution of them will depend upon fortune.
Wherefore let us say no more about these matters for the present.

Returning to the constitution itself, let us seek to 10
determine out of what, and what sort of, elements the state
which is to be happy and well-governed should be composed.
There are two things in which all well-being consists ; one of 2
them is the choice of a right end and aim of action, and
the other the discovery of the actions which are means
towards it ; for the means and the end may agree or disagree.
Sometimes the right end is set before men, but in practice they
fail to attain it ; in other cases they are successful in all the
means, but they propose to themselves a bad end, and sometimes they fail in both. Take, for example, the art of medicine ;
physicians do not always understand the nature of health, and
also the means which they use may not effect the desired end.
In all arts and sciences both the end and the means should be
equally within our control.

The happiness and well-being which all men manifestly 3
desire, some have the power of attaining, but to others, from

[1] Reading νενεμῆσθαι with Bekker's first edition.

VII. 13 some accident or defect of nature, the attainment of them is
1332 a not granted; for a good life requires a supply of external
goods, in a less degree when men are in a good state, in
4 a greater degree when they are in a lower state. Others
again, who possess the condition of happiness, go utterly
wrong from the first in the pursuit of it. But since our
object is to discover the best form of government, that,
namely, under which a city will be best governed, and since
the city is best governed which has the greatest opportunity
of obtaining happiness, it is evident that we must clearly
ascertain the nature of happiness.

5 We have said in the Ethics [1], if the arguments there adduced
are of any value, that happiness is the realization and perfect
exercise of virtue, and this not conditional, but absolute.
6 And I used the term 'conditional' to express that which is
indispensable, and 'absolute' to express that which is good
in itself. Take the case of just actions; just punishments
and chastisements do indeed spring from a good principle, but
they are good only because we cannot do without them—
it would be better that neither individuals nor states should
need anything of the sort—but actions which aim at honour
7 and advantage are absolutely the best. The conditional
action is only the choice [2] of a lesser evil; whereas these are
the foundation and creation of good. A good man may
make the best even of poverty and disease, and the other ills
of life; but he can only attain happiness under the opposite
conditions [3]. As we have already said in the Ethics [4],

---

[1] Cp. N. Eth. i. 7. § 15; x. 6. § 2; and cp. c. 8. § 5, supra.
[2] Retaining the MSS. reading αἵρεσις with Bekker's first edition.
[3] N. Eth. i. 10. § 12–14.
[4] N. Eth. iii. 4. §§ 4, 5; E. E. vii. 15. § 4; M. M. ii. 9. § 3.

the good man is he to whom, because he is virtuous, the **VII. 13** absolute good is his good. It is also plain that his use 8 of other goods must be virtuous and in the absolute sense good. This makes men fancy that external goods are the cause of happiness, yet we might as well say that a brilliant performance on the lyre was to be attributed to the instrument and not to the skill of the performer.

It follows then from what has been said that some things the legislator must find ready to his hand in a state, others he must provide. And therefore we can only say: May 9 our state be constituted in such a manner as to be blessed with the goods of which fortune disposes (for we acknowledge her power): whereas virtue and goodness in the state are not a matter of chance but the result of knowledge and purpose. A city can be virtuous only when the citizens who have a share in the government are virtuous, and in our state all the citizens share in the government; let us then enquire how a man becomes virtuous. For even if we could 10 suppose all the citizens to be virtuous, and not each of them, yet the latter would be better, for in the virtue of each the virtue of all is involved.

There are three things which make men good and virtuous: these are nature, habit, reason[1]. In the first place, every one 11 must be born a man and not some other animal; in the second place, he must have a certain character, both of body and soul. But some qualities there is no use in having at birth, for they are altered by habit, and there are some 1332 b gifts of nature which may be turned by habit to good or bad. Most animals lead a life of nature, although in lesser 12 particulars some are influenced by habit as well. Man

[1] Cp. N. Eth. x. 9. § 6.

VII. 13 has reason, in addition, and man only [1]. Wherefore nature,
habit, reason must be in harmony with one another [for they
do not always agree]; men do many things against habit and
13 nature, if reason persuades them that they ought. We have
already determined what natures are likely to be most easily
moulded by the hands of the legislator [2]. All else is the work
of education; we learn some things by habit and some by
instruction.

14   Since every political society is composed of rulers and
subjects, let us consider whether the relations of one to
the other should interchange or be permanent [3]. For the
education of the citizens will necessarily vary with the answer
2 given to this question. Now, if some men excelled others
in the same degree in which gods and heroes are supposed to
excel mankind in general, having in the first place a great
advantage even in their bodies, and secondly in their minds,
so that the superiority of the governors [4] over their subjects
was patent and undisputed [4], it would clearly be better that
once for all the one class should rule and the others serve [5].
3 But since this is unattainable, and kings have no marked
superiority over their subjects, such as Scylax affirms to be
found among the Indians, it is obviously necessary on many
grounds that all the citizens alike should take their turn of
governing and being governed. Equality consists in the same
treatment of similar persons, and no government can stand
4 which is not founded upon justice. For [if the government
be unjust] every one in the country unites with the governed

---

[1] Cp. i. 2. § 10.   [2] Cp. supra, c. 7. § 4.   [3] Cp. iii. 6. § 9.
[4] Or, taking τοῖς ἀρχομένοις with φανεράν, ' was undisputed and patent
to their subjects.'
[5] Cp. i. 5. § 8; iii. 13. § 13.

in the desire to have a revolution, and it is an impossibility that **VII. 14**
the members of the government can be so numerous as to be
stronger than all their enemies put together.   Yet that governors
should excel their subjects is undeniable.   How all this is to
be effected, and in what way they will respectively share in
the government, the legislator has to consider.   The subject
has been already mentioned [1].   Nature herself has given the 5
principle of choice when she made a difference between old
and young (though they are really the same in kind), of whom
she fitted the one to govern and the others to be governed.
No one takes offence at being governed when he is young,
nor does he think himself better than his governors, especially if he will enjoy the same privilege when he reaches the
required age.

We conclude that from one point of view governors 6
and governed are identical, and from another different.   And
therefore their education must be the same and also different. 1333 a
For he who would learn to command well must, as men say,
first of all learn to obey [2].   As I observed in the first
part of this treatise, there is one rule which is for the sake
of the rulers and another rule which is for the sake of the
ruled [3]; the former is a despotic, the latter a free government. 7
Some commands differ not in the thing commanded, but
in the intention with which they are imposed.   Wherefore,
many apparently menial offices are an honour to the free
youth by whom they are performed; for actions do not differ
as honourable or dishonourable in themselves so much as in the
end and intention of them.   But since we say [4] that the virtue 8
of the citizen and ruler is the same as that of the good man,

---

[1] Cp. c. 9. § 5.   [2] Cp. iii. 4. § 14.
[3] Cp. iii. 6. § 6.   [4] Cp. iii. 4 and 5. § 10.

VII. 14 and that the same person must first be a subject and then a ruler, the legislator has to see that they become good men, and by what means this may be accomplished, and what is the end of the perfect life.

9 Now the soul of man is divided into two parts, one of which has reason in itself, and the other, not having reason in itself, is able to obey reason[1]. And we call a man good because he has the virtues of these two parts. In which of them the end is more likely to be found is no 10 matter of doubt to those who adopt our division; for in the world both of nature and of art the inferior always exists for the sake of the better or superior, and the better or superior is that which has reason. The reason too, in our ordinary way of speaking, is divided into two parts, for 11 there is a practical and a speculative reason[2], and there must be a corresponding division of actions; the actions of the naturally better principle are to be preferred by those who have it in their power to attain to both or to all, for that is always to every one the most eligible which is the highest 12 attainable by him. The whole of life is further divided into two parts, business and leisure[3], war and peace, and all actions into those which are necessary and useful, and those 13 which are honourable. And the preference given to one or the other class of actions must necessarily be like the preference given to one or other part of the soul and its actions over the other; there must be war for the sake of peace, business for the sake of leisure, things useful and necessary for the sake of things honourable. All these

[1] Cp. N. Eth. i. 13. §§ 18, 19.
[2] Cp. N. Eth. vi. 1. § 5; 11. § 4.
[3] N. Eth. x. 7. § 6.

points the statesman should keep in view when he frames his **VII. 14**
laws; he should consider the parts of the soul and their
functions, and above all the better and the end; he should 14
also remember the diversities of human lives and actions.
For men must engage in business and go to war, but leisure 1333 b
and peace are better; they must do what is necessary and
useful, but what is honourable is better. In such principles
children and persons of every age which requires education
should be trained. Whereas even the Hellenes of the 15
present day, who are reputed to be best governed, and the
legislators who gave them their constitutions, do not appear
to have framed their governments with a regard to the best
end, or to have given them laws and education with a view to
all the virtues, but in a vulgar spirit have fallen back on those
which promised to be more useful and profitable. Many 16
modern writers have taken a similar view : they commend the
Lacedaemonian constitution, and praise the legislator for
making conquest and war his sole aim [1], a doctrine which
may be refuted by argument and has long ago been refuted by
facts. For most men desire empire in the hope of accumu- 17
lating the goods of fortune ; and on this ground Thibron and
all those who have written about the Lacedaemonian constitution have praised their legislator, because the Lacedaemonians, by a training in hardships, gained great power.
But surely they are not a happy people now that their empire 18
has passed away, nor was their legislator right. How
ridiculous is the result, if, while they are continuing in the
observances of his laws and no one interferes with them
they have lost the better part of life. These writers further 19

---

[1] Plato, Laws, i. 628, 638.

VII. 14 err about the sort of government which the legislator should
approve, for the government of freemen is noble, and implies
more virtue than despotic government [1].   Neither is a city to
be deemed happy or a legislator to be praised because he
trains his citizens to conquer and obtain dominion over their
20 neighbours, for there is great evil in this.   On a similar
principle any citizen who could, would obviously try to obtain
the power in his own state—the crime which the Lacedaemonians accused king Pausanias of attempting [2], although
he had so great honour already.   No such principle and
no law having this object is either statesmanlike or useful or
21 right.   For the same things are best both for individuals and
for states, and these are the things which the legislator ought
to implant in the minds of his citizens.   Neither should men
study war with a view to the enslavement of those who
do not deserve to be enslaved; but first of all they should
provide against their own enslavement, and in the second
1334 a place obtain empire for the good of the governed, and not for
the sake of exercising a general despotism, and in the third
place they should seek to be masters only over those
22 who deserve to be slaves.   Facts, as well as arguments, prove
that the legislator should direct all his military and other
measures to the provision of leisure and the establishment of
peace.   For most of these military states are safe only while
they are at war [3], but fall when they have acquired their
empire; like unused iron they lose their edge in time of peace.
And for this the legislator is to blame, he never having
taught them how to lead the life of peace.

15   Since the end of individuals and of states is the same, the

[1] Cp. i. 5. § 2.   [2] Cp. v. 1. § 10; 7. § 4.
[3] Cp. ii. 9. § 34.

end of the best man and of the best state must also be **VII. 15**
the same; it is therefore evident that there ought to exist in
both of them the virtues of leisure; for peace, as has been
often repeated, is the end of war, and leisure of toil.   But **2**
leisure and cultivation may be promoted, not only by those
virtues which are practised in leisure, but also by some
of those which are useful to business [1].   For many necessaries of life have to be supplied before we can have leisure.
Therefore a city must be temperate and brave, and able
to endure: for truly, as the proverb says, 'There is no
leisure for slaves,' and those who cannot face danger like men
are the slaves of any invader.   Courage and endurance **3**
are required for business and intellectual virtue for leisure,
temperance and justice for both, more especially in times
of peace and leisure, for war compels men to be just and
temperate, whereas the enjoyment of good fortune and
the leisure which comes with peace tends to make them
insolent.   Those, then, who seem to be the best off and to be **4**
in the possession of every good, have special need of justice
and temperance—for example, those (if such there be, as the
poets say) who dwell in the Islands of the Blest; they above
all will need philosophy and temperance and justice, and all
the more the more leisure they have, living in the midst
of abundance.   There is no difficulty in seeing why the state **5**
that would be happy and good ought to have these virtues.
If it be disgraceful in men not to be able to use the goods of
life, it is peculiarly disgraceful not to be able to use them in
time of peace—to show excellent qualities in action and war,
and when they have peace and leisure to be no better than slaves.

[1] i. e. 'not only by some of the speculative but also by some of the
practical virtues.'

VII. 15 Wherefore we should not practise virtue after the manner of
6 the Lacedaemonians[1].   For they, while agreeing with other
1334 b men in their conception of the highest goods, differ from the
rest of mankind in thinking that they are to be obtained by the
practice of a single virtue.   And since these goods and the
enjoyment of them are clearly greater than the enjoyment
derived from the virtues of which they are the end, we must
now consider how and by what means they are to be
attained.

7   We have already determined that nature and habit and reason
are required[2], and what should be the character of the citizens
has also been defined by us.   But we have still to consider
whether the training of early life is to be that of reason or
habit, for these two must accord, and when in accord they
will then form the best of harmonies.   Reason may make
mistakes and fail in attaining the highest ideal of life, [3] and
8 there may be a like evil influence of habit[3].   Thus much is
clear in the first place, that, as in all other things, generation
starts from a beginning, and that the ends of some beginnings
are related to another end.   Now, in men reason and mind are
the end towards which nature strives, so that the generation
and moral discipline of the citizens ought to be ordered with
9 a view to them.   In the second place, as the soul and body
are two, we see also that there are two parts of the soul, the
rational and the irrational[4], and two corresponding states —
reason and appetite.   And as the body is prior in order of
generation to the soul, so the irrational is prior to the rational.

---

[1] Cp. ii. 9. § 34.   [2] Cp. 13 § 12.

[3] Or, 'and yet a man may be trained by habit as if the reason had not
so erred.'

[4] Cp. N. Eth. i. 13. § 9 ff.

The proof is that anger and will and desire are implanted in **VII. 15** children from their very birth, but reason and understanding ¹⁰ are developed as they grow older. Wherefore, the care of the body ought to precede that of the soul, and the training of the appetitive part should follow : none the less our care of it must be for the sake of the reason, and our care of the body for the sake of the soul [1].

Since the legislator should begin by considering how the **16** frames of the children whom he is rearing may be as good as possible, his first care will be about marriage—at what age should his citizens marry, and who are fit to marry ?   In **2** legislating on this subject he ought to consider the persons and their relative ages, that there may be no disproportion in them, and that they may not differ in their bodily powers, as will be the case if the man is still able to beget children while the woman is unable to bear them, or the woman able to bear while the man is unable to beget, for from these causes arise quarrels and differences between married persons.   Secondly, he must consider the time at which the children will succeed to their parents ; there ought not to be too great an interval of age, for **3** then the parents will be too old to derive any pleasure from their affection, or to be of any use to them.   Nor ought they **1335 a** to be too nearly of an age ; to youthful marriages there are many objections—the children will be wanting in respect to their parents, who will seem to be their contemporaries, and disputes will arise in the management of the household.   Thirdly, and **4** this is the point from which we digressed, the legislator must mould to his will the frames of newly-born children.   Almost all these objects may be secured by attention to one point. Since the time of generation is commonly limited within the **5**

[1] Cp. Plato, Rep. iii. 410.

VII. 16 age of seventy years in the case of a man, and of fifty in the
case of a woman, the commencement of the union should con-
6 form to these periods.   The union of male and female when
too young is bad for the procreation of children ; in all other
animals the offspring of the young are small and ill-developed,
and generally of the female sex, and therefore also in man, as
is proved by the fact that in those cities in which men and
women are accustomed to marry young, the people are small
7 and weak ; in childbirth also younger women suffer more,
and more of them die ; some persons say that this was the
meaning of the response once given to the Troezenians—
['Shear not the young field ']—the oracle really meant that
many died because they married too young; it had nothing to
8 do with the ingathering of the harvest.   It also conduces to
temperance not to marry too soon ; for women who marry
early are apt to be wanton ; and in men too the bodily frame
is stunted if they marry while they are growing (for there is
9 a time when the growth of the body ceases).   Women should
marry when they are about eighteen years of age, and men at
seven-and-thirty [1] ; then they are in the prime of life, and the
10 decline in the powers of both will coincide.   Further, the
children, if their birth takes place at the time that may
reasonably be expected, will succeed in their prime, when the
fathers are already in the decline of life, and have nearly
reached their term of three-score years and ten.

Thus much of the age proper for marriage : the season of
the year should also be considered ; according to our present
custom, people generally limit marriage to the season of winter,
11 and they are right.   The precepts of physicians and natural
philosophers about generation should also be studied by the

---

[1] Omitting ἢ μικρόν.

parents themselves; the physicians give good advice about **VII. 16** the right age of the body, and the natural philosophers about the winds; of which they prefer the north to the south.   1335 b

What constitution in the parent is most advantageous to 12 the offspring is a subject which we will hereafter consider when we speak of the education of children, and we will only make a few general remarks at present.   The temperament of an athlete is not suited to the life of a citizen, or to health, or to the procreation of children, any more than the valetudinarian or exhausted constitution, but one which is in a mean between them.   A man's constitution should be inured to labour, but 13 not to labour which is excessive or of one sort only, such as is practised by athletes; he should be capable of all the actions of a freeman.   These remarks apply equally to both parents.

Women who are with child should be careful of themselves; 14 they should take exercise and have a nourishing diet.   The first of these prescriptions the legislator will easily carry into effect by requiring that they shall take a walk daily to some temple, where they can worship the gods who preside over birth [1]. Their minds, however, unlike their bodies, they ought to keep unexercised, for the offspring derive their natures from their mothers as plants do from the earth.

As to the exposure and rearing of children, let there be a 15 law that no deformed child shall live, but where there are too many (for in our state population has a limit), when couples have children in excess, and the state of feeling is averse to the exposure of offspring, let abortion be procured before sense and life have begun; what may or may not be lawfully done in these cases depends on the question of life and sensation.

And now, having determined at what ages men and women 16

[1] Cp. Plato, Laws, vii. 789.

VII. 16 are to begin their union, let us also determine how long they shall continue to beget and bear offspring for the state[1]; men who are too old, like men who are too young, produce children who are defective in body and mind; the children of very old **17** men are weakly. The limit, then, should be the age which is the prime of their intelligence, and this in most persons, according to the notion of some poets who measure life by periods of seven years, is about fifty[2]; at four or five years later, they should cease from having families; and from that time forward only cohabit with one another for the sake of health, or for some similar reason.

18 As to adultery, let it be held disgraceful for any man or woman to be unfaithful when they are married, and called **1336 a** husband and wife. If during the time of bearing children anything of the sort occur, let the guilty person be punished with a loss of privileges in proportion to the offence[3].

17 After the children have been born, the manner of rearing them may be supposed to have a great effect on their bodily strength. It would appear from the example of animals, and of those nations who desire to create the military habit, that the food which has most milk in it is best suited to human beings; but the less wine the better, if they would escape disease. **2** Also all the motions to which children can be subjected at their early age are very useful. But in order to preserve their tender limbs from distortion, some nations have had recourse to mechanical appliances which straighten their bodies. To accustom children to the cold from their earliest years is also an excellent practice, which greatly conduces to health, and **3** hardens them for military service. Hence many barbarians

---

[1] λειτουργεῖν.   [2] Cp. Solon, Fragm. 25 Bergk.

[3] Cp. Laws, viii. 841.

have a custom of plunging their children at birth into a cold **VII. 17** stream; others, like the Celts, clothe them in a light wrapper only. For human nature should be early habituated to endure all which by habit it can be made to endure; but the process must be gradual. And children, from their natural warmth, may be easily trained to bear cold. Such care should attend them in the first stage of life.

The next period lasts to the age of five; during this no **4** demand should be made upon the child for study or labour, lest its growth be impeded; and there should be sufficient motion to prevent the limbs from being inactive. This can be secured, among other ways, by amusement, but the amusement should not be vulgar or tiring or riotous. The Directors of Education, as **5** they are termed, should be careful what tales or stories the children hear [1], for the sports of children are designed to prepare the way for the business of later life, and should be for the most part imitations of the occupations which they will hereafter pursue in earnest [2]. Those are wrong who [like Plato] in the Laws **6** attempt to check the loud crying and screaming of children, for these contribute towards their growth, and, in a manner, exercise their bodies [3]. Straining the voice has an effect similar to that produced by the retention of the breath in violent exertions. Besides other duties, the Directors of **7** Education should have an eye to their bringing up, and should take care that they are left as little as possible with slaves. For until they are seven years old they must live at home; **1336 b** and therefore, even at this early age, all that is mean and low should be banished from their sight and hearing. Indeed, **8** there is nothing which the legislator should be more careful to

[1] Plato, Rep. ii. 377 ff.   [2] Plato, Laws, i. 643; vii. 799.
[3] Plato, Laws, vii. 792.

VII. 17 drive away than indecency of speech ; for the light utterance
of shameful words is akin to shameful actions. The young
especially should never be allowed to repeat or hear anything of
9 the sort. A freeman who is found saying or doing what is
forbidden, if he be too young as yet to have the privilege of
a place at the public table, should be disgraced and beaten, and
an elder person degraded as his slavish conduct deserves. And
since we do not allow improper language, clearly we should
10 also banish pictures or tales which are indecent. Let the
rulers take care that there be no image or picture representing
unseemly actions, except in the temples of those Gods at
whose festivals the law permits even ribaldry, and whom the
law also permits to be worshipped by persons of mature age
on behalf of themselves, their children, and their wives. But
11 the legislator should not allow youth to be hearers of satirical
Iambic verses or spectators of comedy until they are of an age
to sit at the public tables and to drink strong wine ; by that
time education will have armed them against the evil influences
of such representations.

12 . We have made these remarks in a cursory manner—they
are enough for the present occasion; but hereafter [1] we will
return to the subject and after a fuller discussion determine
whether such liberty should or should not be granted, and in
13 what way granted, if at all. Theodorus, the tragic actor, was
quite right in saying that he would not allow any other actor,
not even if he were quite second-rate, to enter before himself,
because the spectators grew fond of the voices which they first
heard. And the same principle of association applies universally
to things as well as persons, for we always like best whatever
14 comes first. And therefore youth should be kept strangers to

---

[1] Unfulfilled promise (?), but cp. viii. **5.** § **21.**

all that is bad, and especially to things which suggest vice or **VII. 17**
hate. When the five years have passed away, during the two
following years they must look on at the pursuits which they
are hereafter to learn. There are two periods of life into 15
which education has to be divided—from seven to the age of
puberty, and onwards to the age of one-and-twenty. [The 1337 a
poets] who divide ages by sevens[1] are not always right[2] : we
should rather adhere to the divisions actually made by nature ;
for the deficiencies of nature are what art and education seek
to fill up.

Let us then first enquire if any regulations are to be laid 16
down about children, and secondly, whether the care of them
should be the concern of the state or of private individuals—
which latter is in our own day the common custom—and in the
third place, what these regulations should be.

[1] Cp. supra, c. 16. § 17.
[2] Reading οὐ καλῶς, with the MSS. and Bekker's first edition :
or, reading οὐ κακῶς, a conjecture of Muretus, which Bekker has adopted
in his second edition, 'are in the main right ; but we should also observe.
etc.'

BOOK VIII

VIII. 1   No one will doubt that the legislator should direct his attention above all to the education of youth, or that the **2** neglect of education does harm to states. The citizen should be moulded to suit the form of government under which he lives [1]. For each government has a peculiar character which originally formed and which continues to preserve it. The character of democracy creates democracy, and the character of oligarchy creates oligarchy; and always the better the character, the better the government.

Now for the exercise of any faculty or art a previous training and habituation are required; clearly therefore **3** for the practice of virtue. And since the whole city has one end, it is manifest that education should be one and the same for all, and that it should be public, and not private— not as at present, when every one looks after his own children separately, and gives them separate instruction of the sort which he thinks best; the training in things which are of **4** common interest should be the same for all. Neither must we suppose that any one of the citizens belongs to himself, for they all belong to the state, and are each of them a part of the state, and the care of each part is inseparable from the care of the whole. In this particular the Lacedaemonians are to be praised, for they take the greatest pains about their children, and make education the business of the state [2].

2   That education should be regulated by law and should be an affair of state is not to be denied, but what should

[1] Cp. v. 9. §§ 11–16.   [2] Cp. N. Eth. x. 9. § 13.

be the character of this public education, and how young VIII. 2
persons should be educated, are questions which remain to be
considered. For mankind are by no means agreed about the
things to be taught, whether we look to virtue or the best life.
Neither is it clear whether education is more concerned
with intellectual or with moral virtue. The existing prac- 2
tice is perplexing; no one knows on what principle we
should proceed—should the useful in life, or should virtue,
or should the higher knowledge, be the aim of our training;
all three opinions have been entertained. Again, about the 1337 b
means there is no agreement; for different persons, starting with different ideas about the nature of virtue, naturally
disagree about the practice of it. There can be no doubt 3
that children should be taught those useful things which
are really necessary, but not all things; for occupations
are divided into liberal and illiberal; and to young children
should be imparted only such kinds of knowledge as will
be useful to them without vulgarizing them. And any 4
occupation, art, or science, which makes the body or soul or
mind of the freeman less fit for the practice or exercise
of virtue, is vulgar; wherefore we call those arts vulgar 5
which tend to deform the body, and likewise all paid employments, for they absorb and degrade the mind. There are
also some liberal arts quite proper for a freeman to acquire,
but only in a certain degree, and if he attend to them
too closely, in order to attain perfection in them, the same
evil effects will follow. The object also which a man 6
sets before him makes a great difference; if he does or
learns anything for his own sake[1] or for the sake of his
friends, or with a view to excellence, the action will not

[1] Cp. iii. 4. § 13.

VIII. 2 appear illiberal; but if done for the sake of others, the very same action will be thought menial and servile. The received subjects of instruction, as I have already remarked [1], are partly of a liberal and partly of an illiberal character.

3 The customary branches of education are in number four; they are—(1) reading and writing, (2) gymnastic exercises, (3) music, to which is sometimes added (4) drawing. Of these, reading and writing and drawing are regarded as useful for the purposes of life in a variety of ways, and gymnastic exercises are thought to infuse courage. Concerning music **2** a doubt may be raised—in our own day most men cultivate it for the sake of pleasure, but originally it was included in education, because nature herself, as has been often said, requires that we should be able not only to work well, but to use leisure well; for, as I must repeat once and again [2], the **3** first principle of all action is leisure. Both are required, but leisure is better than occupation; and therefore the question must be asked in good earnest, what ought we to do when at leisure? Clearly we ought not to be amusing ourselves, for then amusement would be the end of life. But if this is **4** inconceivable, and yet amid serious occupations amusement is needed more than at other times (for he who is hard at work has need of relaxation, and amusement gives relaxation, whereas occupation is always accompanied with exertion and effort), at suitable times we should introduce amusements, and they should be our medicines, for the emotion which they create in the soul is a relaxation, and 1338 a from the pleasure we obtain rest. Leisure of itself gives pleasure and happiness and enjoyment of life, which are **5** experienced, not by the busy man, but by those who have

---

[1] § 3 supra.   [2] As in vii. 15. §§ 1, 2, and N. Eth. x. 6.

leisure. For he who is occupied has in view some end which **VIII. 3**
he has not attained ; but happiness is an end which all men
deem to be accompanied with pleasure and not with pain.
This pleasure, however, is regarded differently by different
persons, and varies according to the habit of individuals ; the
pleasure of the best man is the best, and springs from
the noblest sources. It is clear, then, that there are branches **6**
of learning and education which we must study with a view
to the enjoyment of leisure, and these are to be valued
for their own sake ; whereas those kinds of knowledge which
are useful in business are to be deemed necessary, and exist
for the sake of other things. And therefore our fathers **7**
admitted music into education, not on the ground either of its
necessity or utility, for it is not necessary, nor indeed useful
in the same manner as reading and writing, which are useful
in money-making, in the management of a household, in the
acquisition of knowledge and in political life, nor like drawing,
useful for a more correct judgment of the works of artists,
nor again like gymnastic, which gives health and strength ;
for neither of these is to be gained from music. There
remains, then, the use of music for intellectual enjoyment in
leisure ; which appears to have been the reason of its introduction, this being one of the ways in which it is thought that
a freeman should pass his leisure ; as Homer says—

' How good is it to invite men to the pleasant feast[1],'
and afterwards he speaks of others whom he describes as
inviting

' The bard who would delight them all[2].'

[1] Or, ' to invite **Thalia** to the feast,' an interpretation of the passage
possibly intended by **Aristotle**, though of course not the original
meaning. [2] Od. xvii. 385.

VIII. 3 And in another place Odysseus says there is no better way of passing life than when

> 'Men's hearts are merry and the banqueters in the hall, sitting in order, hear the voice of the minstrel[1].'

10 It is evident, then, that there is a sort of education in which parents should train their sons, not as being useful or necessary, but because it is liberal or noble. Whether this is of one kind only, or of more than one, and if so, what they are, and how they are to be imparted, must hereafter be 11 determined. Thus much we are now in a position to say that the ancients witness to us; for their opinion may be gathered from the fact that music is one of the received and traditional branches of education. Further, it is clear that children should be instructed in some useful things—for example, in reading and writing—not only for their usefulness, but also because many other sorts of knowledge are acquired through 12 them. With a like view they may be taught drawing, not to prevent their making mistakes in their own purchases, or in order that they may not be imposed upon in the buying 1338 b or selling of articles, but rather because it makes them judges of the beauty of the human form. To be always seeking after the useful does not become free and exalted 13 souls[2]. Now it is clear that in education habit must go before reason, and the body before the mind; and therefore boys should be handed over to the trainer, who creates in them the proper habit of body, and to the wrestling-master, who teaches them their exercises.

4 Of those states which in our own day seem to take the greatest care of children, some aim at producing in them an athletic habit, but they only injure their forms and stunt their growth.

---

[1] Od. ix. 7.   [2] Cp. Plato, Rep. vii. 525 ff.

Although the Lacedaemonians have not fallen into this **VIII. 4**
mistake, yet they brutalize their children by laborious exercises
which they think will make them courageous.   But in truth, **2**
as we have often repeated, education should not be exclusively
directed to this or to any other single end.   And even if we
suppose the Lacedaemonians to be right in their end, they do
not attain it.   For among barbarians and among animals
courage is found associated, not with the greatest ferocity, but
with a gentle and lion-like temper.   There are many races **3**
who are ready enough to kill and eat men, such as the
Achaeans and Heniochi, who both live about the Black Sea [1];
and there are other inland tribes, as bad or worse, who all live
by plunder, but have no courage.   It is notorious that the **4**
Lacedaemonians, while they were themselves assiduous
in their laborious drill, were superior to others, but now they
are beaten both in war and gymnastic exercises.   For their
ancient superiority did not depend on their mode of training
their youth, but only on the circumstance that they trained
them at a time when others did not.   Hence we may **5**
infer that what is noble, not what is brutal, should have the
first place ; no wolf or other wild animal will face a really
noble danger ; such dangers are for the brave man [2].   And **6**
parents who devote their children to gymnastics while
they neglect their necessary education, in reality vulgarize
them ; for they make them useful to the state in one quality
only, and even in this the argument proves them to be inferior
to others.   We should judge the Lacedaemonians not from **7**
what they have been, but from what they are ; for now they
have rivals who compete with their education ; formerly they
had none.

[1] Cp. N. Eth. vii. 5. § 2.   [2] Cp. N. Eth. iii. 6. § 8.

VIII. 4 It is an admitted principle that gymnastic exercises should be employed in education, and that for children they should be of a lighter kind, avoiding severe regimen or painful toil, **8** lest the growth of the body be impaired. The evil of excessive training in early years is strikingly proved by **1339 a** the example of the Olympic victors; for not more than two or three of them have gained a prize both as boys and as men; their early training and severe gymnastic exercises exhausted **9** their constitutions. When boyhood is over, three years should be spent in other studies; the period of life which follows may then be devoted to hard exercise and strict regimen. Men ought not to labour at the same time with their minds and with their bodies[1]; for the two kinds of labour are opposed to one another—the labour of the body impedes the mind, and the labour of the mind the body.

5 Concerning music there are some questions which we have already raised; these we may now resume and carry further; and our remarks will serve as a prelude to this or any other **2** discussion of the subject. It is not easy to determine the nature of music, or why any one should have a knowledge of it. Shall we say, for the sake of amusement and relaxation, like sleep or drinking, which are not good in themselves, but are pleasant, and at the same time 'make care to cease,' **3** as Euripides[2] says? And therefore men rank them with music, and make use of all three—sleep[3], drinking, music— to which some add dancing. Or shall we argue that music conduces to virtue, on the ground that it can form our minds and habituate us to true pleasures as our bodies are made by

---

[1] Cp. Plato, Rep. vii. 537 B.   [2] Bacchae, 380.

[3] Reading (with Bekker's 2nd ed.) ὕπνῳ, a correction which seems necessary, and is suggested by ὕπνου καὶ μέθης above.

gymnastic to be of a certain character? Or shall we say that **VIII. 5**
it contributes to the enjoyment of leisure and mental cultiva- **4**
tion, which is a third alternative? Now obviously youth are
not to be instructed with a view to their amusement, for learning is no pleasure, but is accompanied with pain. Neither is
intellectual enjoyment suitable to boys of that age, for it is
the end, and that which is imperfect cannot attain the perfect
or end. But perhaps it may be said that boys learn music for **5**
the sake of the amusement which they will have when they
are grown up. If so, why should they learn themselves, and
not, like the Persian and Median kings, enjoy the pleasure
and instruction which is derived from hearing others? (for **6**
surely skilled persons who have made music the business
and profession of their lives will be better performers than
those who practise only to learn). If they must learn music,
on the same principle they should learn cookery, which
is absurd. And even granting that music may form the **7**
character, the objection still holds: why should we learn
ourselves? Why cannot we attain true pleasure and form **1339 b**
a correct judgment from hearing others, like the Lacedaemonians?—for they, without learning music, nevertheless can
correctly judge, as they say, of good and bad melodies. Or **8**
again, if music should be used to promote cheerfulness
and refined intellectual enjoyment, the objection still remains—
why should we learn ourselves instead of enjoying the
performances of others? We may illustrate what we are
saying by our conception of the Gods; for in the poets Zeus
does not himself sing or play on the lyre. Nay, we call
professional performers vulgar; no freeman would play or
sing unless he were intoxicated or in jest. But these matters **9**
may be left for the present.

VIII. 5   The first question is whether music is or is not to be a part
of education.   Of the three things mentioned in our discussion, which is it?—Education or amusement or intellectual
enjoyment, for it may be reckoned under all three, and seems
10 to share in the nature of all of them.   Amusement is for the
sake of relaxation, and relaxation is of necessity sweet, for
it is the remedy of pain caused by toil, and intellectual
enjoyment is universally acknowledged to contain an element
not only of the noble but of the pleasant, for happiness
11 is made up of both.   All men agree that music is one of
the pleasantest things, whether with or without song ; as
Musaeus says,

'Song is to mortals of all things the sweetest.'
Hence and with good reason it is introduced into social
gatherings and entertainments, because it makes the hearts of
men glad : so that on this ground alone we may assume that
12 the young ought to be trained in it.   For innocent pleasures
are not only in harmony with the perfect end of life, but they
also provide relaxation.   And whereas men rarely attain the
end, but often rest by the way and amuse themselves, not only
with a view to some good, but also for the pleasure's sake, it
may be well for them at times to find a refreshment in music.
13 It sometimes happens that men make amusement the end,
for the end probably contains some element of pleasure,
though not any ordinary or lower pleasure ; but they mistake
the lower for the higher, and in seeking for the one find the
other, since every pleasure has a likeness to the end of
action[1].   For the end is not eligible, nor do the pleasures
which we have described exist, for the sake of any future
good but of the past, that is to say, they are the alleviation of

[1] Cp. N. Eth. vii. 13. § 6.

past toils and pains.   And we may infer this to be the **VIII. 5**
reason why men seek happiness from common pleasures. 14
But music is pursued, not only as an alleviation of past
toil, but also as providing recreation.   And who can say 15
whether, having this use, it may not also have a nobler one?
In addition to this common pleasure, felt and shared in by all 1340 a
(for the pleasure given by music is natural, and therefore
adapted to all ages and characters), may it not have also
some influence over the character and the soul?   It must 16
have such an influence if characters are affected by it.   And
that they are so affected is proved by the power which
the songs of Olympus and of many others exercise; for
beyond question they inspire enthusiasm, and enthusiasm
is an emotion of the ethical part of the soul.   Besides, when 17
men hear imitations, even unaccompanied by melody or
rhythm, their feelings move in sympathy.   Since, then, music
is a pleasure, and virtue consists in rejoicing and loving and
hating aright, there is clearly nothing which we are so much
concerned to acquire and to cultivate as the power of forming
right judgments, and of taking delight in good dispositions
and noble actions [1].   Rhythm and melody supply imitations 18
of anger and gentleness, and also of courage and temperance
and of virtues and vices in general, which hardly fall short of
the actual affections, as we know from our own experience,
for in listening to such strains our souls undergo a change.
The habit of feeling pleasure or pain at mere representations 19
is not far removed from the same feeling about realities [2]; for
example, if any one delights in the sight of a statue for
its beauty only, it necessarily follows that the sight of

[1] Cp. Plato, Rep. iii. 401, 402; Laws, ii. 658, 659.
[2] Cp. Plato, Rep. iii. 395.

VIII. 5 the original will be pleasant to him.   No other sense, such
  20 as taste or touch, has any resemblance to moral qualities;
     in sight only there is a little, for figures are to some extent of
     a moral character, and [so far] all participate in the feeling
     about them.   Again, figures and colours are not imitations,
  21 but signs of moral habits, and these signs occur only when the
     body is under the influence of emotions.   The connexion of
     them with morals is slight, but in so far as there is any,
     young men should be taught to look, not at the works
     of Pauson, but at those of Polygnotus[1], or any other painter
     or statuary who expresses moral ideas.   On the other hand,
  22 even in mere melodies[2] there is an imitation of character, for
     the musical modes differ essentially from one another,
     and those who hear them are differently affected by each.
1340 b Some of them make men sad and grave, like the so-called
     Mixolydian, others enfeeble the mind, like the relaxed
     harmonies, others, again, produce a moderate and settled
     temper, which appears to be the peculiar effect of the Dorian;
  23 the Phrygian inspires enthusiasm.   The whole subject
     has been well treated by philosophical writers on this branch
     of education, and they confirm their arguments by facts.
     The same principles apply to rhythms[3]: some have a
     character of rest, others of motion, and of these latter again,
  24 some have a more vulgar, others a nobler movement.   Enough
     has been said to show that music has a power of forming the
     character, and should therefore be introduced into the education
  25 of the young.   The study is suited to the stage of youth, for
     young persons will not, if they can help, endure anything which
     is not sweetened by pleasure, and music has a natural sweet-

---

[1] Cp. Poet. 2. § 2; 6. § 15.   [2] Cp. Plato, Rep. iii. 398, 399.
               [3] Rep. iii. 399 E, 400.

ness.   There seems to be in us a sort of affinity to harmonies **VIII. 5**
and rhythms, which makes some philosophers say that the soul
is a harmony, others, that she possesses harmony.

And now we have to determine the question which **6**
has been already raised[1], whether children should be
themselves taught to sing and play or not.   Clearly there is
a considerable difference made in the character by the actual
practice of the art.   It is difficult, if not impossible, for
those who do not perform to be good judges of the performance of others[2].   Besides, children should have something **2**
to do, and the rattle of Archytas, which people give to their
children in order to amuse them and prevent them from
breaking anything in the house, was a capital invention,
for a young thing cannot be quiet.   The rattle is a toy suited
to the infant mind, and [musical] education is a rattle or toy
for children of a larger growth.   We conclude then that they **3**
should be taught music in such a way as to become not only
critics but performers.

The question what is or is not suitable for different ages
may be easily answered; nor is there any difficulty in
meeting the objection of those who say that the study of
music is vulgar.   We reply (1) in the first place, that they **4**
who are to be judges must also be performers, and that they
should begin to practise early, although when they are older
they may be spared the execution; they must have learned
to appreciate what is good and to delight in it, thanks to
the knowledge which they acquired in their youth.   As to **5**
(2) the vulgarizing effect which music is supposed to exercise,
this is a question [of degree], which we shall have no
difficulty in determining, when we have considered to what

[1] c. 5. §§ 5–8.   [2] Cp. supra, c. 5. § 7.

VIII. 6 extent freemen who are being trained to political virtue should pursue the art, what melodies and what rhythms they 1341 a should be allowed to use, and what instruments should be employed in teaching them to play, for even the instrument 6 makes a difference.   The answer to the objection turns upon these distinctions; for it is quite possible that certain methods of teaching and learning music do really have a degrading effect.   It is evident then that the learning of music ought not to impede the business of riper years, or to degrade the body or render it unfit for civil or military duties, whether for the early practice or for the later study of them.

7   The right measure will be attained if students of music stop short of the arts which are practised in professional contests, and do not seek to acquire those fantastic marvels of execution which are now the fashion in such contests, and from these 8 have passed into education.   Let the young pursue their studies until they are able to feel delight in noble melodies and rhythms, and not merely in that common part of music in which every slave or child and even some animals find pleasure.

From these principles we may also infer what instruments 9 should be used.   The flute, or any other instrument which requires great skill, as for example the harp, ought not to be admitted into education, but only such as will make intelligent students of music or of the other parts of education. Besides, the flute is not an instrument which has a good moral effect; it is too exciting.   The proper time for using it is when the performance aims not at instruction, but at the relief 10 of the passions [1].   And there is a further objection; the impediment which the flute presents to the use of the voice detracts from its educational value.   The ancients therefore

[1] Cp. c. 7. § 3.

were right in forbidding the flute to youths and freemen, **VIII. 6** although they had once allowed it. For when their wealth gave 11 them greater leisure, and they had loftier notions of excellence, being also elated with their success, both before and after the Persian War, with more zeal than discernment they pursued every kind of knowledge, and so they introduced the flute into education. At Lacedaemon there was a Choragus who led 12 the Chorus with a flute, and at Athens the instrument became so popular that most freemen could play upon it. The popularity is shown by the tablet which Thrasippus dedicated when he furnished the Chorus to Ecphantides. Later experience enabled men to judge what was or what was not really conducive to virtue, and they rejected both the flute and several 13 other old-fashioned instruments, such as the Lydian harp, the many-stringed lyre, the 'heptagon,' 'triangle,' 'sambuca,' and 1341 b the like—which are intended only to give pleasure to the hearer, and require extraordinary skill of hand [1]. There is a meaning also in the myth of the ancients, which tells how Athene invented the flute and then threw it away. It was 14 not a bad idea of theirs, that the Goddess disliked the instrument because it made the face ugly ; but with still more reason may we say that she rejected it because the acquirement of flute-playing contributes nothing to the mind, since to Athene we ascribe knowledge and art.

Accordingly we reject the professional instruments and also 15 the professional mode of education in music—and by professional we mean that which is adopted in contests, for in this the performer practises the art, not for the sake of his own improvement, but in order to give pleasure, and that of a vulgar sort, to his hearers. For this reason the execution of such

[1] Cp. Plato, Rep. iii. **399 D**.

VIII. 6 music is not the part of a freeman but of a paid performer, and
16 the result is that the performers are vulgarized, for the end at
which they aim is bad[1]. The vulgarity of the spectator tends
to lower the character of the music and therefore of the performers ; they look to him—he makes them what they are, and
fashions even their bodies by the movements which he expects
them to exhibit.

7   We have also to consider rhythms and harmonies. Shall we
use them all in education or make a distinction ? and shall the
distinction be that which is made by those who are engaged in
education, or shall it be some other?   For we see that music
is produced by melody and rhythm, and we ought to know
what influence these have respectively on education, and
whether we should prefer excellence in melody or excellence in
2 rhythm.   But as the subject has been very well treated by
many musicians of the present day, and also by philosophers
who have had considerable experience of musical education, to
these we would refer the more exact student of the subject ; we
shall only speak of it now after the manner of the legislator,
having regard to general principles.

3   We accept the division of melodies proposed by certain
philosophers into ethical melodies, melodies of action, and
passionate or inspiring melodies, each having, as they say, a
mode or harmony corresponding to it.   But we maintain
further that music should be studied, not for the sake of one,
but of many benefits, that is to say, with a view to (1)
education, (2) purgation (the word ' purgation ' we use at present
without explanation, but when hereafter we speak of poetry [2], we
will treat the subject with more precision); music may also

---

[1] Cp. Plato, Laws, iii. 700.
[2] Cp. Poet. c. 6, though the promise is really unfulfilled

serve (3) for intellectual enjoyment, for relaxation and for VIII. 7
recreation after exertion. It is clear, therefore, that all the 1342 a
harmonies must be employed by us, but not all of them in the
same manner. In education ethical melodies are to be preferred,
but we may listen to the melodies of action and passion when
they are performed by others. For feelings such as pity and 4
fear, or, again, enthusiasm, exist very strongly in some souls,
and have more or less influence over all. Some persons fall
into a religious frenzy, whom we see disenthralled by the use of
mystic melodies, which bring healing and purgation to the soul.
Those who are influenced by pity or fear and every emotional 5
nature have a like experience, others in their degree are stirred
by something which specially affects them, and all are in a
manner purged and their souls lightened and delighted. The
melodies of purgation likewise give an innocent pleasure to
mankind. Such are the harmonies and the melodies in which 6
those who perform music at the theatre should be invited to
compete. But since the spectators are of two kinds—the
one free and educated, and the other a vulgar crowd composed
of mechanics, labourers and the like—there ought to be 7
contests and exhibitions instituted for the relaxation of the
second class also. And the melodies will correspond to their
minds; for as their minds are perverted from the natural state,
so there are exaggerated and corrupted harmonies which are
in like manner a perversion. A man receives pleasure from
what is natural to him, and therefore professional musicians
may be allowed to practise this lower sort of music before an
audience of a lower type. But, for the purpose of education, 8
as I have already said, those modes and melodies should be
employed which are ethical, such as the Dorian; though we
may include any others which are approved by philosophers

VIII. 7 who have had a musical education. The Socrates of the
   9 Republic [1] is wrong in retaining only the Phrygian mode along
 1342 b with the Dorian, and the more so because he rejects the flute;
      for the Phrygian is to the modes what the flute is to musical
      instruments—both of them are exciting and emotional.
   10 Poetry proves this, for Bacchic frenzy and all similar emotions
      are most suitably expressed by the flute, and are better set to
      the Phrygian than to any other harmony. The dithyramb, for
   11 example, is acknowledged to be Phrygian, a fact of which the
      connoisseurs of music offer many proofs, saying, among other
      things, that Philoxenus, having attempted to compose his
      Tales [2] as a dithyramb in the Dorian mode, found it impossible,
   12 and fell back into the more appropriate Phrygian. All men
      agree that the Dorian music is the gravest and manliest. And
      whereas we say that the extremes should be avoided and the
      mean followed, and whereas the Dorian is a mean between the
      other harmonies [the Phrygian and the Lydian [3]], it is evident
      that our youth should be taught the Dorian music.

   13   Two principles have to be kept in view—what is possible,
      what is becoming : at these every man ought to aim. But
      even these are relative to age; the old, who have lost their
      powers, cannot very well sing the severe melodies, and nature
      herself seems to suggest that their songs should be of the
   14 more relaxed kind. Wherefore the musicians likewise blame
      Socrates, and with justice, for rejecting the relaxed harmonies
      in education under the idea that they are intoxicating ; not in the
      ordinary sense of intoxication (for wine rather tends to excite
      men), but because they have no strength in them. And so

---

[1] Plato, Rep. iii. 399.
[2] Retaining the MS. reading μύθους. Cp. Poet. c. 2. § 7.
[3] Cp. c. 5. § 22.

with a view to a time of life when men begin to grow old, **VIII. 7**
they ought to practise the gentler harmonies and melodies as
well as the others.   And if there be any harmony, such as the 15
Lydian above all others appears to be, which is suited to
children of tender age, and possesses the elements both of order
and of education, clearly [we ought to use it, for] education
should be based upon three principles—the mean, the possible,
the becoming, these three.

INDEX

§ 3; not a perversion, iv. 8, § 1; analogous to oligarchy (1) because the few rule, v. 7, § 1; (2) because birth and education commonly accompany wealth, iv. 8, § 3;—to royalty as a government of the best, ib. 10, § 2; preferable to royalty, because the good are more than one, iii. 15, § 10; how distinguished from oligarchy and constitutional government, iv. 7; 8; 14, § 10; v. 7, §§ 5–9 (cp. ii. 11, §§ 5–10); usually degenerates into oligarchy, iii. 7, § 5; 15, § 11; iv. 2, § 2; v. 7, § 7; 8, § 7;—causes of revolutions in aristocracies, v. 7; the means of their preservation, ib. 8, §§ 5–7; aristocracy less stable than constitutional government, ib. 7, § 6; liable to danger because the rich have too much power, ib. 12, § 6; might be combined with democracy if the magistrates were unpaid and office open to all, ib. 8, § 17 (cp. vi. 4, § 6);—magistracies peculiar to aristocracy, iv. 15, § 10; vi. 8, §§ 22, 24; aristocratical modes of appointing magistrates and judges, iv. 15, §§ 20, 21; 16, § 8; practice of trying all suits by the same magistrates, aristocratical, ii. 11, § 8; iii. 1, § 10;—the people naturally suited to an aristocracy, iii. 17, §§ 3–7.

Aristogeiton, conspiracy of Harmodius and, v. 10, § 15.

Aristophanes, ii. 4, § 6.

Arrhibaeus, king of the Lyncestians, v. 10, § 17.

Art, works of, wherein different from realities, iii. 11, § 4.

Artapanes, v. 10, § 21.

Artisan, the employments of the, devoid of moral excellence, i. 13, §§ 13, 14; iii. 5, § 5; vi. 4, § 12; vii. 9, §§ 3, 7; artisans sometimes public slaves, ii. 7, § 22; only admitted to office in democracies, iii. 4, § 12; often acquire wealth, ib. 5, § 6; the question whether they are citizens, ib. 5; necessary to the existence of the state, iv. 4, §§ 9, 21; not a part of the state, vii. 4, § 6; should be debarred from the 'Freemen's Agora,' ib. 12, § 3.

Arts, the, require instruments, both living and lifeless, i. 4; some arts subservient to others, ib. 8, § 2; 10, §§ 1–4; the arts have a limit in their means though not in their end, ib. 8, § 14; 9, § 13; both the means and the end ought to be within our control, vii. 13, § 2; amount of knowledge which a freeman is permitted in the arts, i. 11, § 1; viii. 2, § 5; degrees of excellence in them, i. 11, § 6; viii. 2, §§ 5, 6; changes in, advantageous, ii. 8, § 18; iii. 15, § 4; the analogy of, not to be extended to the laws, ii. 8, § 24; iii. 15, § 4; exist for the benefit of those under them, iii. 6, §§ 7–9; by whom should the artist be judged? ib. 11, §§ 10–14 (cp. viii. 6, §§ 1–4); the arts aim at some good, iii. 12, § 1; justice of the different claims to political superiority illustrated from the arts, ib. 12, §§ 4–8; law of proportion in the arts, ib. 13, § 21; the problems of the arts, an illustration of the problems of politics, iv. 1, §§ 1–4; the arts have to supply the deficiencies of Nature, vii. 17, § 15.

Asia, ii. 10, § 3; iv. 3, § 3; the Asiatics better fitted for slavery

not to be citizens, iii. 5; vii. 9, §3; nor the sailors, vii. 6, §§ 7, 8; is the life of the citizen the best? ib. 2; 3; the character necessary in the citizens, ib. 7; their habit of body, ib. 16, § 12; viii. 3, § 13; 4.

Citizenship, rights of, conferred on strangers in early times at Sparta, ii. 9, § 17; lost at Sparta, by failure to contribute to the common meals, ib. § 32; 10, § 7; given to persons of illegitimate birth in extreme democracies, iii. 5, § 7; vi. 4, § 16; exclusion from, sometimes concealed, iii. 5, § 9; easily pretended in a large state, vii. 4, § 14.

City, the: *see* State.

Clazomenae, v. 3, § 15.

Cleander, tyrant of Gela, v. 12, § 13.

Cleisthenes, tyrant of Sicyon, v. 12, §§ 1, 12.

—, the Athenian, iii. 2, § 3; vi. 4, § 18.

Cleomenes (king of Sparta), v. 3, § 7.

Cleopatra (the widow of Perdiccas), v. 10, § 17.

Cleotimus, leader of a revolution at Amphipolis, v. 6, § 8.

Clubs; at Carthage, ii. 11, § 3; at Abydos, v. 6, §§ 6, 13; hated by tyrants, ii. 11, § 5.

Cnidus, v. 6, §§ 4, 16.

Codrus, king of Athens, v. 10, § 8.

Colonies, of Carthage, ii. 11, § 15; vi. 5, § 9; oligarchies formed in colonies by the first settlers, iv. 4, § 5; dissensions in, a cause of revolutions, v. 3, §§ 11-14.

Colophon, of, iv. 4, § 5; v. 3, § 15.

Commerce, divisions of, i. 11, § 3; its advantages and disadvantages, vii. 6;—commercial treaties, iii. 9, § 6.

Common meals, hostility of the tyrant to, v. 11, § 5; first established in Italy, vii. 10, §§ 1-8; how they should be arranged, ib. §§ 10-12; the young not allowed to share in them, ib. 17, § 11;—of the magistrates, vi. 2, § 7; vii. 12, § 1; of the priests, vii. 12, § 6;—(at Carthage), ii. 11, § 3;—(in Crete), ib. 5, § 15; the original of the Spartan, ib. 10, § 5; maintained at the public cost, ib. §§ 7-10;—(at Sparta), make property to some degree common, ib. 5, § 15; badly regulated, ib. 9, §§ 31, 32; 10, § 7; anciently called 'andria,' ib. 10, § 5.

Community of women and children, the, proposed by Plato, ii. 1, § 3; arguments against, ii. 3; 4;—of property, ib. 5; vii. 10, § 9.

Confederacy, difference between a, and a state, ii. 2, § 3; iii. 9, §§ 6-8.

Constitution, regard must be had to the, in education, i. 13, § 15; v. 9, §§ 11-15; viii. 1; the best constitution supposed by some to be a combination of all existing forms, ii. 6, § 17 (cp. iv. 1, § 6; 7, § 4; 9, § 7); the permanence of a constitution only secured by the consent of all classes, ii. 9, § 22; iv. 9, § 10; 12, § 6; v. 8, § 5; 9, §§ 5-10; vi. 6, § 2; 7, § 4; older constitutions more simple than later, ii. 10, § 1; contentment with a constitution not always a proof of its excellence, ib. 10, § 12 (*but* cp. c. 11, §§ 2, 15); in each constitution the citizen different, iii. 1, § 9; 5, § 5; 13, § 12;

character and powers of the assembly, ib. 14, §§ 1-7 ;—the best material of a democracy, ib. 6, § 2 ; vi. 4, § 1 ; the position suitable to a democracy, vii. 11, § 5 ; democracy always supported by the sailors and light armed, vi. 7, §§ 1, 2.

Derdas (? King of Elymaea), v. 10, § 16.

Devices, political, of oligarchies and democracies, iv. 13, §§ 1-8 ; their inutility, v. 8, § 4.

Diagoras, an Eretrian, v. 6, § 14.

Dicaea, 'the Pharsalian mare,' ii. 3, § 9.

Dicasteries, the Athenian, ii. 12, § 4.

Dictators : *see* Aesymnetes.

Diocles, ii. 12, §§ 8-11.

Dion, v. 10, §§ 23, 28, 31, 32.

Dionysius the Elder, i. 11, §§ 11, 12 ; iii. 15, § 16 ; v. 5, §§ 8, 10 ; 7, § 10 ; 10, § 6 ; 11, § 10.

Dionysius the Younger, v. 10, §§ 23, 28, 31, 32.

Diophantus, ii. 7, § 23.

Directors of Education, vii. 17, §§ 5, 7 ; of Gymnastics, vi. 8, § 22.

Dorian Harmony, the : *see* Harmony.

Dowries, ii. 7, § 3 ; 9, § 15.

Doxander, v. 4, § 6.

Draco, ii. 12, § 13.

Drawing, a branch of education, viii. 3, §§ 1, 12.

Dynasty, or Family Oligarchy : *see* Oligarchy.

Ecphantides (the ancient comic poet), viii. 6, § 12.

Education, may be directed to a wrong end, ii. 7, §§ 8, 9 ; must have regard to the constitution, i. 13, § 15 ; v. 9, § 11 ; viii. 1 ; the great means

of uniting the state, ii. 5, §§ 18-21 ; special, for the ruler, iii. 4, § 8 (cp. vii. 14, § 6) ; confers a claim to pre-eminence in the state, iii. 13, § 1 (cp. c. 9, §§ 14, 15 ; 12, §§ 8, 9 ; iv. 8, §§ 2-5) ; excellence of the Spartan education, iv. 9, § 7 ; viii. 1, § 4 (*but* cp. viii. 4, §§ 1-7) ; bad education of the rich, iv. 11, § 6 ; v. 9, § 13 ; hostility of the tyrant to education, v. 11, § 5 ; education necessary to supplement habit, vii. 13, § 13 ; 17, § 15 ; the special business of the legislator, viii. 1, § 1 : wrong notions of education prevalent in Hellas, vii. 14, § 15 ; viii. 1, § 3 ; 4, § 6 ; the periods of education, vii. 17 ; viii. 4, §§ 7-9 ; necessity of a common system of education, viii. 1, § 3 (cp. ii. 7, § 8 ; and iv. 9, § 7) ; should education have an ethical or a practical aim ? viii. 2 ; 3 ; 5 ; should it include music ? ib. 3 ; 5 ; 6 ; what instruments and harmonies are to be used ? ib. 6, §§ 8-16 ; 7 ; education not to be directed to a single end, ib. 4, § 2 ; the proper place of gymnastics in education, ib. 3, § 13 ; 4 ; the education of mind and body not to be carried on together, ib. 4, § 9 ; writers upon musical education, ib. 5, § 23 ; 7, §§ 2, 3, 8, 11, 14 ; musical education a kind of rattle to older children, ib. 6, § 2 ; the three principles of education, ib. 7, § 15 :—Directors of Education, vii. 17, §§ 5, 7.

Egypt, iii. 15, § 4 ; v. 11, § 9 ; vii. 10, §§ 1-6, 8.

Eleven, the, at Athens, vi. 8, § 11.

Elis, v. 6, § 11.

Elymaea, v. 10, § 17.

art of money-making, i. 8, § 3;
10, § 3; 11, § 2.

Iapygia, v. 3, § 7; vii. 10, § 5.
Iberians, the, vii. 2, § 11.
India, vii. 14, § 3.
Inheritance, sale of an, forbidden,
ii. 7, § 6; (at Sparta), ib. 9,
§ 14 (cp. v. 8, § 20); the division of an, may be a cause of
revolution, v. 4, § 4.
Instruments, best when made for
one use, i. 2, § 3; may be either
living or lifeless, ib. 4, § 2; are
used either in production or in
action, ib. §§ 4–6; are never
unlimited in the arts, ib. 8,
§§ 14, 15; the slave a living
instrument, ib. 4, §§ 2, 6.
Ionian, v. 10, § 6.
Ionian Gulf, the, vii. 10, § 5.
Iphiades, a party leader at
Abydos, v. 6, § 14.
Istros, v. 6, § 2.
Italus, king of Oenotria, vii. 10,
§ 3.
Italy, vii. 10, §§ 2–6.

Jason, tyrant of Pherae, iii. 4, § 9.
Judges, not allowed to commu-
nicate with each other, ii. 8,
§ 13; should not hold office for
life, ib. 9, § 25; necessary, even
in the first beginnings of the
state, iv. 4, §§ 13, 14; the
various modes of appointing
them, ib. 16, §§ 5–7; provision
for an equal division of opinion
among judges, vi. 3, § 6; those
who inflict penalties to be
different from those who see to
their execution, ib. 8, §§ 8–11.
Justice, the sense of, peculiar to
man, i. 2, § 12; the bond of
men in states, ib. § 16; iii. 12,
§ 9; 13, § 3; (cp. iv. 4, § 13);
sometimes defined as benevo-

lence, i. 6, § 4; different in men
and women, ib. 13, §§ 3, 9; in
the ruler and the subject, ib.
§§ 2–8; iii. 4, §§ 16–18; consists in equality, iii. 9, § 1; 12,
§ 1; 13, § 12; vii. 14, § 3;
cannot be the destruction of the
state, iii. 10, § 2; cannot be
united with the love of conquest,
vii. 2, §§ 7–18; selfishness of
the ordinary notions of justice,
vi. 3, § 6; vii. 2, § 14; all claims
to rule based upon partial and
relative justice only, iii. 9,
§§ 1–6, 15; v. 1, §§ 2–6; 9,
§ 1; vi. 2, § 2; 3, §§ 1–4.

King, the, not the same with the
statesman, i. 1, § 2; ought to
be chosen for merit (as at
Carthage), ii. 9, § 29; 11, § 4;
receives a special education, iii.
4, § 8; may be justified in putting down his rivals, ib. 13,
§ 22; v. 11, § 27; is the
champion of the better classes
against the people, v. 10, § 3;
often supreme in religious
matters, iii. 14, § 13; vi. 8,
§ 20; should he have a military
force? iii. 15, §§ 14–16; is
guarded by the citizens, ib. 14,
§ 7; v. 10, § 10.
King, the true, or natural superior of the citizens, iii. 13,
§§ 13, 24, 25; 17, §§ 5–8; vii.
3, § 6; unknown in later Hellas,
v. 10, § 37. [*See* Royalty.]
King, a, the Gods why supposed
to be under, i. 2, § 7; 12, § 3.
Kings, the, of Crete (in ancient
times), ii. 10, § 6; of Carthage,
ib. 11, §§ 3–6, 9, 10; of Macedonia, v. 10, § 8; of the Molossians, ib.; 11, § 2; of Persia,
viii. 5, § 5; of Sparta [*see* Lace-
daemon]:—Kings, the ancient,

animals created for his sake, ib. 8, § 12 :—Man, the virtue of the, different from that of the woman, ib. 13, §§ 3, 9-11 ; iii. 4, § 16 :—Men are unlimited in their desires, i. 9, §§ 16-18 ; ii. 7, §§ 8, 19 ; are wicked by nature, ii. 5, § 12 ; are more desirous of gain than of honour, iv. 13, § 8 ; v. 8, § 16 ; vi. 4, § 3 ; are satisfied with a moderate amount of virtue, vii. 1, § 5 :—Men, the first, were ordinary, foolish people, ii. 8, § 21.

Mantinea, battle of, v. 4, § 9 ; government by representation at, vi. 4, § 4.

Marriage, regulations respecting, vii. 16 ;—the marriage relation, i. 2, § 2 ; 3, §§ 1-3 ; 12 ; iii. 4, § 6.

Massalia, v. 6, §§ 2, 3 ; vi. 7, § 4.

Master, the, in relation to the slave, i. 2, §§ 2-5 ; 3, §§ 1-3 ; 12, § 1 ; 13, §§ 7, 12-14 ; has a common interest with the slave, ib. 6, § 10 ; iii. 6, § 6 ; vii. 14, § 6 ; ought to train the slave in virtue, i. 13, § 14 ;— the science peculiar to, ib. 3, § 4 ; 7, §§ 2-5 ; 13, § 14 ;—the rule of, ib. 3, § 4 ; iii. 4, § 11 ; vii. 14, § 6 ; wrongly supposed [by Plato] to be different from political rule, i. 1, § 2 ; 3, § 4.

Mean, importance of the, in states, iv. 11 ; v. 9, § 6 ; in education, viii. 6, § 7 ; 7, § 15.

Mechanic, the: *see* Artisan.

Medes, the, iii. 13, § 19 ; viii. 5, § 5.

Medicine, i. 9, §§ 13, 17 ; 10, §§ 3, 4 ; ii. 8, § 18. (*See* Physician.)

Megacles, v. 10, § 19.

Megara, iii. 9, § 9 ; iv. 15, § 15 ; v. 3, § 5 ; 5, §§ 4, 9.

Messenian War, the (Second), v. 7, § 3.

Messenians, the, ii. 9, §§ 3, 11.

Metics : *see* Aliens.

Midas, i. 9, § 11.

Middle class, virtues of the, iv. 11 ; 12 ; the middle-class state the best, ib. 11, §§ 8-15 ; 12, § 4 ; v. 8, § 14 ; 9, § 6 ; smallness of the middle class in ancient states, iv. 13, § 11.

Might and right, i. 6, § 3 ; vi. 3, § 6 ; vii. 2, § 13.

Miletus, i. 11, § 9 ; v. 5, § 8.

Minos, ii. 10, § 3 ; vii. 10, §§ 2, 6.

Mithridates (? Satrap of Pontus), v. 10, § 25.

Mitylene, iii. 14, § 10 ; v. 4, §§ 5, 6 ; 10, § 19.

Mixo-Lydian Harmony, the: *see* Harmony.

Mnaseas, a Phocian, v. 4, § 7.

Mnason, a Phocian, v. 4, § 7.

Moderation in politics, necessary for the salvation of the state, iv. 11, §§ 16-19 ; v. 9, § 6 ; vi. 5, § 2.

Molossians, the, in Epirus, v. 10, § 8 ; 11, § 2.

Monarchy, arguments for and against, iii. 15-17.

Monarchy : *see* King, Royalty, *and* Tyranny.

Money, origin of, i. 9, § 8 ; its conventional nature, ib. § 11 ; ought not to be made from money, ib. 10, § 5.

Money-making, the art of, how related to household management, i. 3, § 3 ; 8, §§ 1, 2 ; 9, §§ 1, 12-18 ; 10, §§ 1-4 : the natural kind, ib. 8, §§ 3-15 ; 9, §§ 1-8 ; 10, §§ 1-4 ; 11, §§ 1, 2 ; the unnatural, ib. 9, § 1 foll. ;

of revolutions, v. 1, § 16; 4, § 1; 6, § 5; 8, § 9; form a democracy among themselves, ib. 8, § 6; should be humane to the subject classes, iv. 13, § 8; vi. 5, §§ 5-11.

Notium, v. 3, § 15.

Obedience, the necessary preliminary to command, iii. 4, §§ 10, 14; vii. 9, § 6; 14, § 6.

Odysseus, viii. 3, § 9.

Oenophyta, battle of, v. 3, § 5.

Oenotrians, the (in Southern Italy), vii. 10, §§ 3-5.

Office, the 'indefinite,' in which all the citizens share, iii. 1, §§ 6-12; 2, § 5.

Office, lust of mankind for, iii. 6, § 10; oligarchical tricks to keep the poor from, iv. 13, §§ 1-4; justice of the various claims to, iii. 10-13 :—Offices, the, of the state, posts of honour, ib. 10, § 4; their distribution, iv. 15; vi. 8; their organization determines the character of each constitution, iv. 1, § 10; 3, § 5; in small states must be combined, in large ones specialized, ii. 11, § 14; iv. 15, §§ 5-7; vi. 8, § 2; in democracies restricted to six months' tenure, v. 8, § 6; (cp. vi. 2, § 5); and rarely held more than once by the same person, iii. 1, § 6; vi. 2, § 5; should be divided into two classes, v. 8, § 21; vi. 5, § 11.

Offices, sale of, and pluralism, at Carthage, ii. 11, §§ 10, 13.

Oligarchy, the government of the few for their private interests, iii. 6, § 2; 8, § 3;—or, more correctly, of the wealthy, ib. 7, § 5; 8, §§ 6, 7; iv. 4, §§ 1-6, 19; 8, § 7; 11, §§ 16-19; v. 1, § 3; vi. 2, § 7; Plato wrong in think-

ing that an oligarchy can ever be called 'good,' iv. 2, § 3; oligarchy the perversion of aristocracy, iii. 7, § 5; 15, § 12; iv. 2, § 2; how distinguished from it, ii. 11, §§ 5-10; iv. 5, § 1; 7; 8, §§ 2-10; 14, § 10; v. 7, §§ 5-8; popularly supposed, like aristocracy, to be a 'government of the best,' iv. 8, § 4; v. 1, § 14; analogous to tyranny in love of wealth, v. 10, § 11; has more forms than one, iv. 1, § 8; 4, §§ 20-22; 12, § 3; 13, § 12; the forms enumerated, ib. 5, §§ 1-3; 6, §§ 7-11; 14, §§ 8-11; vi. 6; oligarchy less stable than democracy, iv. 11, § 14; v. 1, § 15; 7, § 6; the shortest lived of all forms of governments, excepting tyranny, v. 12, § 1 (cp. vi. 6, § 4); the extreme form apt to pass into tyranny, iv. 11, § 11; v. 10, § 5; 12, § 13; the causes of revolutions in oligarchies, v. 3, § 14; 6; 12, §§ 15-18; the means of their preservation, ib. 6, § 9; 8, §§ 5-21; 9; vi. 6, § 5; 7;—the Lacedaemonians the champions of oligarchy in Hellas, iv. 11, § 18; v. 7, § 14; —the people to whom oligarchy is suited, iv. 2, § 4; 12, § 3;—the military strength of oligarchy derived from cavalry and heavy infantry, ib. 3, § 3; 13, § 10; vi. 7, § 1;—oligarchical modes of appointing magistrates and judges, ii. 6, §§ 19, 20; iv. 14, §§ 7-11; 15, §§ 14-21; 16, § 8; magistracies peculiar to oligarchy, iv. 14, § 14; 15, § 11; vi. 8, §§ 17, 24;—luxury of the women in oligarchies, iv. 15, § 13; bad education of the children, ib. 11, § 6; v. 9,

13, § 8 ; **v. 8**, § 16 ; vi. 4, § 2 ;
Solon wrong in thinking that
'no bound has been fixed to
riches,' i. 8, § 14. *See* Wealth.
Royalty, the form of government
in which one rules for the best,
iii. 7, § 3 ; v. 10, § 3 ; analogous
to aristocracy, **v.** 10, §§ 2, 7 ;
opposed to tyranny, iii. 7, § 5 ;
iv. 2, § 2 ; v. 10, § 2 ; is it
better than the rule of the law ?
iii. 15 ; 16 ; arose (1) from the
government of families by the
eldest, i. 2, § 6 ; 7, § 1 ; 12, § 3 ;
(2) from services rendered by the
first chiefs, iii. 14, § 12 ; 15, § 11 ;
v. 10, §§ 3, 8 ; (3) from the
weakness of the middle and
lower classes, iv. 13, § 11 ; once
existed in Crete, ii. 10, § 6 ; has
various forms : (1) the Lacedaemonian (which is only a generalship for life), ii. 9, § 33 ; iii. 14,
§§ 3, 14 ; 15, §§ 1, 2 ; 16, § 1 ;
(2) the despotic (among Barbarians), iii. 14, §§ 6, 14 ; iv.
10, § 2 ; (3) the ancient Dicta-
torships, iii. 14, §§ 8, 14 ; iv.
10, § 2 ; (4) the monarchies of
the heroic age, iii. 14, §§ 11-14 ;
(5) the absolute monarchy, ib.
§ 15 ;—the people to whom
royalty is suited, ib. c. 17 ;
—causes of revolutions in monarchies, v. 10 ; means of their
preservation, ib. 11, §§ 1-3 ;
royalty more often destroyed
from within than from without,
ib. 10, § 36 ; true royalty unknown in later Hellas, ib. § 37 ;
vii. 14, § 3. *See* King, Monarchy.
Rule ; the various kinds of rule
essentially different from each
other, i. 1, § 2 ; 3, § 4 ; 5, § 6 ;
7, § 1 ; 12 ; 13, §§ 4-8 ; iii. 6,
§§ 5-7 ; vii. 3, § 2 ; 14, § 6 ;
the distinction between the

ruler and the ruled found
throughout nature, i. 2, § 2 ; 5,
§§ 2-7 ; the better the ruled,
the better the rule, ib. 5, §§ 2,
7 ; v. 11, § 34 ; the rule of freemen better than despotic authority, vii. 14, § 19 ; rule over
others, not the highest object of
the legislator, ib. 14, §§ 14-22 ;
rule must be learnt by obedience,
iii. 4, §§ 10, 14 ; vii. 9, § 6 ;
14, § 6.
Ruler, the, ought to have moral
virtue in perfection, i. 13, § 8 ;
the virtue peculiar to him, iii. 4,
§ 17 ; must learn to govern by
obedience, ii. 11, § 14 ; iii. 4,
§ 14 ; vii. 9, § 6 ; 14, § 6 ; the
rulers ought to remain the same,
ii. 2, §§ 4-8 ; vii. 14, § 2 ;
dangers arising from this
arrangement, ii. 5, §§ 24-27 ;
vii. 14, § 3 ; the difficulty solved,
if the elder rule, and the younger
obey, vii. 9, § 5 ; 14, § 5.

Salamis, victory of, v. 4, § 8.
Samos, iii. 13, § 19 ; v. 3, § 12 ;
11, § 9.
Sardanapalus, v. 10, § 22.
Science, the, of the statesman, i.
1, § 2 ; 10, § 1 ; iii. 12, § 1 ;
iv. 1, § 3 ;—of the master, i. 3,
§ 4 ; 7, §§ 2, 4 ;—of the slave,
ib. 7, §§ 2, 3 ; in all sciences the
whole must be resolved into the
parts, ib. 1, § 3 ; every science
capable of improvement, ii. 8,
§ 18 ; the philosophical student
of science must not neglect any
detail, iii. 8, § 1 ; all sciences
aim at some good, ib. 12, § 1 ;—
the political science the highest
of all sciences, iii. 12, § 1 ; aims
at the good of the state, vii. 2,
§ 4 ; the subjects which it includes, iv. 1, §§ 3-11.

the relations of husband and wife, father and child, master and slave, ruler and subject, ib. 2; 13, § 15; formed of a union of villages, ib. 2, § 8; exists for the sake of a good life, ib. ; iii. 9, §§ 6–14; iv. 4, § 11; vii. 1, § 1; 8, §§ 4, 8;—not for the sake of alliance and security, iii. 9, §§ 6–14; is distinguished from an alliance because it has an ethical aim, ii. 2, § 3; iii. 9, § 8;—from a nation, because it is made up of different elements, ii. 2, § 3; is not necessarily formed by a number of persons residing together, iii. 3, § 3; 9, §§ 9–12; (*but* cp. ii. 1, § 2); is a work of nature, i. 2, §§ 8, 9; prior to the family or the individual, ib. § 12; 13, § 15 :— composed of dissimilar parts or elements, ii. 2, § 3; iii. 1, § 2; 4, §§ 6–8; iv. 3, § 1; 4, § 7; 12, §§ 1–4; v. 1, §§ 12–15; 3, § 6; vii. 8; the parts not to be identified with the conditions of the state, vii. 8, § 1; the parts and conditions enumerated, iv. 3, §§ 1–6; 4, §§ 7–20; vii. 8, § 7 ;—compared to the parts of animals, iv. 4, §§ 7–9 :—the state depends for its identity mainly on the sameness of the constitution, iii. 3; must be able to defend itself, ii. 6, § 7; 7, §§ 14–17; 10, § 15; iii. 12, § 9; iv. 4. § 10; vii. 4, § 6; 15, § 2; should be self-sufficing, i. 2, § 8; ii. 2, § 8; vii. 4, § 11; 5, § 1; 8, § 8; should not exceed a certain size, ii. 6, § 6; iii. 3, §§ 4–7; vii. 4; 5, § 1 ;—has the same virtue, and therefore the same life and end, as the individual, vii. 1–3; 13–15; may, like an individual, be wanting in self-discipline, v.

9, § 12; must have the virtues of leisure, vii. 15, § 1; can lead a life of virtuous activity isolated from others, ib. 2, § 16; 3, §§ 8–10; is not made happier by conquest, ib. 2; 3; 14, §§ 14–22; rests upon justice, i. 2, § 16; vii. 14, § 3; must have a care of virtue, iii. 9, § 8; vii. 13, § 9 (cp. iv. 7, § 4); must be happy, not in regard to a portion of the citizens, but to them all, ii. 5, § 27; vii. 9, § 7; is united by friendship among the citizens, ii. 5, § 6; iii. 9, § 13; iv. 11, § 7; v. 11, § 5 (cp. vi. 5, § 7); must pay great regard to education, i. 13, § 15; ii. 7, § 8; v. 9, § 11; viii. 1 :—must not be left to fortune, ii. 11, §§ 15, 16; vii. 13, § 9; is not the growth of a day, v. 3, § 11; is preserved by the principle of compensation, ii. 2, §§ 4–7; is sometimes left at the mercy of the army by the violence of faction, v. 6, § 13; its permanence can only be secured by the toleration of all elements, ii. 9, § 22; iv. 9, § 10; 12, § 1; v. 8, § 5; 9, § 5; vi. 6, § 2; any state, however ill-constituted, may last a few days, vi. 5, § 1: —the various claims to authority in the state, iii. 9, §§ 1–5, 14; 10; 12; 13; iv. 8, § 9; vi. 3, §§ 1–4; what share in the state may be allowed to the ordinary citizen? iii. 11, §§ 6–8; iv. 13, §§ 5–8; vi. 4, § 5; 7, § 5 (cp. ii. 12, § 5).

State, the ideal, of Aristotle, would require (1) a defensible position, vii. 5, § 3; (2) a moderate naval force, ib. §§ 6–9; (3) courageous and intelligent citizens, ib. 7; (4) the exclusion

Index 353

country,' ib. §§ 17-33; must be on his guard against assassins, especially against those who think that they have been insulted, ib. § 30; must conciliate the poor or the rich, whichever is the stronger, ib. § 32.

Tyrants, the, of Hellenic cities put down by the Lacedaemonians, iii. 2, § 3; v. 10, § 30; of Sicily, by the Syracusans, v. 10, § 30.

Tyrants, most of the ancient, originally demagogues, v. 5, § 6; 10, § 4; sometimes great magistrates, or kings, ib. 5, § 8; 10, § 5.

Tyrrhenians, the, iii. 9, § 6.

Tyrtaeus, v. 7, § 4.

Usury, the most unnatural mode of money-making, i. 10, § 5; 11, § 3.

Utility, too much regarded by Hellenic legislators, vii. 14, § 15; is not the sole aim of education, viii. 2, § 3; 3, § 11; is not sought after by men of noble mind, ib. 3, § 12.

Village, the, a colony of the family, i. 2, § 6; the state a union of villages, ib. § 8.

Virtue, the especial characteristic of aristocratical governments, ii. 11, §§ 5-10; iv. 7; v. 7, §§ 5-7; often allied to force, i. 6, § 3; more a concern of household management than wealth, ib. 13, § 1; depends upon the supremacy of the rational principle in the soul, ib. § 6; vii. 14, § 9; 15, § 9; cannot be included under a general definition, i. 13, § 10; must be taught to the slave by his master, ib. § 12; ought to be the aim and care

of the state, iii. 9, §§ 6-8; vii. 13, § 9 (cp. iv. 7, § 4); gives a claim to superiority in the state, iii. 9, §§ 14, 15; 13, § 1; has many kinds, ib. 7, § 4; cannot ruin those who possess her, ib. 10, § 2; is a mean, iv. 11, § 3; how far required in the great officers of state, v. 9, §§ 1-4; must be at least pretended by the tyrant, ib. 11, §§ 25, 34; is regarded as a secondary object by mankind, vii. 1, § 5:—cannot be separated from happiness, vii. 1, § 3; 2, § 2; 3, § 1; 8, § 5; 9, § 3; 13, § 5; results from nature, habit, and reason, ib. 13, §§ 10-13; 15, §§ 7-10; is not a matter of chance, ib. 13, § 9; how far consistent with the political life, ib. 2; 3; should it be made the aim of education? viii. 2; consists in hating and loving and rejoicing aright, ib. 5, § 17:—should not (as is done by the Lacedaemonians) be supposed inferior to external goods, ii. 9, § 35 (cp. vii. 1, § 5); nor be practised with a view to the single object of success in war, ii. 9, § 34; vii. 2, § 9; 14, § 16; 15, § 6:—the virtue proper to the slave, the woman, the child, i. 13, §§ 1-3; of the ruler and the subject different, ib. §§ 4-6; iii. 4, §§ 7-18; of the ruler, practical wisdom, of the subject, true opinion, iii. 4, § 18; of men and women not the same, i. 13, §§ 3, 9-11; iii. 4, § 16; less required in the artisan than the slave, i. 13, § 12 (cp. vii. 9, § 7); of the citizen relative to the constitution, iii. 4, §§ 1-7; iv. 7, § 3; v. 9, § 1; of the good man absolute, iii. 4, §§ 1-7; vii. 13, § 7; of the good citizen:

—is it identical with that of the good man? iii. 4; 5, § 10; 18; vii. 14, § 8; of the citizen in the perfect state, iii. 4, § 5; 13, § 12; iv. 7, § 2.

Virtue, military, is found in the masses, iii. 7, § 4; the social, is justice, i. 2, § 16; iii. 13, § 3.

Virtues, the, of women and children important to the state, i. 13. § 15; ii. 9, § 5; of the state and the individual the same, vii. 1, § 12; of the military life, ii. 9, §§ 11, 34; vii. 15, § 3; of leisure, vii. 15, § 1.

War, a part of the art of acquisition when directed against wild beasts and against men who are intended by nature to be slaves, i. 7, § 5; 8, § 12; vii. 2, § 15; 14, § 21; exists for the sake of peace, vii. 14, §§ 13, 22; 15, § 1; a school of virtue, ii. 9, § 11; a remedy against the dangers of prosperity, vii. 15, § 3; constant war a part of tyrannical policy, v. 11, § 10; success in war the sole object of the Lacedaemonian and Cretan constitutions, ii. 9, §§ 34, 35; vii. 2, § 9; 14, § 16; 15, § 6; progress in war:—invention of tactics, iv. 13, § 10;—of siege machines, vii. 11, § 9; improvement of fortifications, ib. § 12.

War, captives taken in, ought they to be made slaves? i. 6, §§ 1–8.

War, the Peloponnesian; losses of the Athenian nobility, v. 3, § 7; battle of Oenophyta, ib. § 5;—capture of Mitylene, ib. 4, § 6;—battle of Mantinea, ib. § 9;—the Sicilian expedition, ib.;—the Four Hundred at

Athens, ib. § 13; 6, § 6;—the Thirty, ib. 6, § 6.

War, the Persian, v. 3, § 7; 4, §§ 4, 8; 7, § 4; effect of, upon Athens, ii. 12, § 5; v. 4, § 8; viii. 6, § 11:—the Sacred, v. 4, § 7.

Wealth, always antagonistic to poverty, iv. 4, § 19; forms an element of the state, ii. 7, § 16; iv. 4, § 15; vii. 8, §§ 7, 9; includes many varieties, i. 8, § 3; iv. 3, § 2; [the true kind] has a limit, i. 8, § 14; 9, §§ 1, 12; popularly confused with coin, ib. 9, §§ 10, 14; not so much a concern of household management as virtue, ib. 13, § 1; must be used with both temperance and liberality, ii. 6, § 8; vii. 5, § 1.

Wealth, too highly valued at Sparta and Carthage, ii. 9, §§ 7, 13; 11, §§ 8–12; iv. 7, § 4; the chief characteristic of oligarchy, ii. 11, § 9; iii. 8, § 7; iv. 4. §§ 3, 19; v. 10, § 11; vi. 2, § 7; confers a claim to superiority in the state, iii. 9, §§ 4–6, 15; 12, §§ 8, 9; 13, §§ 1–5; popularly associated with good birth and education, iv. 8, §§ 4, 8; v. 7, § 1. *See* Riches.

Wealthy, the, have the external advantages of which the want tempts men to crime, ii. 7, § 10; iv. 8, § 3; are apt to be spoiled by the luxury in which they are reared, iv. 11, § 6; v. 9, § 13; form one of the classes necessary to the state, iv. 14, § 15; vii. 8, §§ 7, 9. *See* Rich.

Whole, the, must be resolved into its parts, i. 1, § 3; 8, § 1; prior and therefore superior to the parts, ib. 2, §§ 12–14; iii. 17, § 7; the part belongs entirely to the whole, i. 4, § 5; every

DOVER·THRIFT·EDITIONS

POETRY

La Vita Nuova, Dante Alighieri. 56pp. 0-486-41915-0

101 Great American Poems, The American Poetry & Literacy Project (ed.). (Available in U.S. only.) 96pp. 0-486-40158-8

English Romantic Poetry: An Anthology, Stanley Appelbaum (ed.). 256pp. 0-486-29282-7

Bhagavadgita, Bhagavadgita. 112pp. 0-486-27782-8

The Book of Psalms, King James Bible. 128pp. 0-486-27541-8

Imagist Poetry: An Anthology, Bob Blaisdell (ed.). 176pp. (Available in U.S. only.) 0-486-40875-2

Blake's Selected Poems, William Blake. 96pp. 0-486-28517-0

Songs of Innocence and Songs of Experience, William Blake. 64pp. 0-486-27051-3

The Classic Tradition of Haiku: An Anthology, Faubion Bowers (ed.). 96pp. 0-486-29274-6

To My Husband and Other Poems, Anne Bradstreet (Robert Hutchinson, ed.). 80pp. 0-486-41408-6

Best Poems of the Brontë Sisters (ed. by Candace Ward), Emily, Anne, and Charlotte Brontë. 64pp. 0-486-29529-X

Sonnets from the Portuguese and Other Poems, Elizabeth Barrett Browning. 64pp. 0-486-27052-1

My Last Duchess and Other Poems, Robert Browning. 128pp. 0-486-27783-6

Poems and Songs, Robert Burns. 96pp. 0-486-26863-2

Selected Poems, George Gordon, Lord Byron. 112pp. 0-486-27784-4

Jabberwocky and Other Poems, Lewis Carroll. 64pp. 0-486-41582-1

Selected Canterbury Tales, Geoffrey Chaucer. 144pp. 0-486-28241-4

The Rime of the Ancient Mariner and Other Poems, Samuel Taylor Coleridge. 80pp. 0-486-27266-4

The Cavalier Poets: An Anthology, Thomas Crofts (ed.). 80pp. 0-486-28766-1

Selected Poems, Emily Dickinson. 64pp. 0-486-26466-1

Selected Poems, John Donne. 96pp. 0-486-27788-7

Selected Poems, Paul Laurence Dunbar. 80pp. 0-486-29980-5

"The Waste Land" and Other Poems, T. S. Eliot. 64pp. (Available in U.S. only.) 0-486-40061-1

The Rubáiyát of Omar Khayyám: First and Fifth Editions, Edward FitzGerald. 64pp. 0-486-26467-X

A Boy's Will and North of Boston, Robert Frost. 112pp. (Available in U.S. only.) 0-486-26866-7

The Road Not Taken and Other Poems, Robert Frost. 64pp. (Available in U.S. only.) 0-486-27550-7

The Garden of Heaven: Poems of Hafiz, Hafiz. 112pp. 0-486-43161-4

Hardy's Selected Poems, Thomas Hardy. 80pp. 0-486-28753-X

A Shropshire Lad, A. E. Housman. 64pp. 0-486-26468-8

Lyric Poems, John Keats. 80pp. 0-486-26871-3

Gunga Din and Other Favorite Poems, Rudyard Kipling. 80pp. 0-486-26471-8

Snake and Other Poems, D. H. Lawrence. 64pp. 0-486-40647-4

DOVER·THRIFT·EDITIONS

PLAYS

LIFE IS A DREAM, Pedro Calderón de la Barca. 96pp. 0-486-42124-4
H. M. S. PINAFORE, William Schwenck Gilbert. 64pp. 0-486-41114-1
THE MIKADO, William Schwenck Gilbert. 64pp. 0-486-27268-0
SHE STOOPS TO CONQUER, Oliver Goldsmith. 80pp. 0-486-26867-5
THE LOWER DEPTHS, Maxim Gorky. 80pp. 0-486-41115-X
A DOLL'S HOUSE, Henrik Ibsen. 80pp. 0-486-27062-9
GHOSTS, Henrik Ibsen. 64pp. 0-486-29852-3
HEDDA GABLER, Henrik Ibsen. 80pp. 0-486-26469-6
PEER GYNT, Henrik Ibsen. 144pp. 0-486-42686-6
THE WILD DUCK, Henrik Ibsen. 96pp. 0-486-41116-8
VOLPONE, Ben Jonson. 112pp. 0-486-28049-7
DR. FAUSTUS, Christopher Marlowe. 64pp. 0-486-28208-2
TAMBURLAINE, Christopher Marlowe. 128pp. 0-486-42125-2
THE IMAGINARY INVALID, Molière. 96pp. 0-486-43789-2
THE MISANTHROPE, Molière. 64pp. 0-486-27065-3
RIGHT YOU ARE, IF YOU THINK YOU ARE, Luigi Pirandello. 64pp. (Not available in Europe or United Kingdom.) 0-486-29576-1
SIX CHARACTERS IN SEARCH OF AN AUTHOR, Luigi Pirandello. 64pp. (Not available in Europe or United Kingdom.) 0-486-29992-9
PHÈDRE, Jean Racine. 64pp. 0-486-41927-4
HANDS AROUND, Arthur Schnitzler. 64pp. 0-486-28724-6
ANTONY AND CLEOPATRA, William Shakespeare. 128pp. 0-486-40062-X
AS YOU LIKE IT, William Shakespeare. 80pp. 0-486-40432-3
HAMLET, William Shakespeare. 128pp. 0-486-27278-8
HENRY IV, William Shakespeare. 96pp. 0-486-29584-2
JULIUS CAESAR, William Shakespeare. 80pp. 0-486-26876-4
KING LEAR, William Shakespeare. 112pp. 0-486-28058-6
LOVE'S LABOUR'S LOST, William Shakespeare. 64pp. 0-486-41929-0
MACBETH, William Shakespeare. 96pp. 0-486-27802-6
MEASURE FOR MEASURE, William Shakespeare. 96pp. 0-486-40889-2
THE MERCHANT OF VENICE, William Shakespeare. 96pp. 0-486-28492-1
A MIDSUMMER NIGHT'S DREAM, William Shakespeare. 80pp. 0-486-27067-X
MUCH ADO ABOUT NOTHING, William Shakespeare. 80pp. 0-486-28272-4
OTHELLO, William Shakespeare. 112pp. 0-486-29097-2
RICHARD III, William Shakespeare. 112pp. 0-486-28747-5
ROMEO AND JULIET, William Shakespeare. 96pp. 0-486-27557-4
THE TAMING OF THE SHREW, William Shakespeare. 96pp. 0-486-29765-9
THE TEMPEST, William Shakespeare. 96pp. 0-486-40658-X
TWELFTH NIGHT; OR, WHAT YOU WILL, William Shakespeare. 80pp. 0-486-29290-8
ARMS AND THE MAN, George Bernard Shaw. 80pp. (Not available in Europe or United Kingdom.) 0-486-26476-9
HEARTBREAK HOUSE, George Bernard Shaw. 128pp. (Not available in Europe or United Kingdom.) 0-486-29291-6
PYGMALION, George Bernard Shaw. 96pp. (Available in U.S. only.) 0-486-28222-8
THE RIVALS, Richard Brinsley Sheridan. 96pp. 0-486-40433-1
THE SCHOOL FOR SCANDAL, Richard Brinsley Sheridan. 96pp. 0-486-26687-7
ANTIGONE, Sophocles. 64pp. 0-486-27804-2
OEDIPUS AT COLONUS, Sophocles. 64pp. 0-486-40659-8
OEDIPUS REX, Sophocles. 64pp. 0-486-26877-2

DOVER · THRIFT · EDITIONS

FICTION

THE QUEEN OF SPADES AND OTHER STORIES, Alexander Pushkin. 128pp. 0-486-28054-3

THE STORY OF AN AFRICAN FARM, Olive Schreiner. 256pp. 0-486-40165-0

FRANKENSTEIN, Mary Shelley. 176pp. 0-486-28211-2

THE JUNGLE, Upton Sinclair. 320pp. (Available in U.S. only.) 0-486-41923-1

THREE LIVES, Gertrude Stein. 176pp. (Available in U.S. only.) 0-486-28059-4

THE BODY SNATCHER AND OTHER TALES, Robert Louis Stevenson. 80pp. 0-486-41924-X

THE STRANGE CASE OF DR. JEKYLL AND MR. HYDE, Robert Louis Stevenson. 64pp. 0-486-26688-5

TREASURE ISLAND, Robert Louis Stevenson. 160pp. 0-486-27559-0

GULLIVER'S TRAVELS, Jonathan Swift. 240pp. 0-486-29273-8

THE KREUTZER SONATA AND OTHER SHORT STORIES, Leo Tolstoy. 144pp. 0-486-27805-0

THE WARDEN, Anthony Trollope. 176pp. 0-486-40076-X

FATHERS AND SONS, Ivan Turgenev. 176pp. 0-486-0073-5

ADVENTURES OF HUCKLEBERRY FINN, Mark Twain. 224pp. 0-486-28061-6

THE ADVENTURES OF TOM SAWYER, Mark Twain. 192pp. 0-486-40077-8

THE MYSTERIOUS STRANGER AND OTHER STORIES, Mark Twain. 128pp. 0-486-27069-6

HUMOROUS STORIES AND SKETCHES, Mark Twain. 80pp. 0-486-29279-7

AROUND THE WORLD IN EIGHTY DAYS, Jules Verne. 160pp. 0-486-41111-7

CANDIDE, Voltaire (François-Marie Arouet). 112pp. 0-486-26689-3

GREAT SHORT STORIES BY AMERICAN WOMEN, Candace Ward (ed.). 192pp. 0-486-28776-9

"THE COUNTRY OF THE BLIND" AND OTHER SCIENCE-FICTION STORIES, H. G. Wells. 160pp. (Not available in Europe or United Kingdom.) 0-486-29569-9

• THE ISLAND OF DR. MOREAU, H. G. Wells. 112pp. (Not available in Europe or United Kingdom.) 0-486-29027-1

THE INVISIBLE MAN, H. G. Wells. 112pp. (Not available in Europe or United Kingdom.) 0-486-27071-8

THE TIME MACHINE, H. G. Wells. 80pp. (Not available in Europe or United Kingdom.) 0-486-28472-7

THE WAR OF THE WORLDS, H. G. Wells. 160pp. (Not available in Europe or United Kingdom.) 0-486-29506-0

ETHAN FROME, Edith Wharton. 96pp. 0-486-26690-7

SHORT STORIES, Edith Wharton. 128pp. 0-486-28235-X

THE AGE OF INNOCENCE, Edith Wharton. 288pp. 0-486-29803-5

THE PICTURE OF DORIAN GRAY, Oscar Wilde. 192pp. 0-486-27807-7

JACOB'S ROOM, Virginia Woolf. 144pp. (Not available in Europe or United Kingdom.) 0-486-40109-X

MONDAY OR TUESDAY: Eight Stories, Virginia Woolf. 64pp. (Not available in Europe or United Kingdom.) 0-486-29453-6

NONFICTION

POETICS, Aristotle. 64pp. 0-486-29577-X

POLITICS, Aristotle. 368pp. 0-486-41424-8

NICOMACHEAN ETHICS, Aristotle. 256pp. 0-486-40096-4

MEDITATIONS, Marcus Aurelius. 128pp. 0-486-29823-X

THE LAND OF LITTLE RAIN, Mary Austin. 96pp. 0-486-29037-9

THE DEVIL'S DICTIONARY, Ambrose Bierce. 144pp. 0-486-27542-6

THE ANALECTS, Confucius. 128pp. 0-486-28484-0

CONFESSIONS OF AN ENGLISH OPIUM EATER, Thomas De Quincey. 80pp. 0-486-28742-4

THE SOULS OF BLACK FOLK, W. E. B. Du Bois. 176pp. 0-486-28041-1

DOVER · THRIFT · EDITIONS

NONFICTION

NARRATIVE OF THE LIFE OF FREDERICK DOUGLASS, Frederick Douglass. 96pp. 0-486-28499-9

SELF-RELIANCE AND OTHER ESSAYS, Ralph Waldo Emerson. 128pp. 0-486-27790-9

THE LIFE OF OLAUDAH EQUIANO, OR GUSTAVUS VASSA, THE AFRICAN, Olaudah Equiano. 192pp. 0-486-40661-X

THE AUTOBIOGRAPHY OF BENJAMIN FRANKLIN, Benjamin Franklin. 144pp. 0-486-29073-5

TOTEM AND TABOO, Sigmund Freud. 176pp. (Not available in Europe or United Kingdom.) 0-486-40434-X

LOVE: A Book of Quotations, Herb Galewitz (ed.). 64pp. 0-486-40004-2

PRAGMATISM, William James. 128pp. 0-486-28270-8

THE STORY OF MY LIFE, Helen Keller. 80pp. 0-486-29249-5

TAO TE CHING, Lao Tze. 112pp. 0-486-29792-6

GREAT SPEECHES, Abraham Lincoln. 112pp. 0-486-26872-1

THE PRINCE, Niccolò Machiavelli. 80pp. 0-486-27274-5

THE SUBJECTION OF WOMEN, John Stuart Mill. 112pp. 0-486-29601-6

SELECTED ESSAYS, Michel de Montaigne. 96pp. 0-486-29109-X

UTOPIA, Sir Thomas More. 96pp. 0-486-29583-4

BEYOND GOOD AND EVIL: Prelude to a Philosophy of the Future, Friedrich Nietzsche. 176pp. 0-486-29868-X

THE BIRTH OF TRAGEDY, Friedrich Nietzsche. 96pp. 0-486-28515-4

COMMON SENSE, Thomas Paine. 64pp. 0-486-29602-4

SYMPOSIUM AND PHAEDRUS, Plato. 96pp. 0-486-27798-4

THE TRIAL AND DEATH OF SOCRATES: Four Dialogues, Plato. 128pp. 0-486-27066-1

A MODEST PROPOSAL AND OTHER SATIRICAL WORKS, Jonathan Swift. 64pp. 0-486-28759-9

CIVIL DISOBEDIENCE AND OTHER ESSAYS, Henry David Thoreau. 96pp. 0-486-27563-9

WALDEN; OR, LIFE IN THE WOODS, Henry David Thoreau. 224pp. 0-486-28495-6

NARRATIVE OF SOJOURNER TRUTH, Sojourner Truth. 80pp. 0-486-29899-X

THE THEORY OF THE LEISURE CLASS, Thorstein Veblen. 256pp. 0-486-28062-4

DE PROFUNDIS, Oscar Wilde. 64pp. 0-486-29308-4

OSCAR WILDE'S WIT AND WISDOM: A Book of Quotations, Oscar Wilde. 64pp. 0-486-40146-4

UP FROM SLAVERY, Booker T. Washington. 160pp. 0-486-28738-6

A VINDICATION OF THE RIGHTS OF WOMAN, Mary Wollstonecraft. 224pp. 0-486-29036-0

All books complete and unabridged. All 5³⁄₁₆" x 8¼", paperbound. Available at your book dealer, online at **www.doverpublications.com**, or by writing to Dept. GI, Dover Publications, Inc., 31 East 2nd Street, Mineola, NY 11501. For current price information or for free catalogs (please indicate field of interest), write to Dover Publications or log on to **www.doverpublications.com** and see every Dover book in print. Dover publishes more than 500 books each year on science, elementary and advanced mathematics, biology, music, art, literary history, social sciences, and other areas.